GREEK RHETORIC UNDER CHRISTIAN EMPERORS

A History of Rhetoric

Volume I: *The Art of Persuasion in Greece* (1963)

Volume II: *The Art of Rhetoric in the Roman World* (1972)

Volume III: *Greek Rhetoric under Christian Emperors* (1983)

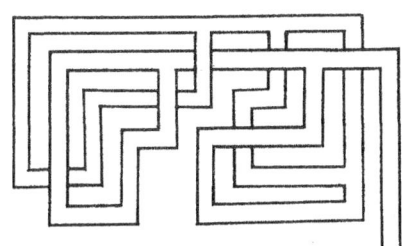

GREEK RHETORIC UNDER CHRISTIAN EMPERORS

GEORGE A. KENNEDY

WIPF & STOCK · Eugene, Oregon

Wipf and Stock Publishers
199 W 8th Ave, Suite 3
Eugene, OR 97401

Greek Rhetoric Under Christian Emperors
By Kennedy, George Alexander
Copyright©1983 by Kennedy, George Alexander
ISBN 13: 978-1-55635-980-4
Publication date 4/30/2008
Previously published by Princeton University Press, 1983

FOR KENNETH AND DOUG

Contents

Bibliographical Abbreviations	xi
Foreword	xv

CHAPTER ONE

Introduction: Forms and Functions of Secular Speech in Later Antiquity	3
Judicial Oratory	6
Deliberative Oratory	19
Epideictic Oratory	23
Julian the Apostate	27
Themistius	32
Synesius of Cyrene	35
Atticism	45

CHAPTER TWO

Later Greek Rhetorical Theory	52
Progymnasmata	54
Stasis	73
Invention	86
Ideas	96
Method	101
Sopatros	104
Syrianus	109
Marcellinus	112
George of Alexandria	115
Prolegomena	116
Figures of Speech	123
Neoplatonic Commentaries on the *Phaedrus* and the *Gorgias*	126

CONTENTS

CHAPTER THREE
The Schools of the Sophists — 133

- The Sophists of Athens — 135
- Himerius — 141
- The Schools of Antioch — 149
- Libanius — 150
- The Schools of Constantinople — 163
- Athenian Schools in the Fifth Century — 167
- The School of Gaza — 169
- The Decline of the Schools — 177

CHAPTER FOUR
Christianity and Rhetoric — 180

- Eusebius — 186
- The Arian Controversy — 197
- Asterius the Sophist — 207
- Athanasius — 208
- Gregory of Nazianzus — 215
- Basil the Great and Gregory of Nyssa — 239
- John Chrysostom — 241
- Theodore of Mopsuestia — 254
- Isidore of Pelusium — 256
- Cyril of Alexandria — 257
- The Council of Ephesus — 258
- The Tome of Pope Leo — 261

CHAPTER FIVE
Rhetoric in Byzantium, 600-900 — 265

- Early Byzantine Oratory — 267
- Early Byzantine Education — 273
- Photius — 278
- Arethas — 287

CONTENTS

CHAPTER SIX
Some Features of Rhetoric in Byzantium, 900-1300   291
   Michael Psellus   296
   Middle Byzantine Rhetoricians   306
   The Later Byzantine Period   320

Additional Bibliography   327

Index   331

Corrections to the First Printing

P. 70, n. 18, Replace the reference to the *Ohio Journal of Religious Studies* with the following: Abraham J. Malherbe, *Ancient Epistolary Theorists*. Atlanta: Scholars Press, 1988.

P. 70, n. 29: For a French translation of Longinus' *Art of Rhetoric*, see *Longin: Fragments, Art rhétorique; Rufus: Art rhétorique*, ed. and trasl. by Michael Patillon. Paris: Les Belles Lettres 2001, pp. 58–133.

P. 86. n. 37: For an English translation of *On Invention*, see Additional Bibliography, above, ch. 2.

P. 88, line 6–7: The term *prokataskeue* occurs in Dionysius of Halicarnassus, *Lysias* 15 and Isaeus 3.15.

P. 96, n. 40: For a translation of Hermogenes' *On Ideas* see Wooten, *Hermogenes On Ideas of Style* in the Additional Bibliography, above, ch. 2.

P. 102, n. 42: For a translation of *On Method*, see Additional Bibliography, above, ch. 2.

P. 105: line 16: *prophorikos,* not *prosphorikos*

P. 129, line 9: "occasional"

P. 147, line 8: "Dionysus" not "Dionysius"

P. 238, line 19, "eleventh" not "ninth century"

P. 239, line 4: "Georgian" (language) not "Georgic"

P. 240, n. 92: Basil, "pp. 363–345" not "249–348"

P. 241, line 2: "St. Ephaem Syrus" not "Styrus"

P. 249, n. 107: *Rendiconti dell' Istituto Lombardo* …

P. 254, line 13: "Council" not "Coucil"; line 9 from the bottom: "Theodore" not "John"

P. 264, line 18: *synegoria*, not *synegeria*

P. 268, line 14: "encouraged" not "ecouraged"

Bibliographical Abbreviations

APG	George Kennedy, *The Art of Persuasion in Greece*, Princeton University Press, 1963.
ARRW	George Kennedy, *The Art of Rhetoric in the Roman World*, Princeton University Press, 1972.
BZ	*Byzantinische Zeitschrift*, Munich: Beck.
CPh	*Classical Philology*, University of Chicago Press.
CR & CST	George A. Kennedy, *Classical Rhetoric and Its Christian and Secular Tradition from Ancient to Modern Times*, Chapel Hill: University of North Carolina Press, 1980.
Gloeckner	Stephanus Gloeckner, "Quaestiones Rhetoricae. Historiae Artis Rhetoricae Qualis Fuerit Aevo Imperatorio Capita Selecta," *Breslauer Philologische Abhandlungen*, VIII, 2, Breslau: Marcus, 1901.
GRBS	*Greek, Roman, and Byzantine Studies*, Chapel Hill: University of North Carolina Press.
HSCPh	*Harvard Studies in Classical Philology*, Cambridge: Harvard University Press.
Hunger	Herbert Hunger, *Die hochsprachliche profane Literatur der Byzantiner*, 2 vols. (Byzantinisches Handbuch v, 1-2 = Handbuch der Altertumswissenschaft XII, 5, 1-2), Munich: Beck, 1978.

BIBLIOGRAPHICAL ABBREVIATIONS

Krumbacher — Karl Krumbacher, *Geschichte der byzantinischen Literatur von Justinian bis zum Ende des oströmischen Reiches (527-1453)*, 2 vols. (Handbuch der Altertumswissenschaft IX, 1) 1897; reprinted, New York: Burt Franklin, 1970.

Kustas — George L. Kustas, *Studies in Byzantine Rhetoric* (Analecta Vlatadon XVII), Thessaloniki: Patriarchal Institute for Patristic Studies, 1973.

Lausberg — Heinrich Lausberg, *Handbuch der literarischen Rhetorik. Eine Grundlegung der Literaturwissenschaft*, 2 vols., Munich: Hueber, 1960.

LCL — The Loeb Classical Library, Cambridge: Harvard University Press; London: Heinemann.

Martin — Josef Martin, *Antike Rhetorik, Technik und Methode* (Handbuch der Altertumswissenschaft II, 3), Munich: Beck, 1974.

OCD² — *The Oxford Classical Dictionary*, ed. N.G.L. Hammond and H. H. Scullard, 2nd ed., Oxford: Clarendon Press, 1970.

PG — *Patrologiae Cursus Completus, Series Graeca*, ed. J.-P. Migne.

PhW — *Philologische Wochenschrift*, Leipzig: Reisland, 1881-1944.

PL — *Patrologiae Cursus Completus, Series Latina*, ed. J.-P. Migne.

PS — *Prolegomenon Sylloge*, ed. Hugo Rabe, Leipzig: Teubner, 1935.

BIBLIOGRAPHICAL ABBREVIATIONS

Quasten	Johannes Quasten, *Patrology*, 3 vols., Westminster Md.: The Newman Press, 1950.
R-E	*Paulys Real-Encyclopädie der klassischen Altertumswissenschaft*, 34 vols., 15 supplements, Munich: Druckenmüller, 1894-1977.
RhM	*Rheinisches Museum*, Frankfurt: Sauerländer.
RLM	*Rhetores Latini Minores*, ed. Karl Halm, Leipzig, 1863; reprinted Frankfurt: Minerva, 1964.
Schmid-Stählin	*Wilhelm von Christs Geschichte der griechischen Literatur*, ed. Wilhelm Schmid and Otto Stählin, Vol. 2: *Die nachklassische Periode der griechischen Literatur*, Part 2: *Von 100 bis 530 nach Christus* (Handbuch der Altertumswissenschaft VII, 2, 2), 6th ed., Munich: Beck, 1924.
SLN & PNF	A *Select Library of Nicene and Post-Nicene Fathers of the Christian Church*, ed. Philip Schaff and Henry Wace, New York, 1890-1900; reprinted Grand Rapids, Mich.: Eerdmanns, 1955.
Spengel	*Rhetores Graeci*, ed. Leonard Spengel, 3 vols., Leipzig, 1853-56; reprinted Frankfurt: Minerva, 1966. Note: Vol. I was reedited by Caspar Hammer, Leipzig: Teubner, 1894. Since this edition has not been reprinted and is not widely available, references to Vol. I are to the first edition of Spengel except where otherwise noted.

BIBLIOGRAPHICAL ABBREVIATIONS

TAPhA *Transactions of the American Philological Association*, Chico, Calif.: Scholars Press.

Walz *Rhetores Graeci*, ed. Christian Walz, 9 vols., 1832-36; reprinted Osnabrück: Zeller, 1968.

Unless otherwise noted, translations in this volume are by the author. Centuries of the Christian era are referred to in the text with initial capital letters (e.g., Fourth Century); centuries before Christ are not capitalized.

Foreword

This volume, like its two predecessors, is primarily addressed to students of the classics and of speech, but should appeal to some interested in philosophy, especially Neoplatonism, in the history of the Church, and in Byzantine studies. When I first began my studies of rhetoric thirty years ago the subject was often ignored or denigrated. This is no longer true, and I hope that this series has contributed to and will continue to encourage the understanding of a fundamental human faculty.

Since rhetoric was regarded as a somewhat questionable art in the middle of the Twentieth Century, I have occasionally been asked about the genesis of my interest in it, and this is a convenient place to reply. My family took a keen interest in public affairs while I was growing up. Among my earliest memories are the voices of Franklin D. Roosevelt and Adolf Hitler, but most of all the great speeches of Winston Churchill over the crackling wireless as events of World War II ebbed and flowed. One of my favorite occupations as a boy was to sit in the gallery of the Connecticut House of Representatives, in which my great-grandfather, grandfather, two great-uncles, an uncle, and a cousin had served. It was not, perhaps, the home of the greatest oratory, but I observed some effective use of ethos and learned that things could be said on both sides of a question. I was also taken to church, where I became an early, if sometimes impatient, critic of the eloquence of the pulpit. My own first appearance as a public orator came when I delivered an encomium of the Mississippi River (which I had never seen) before the graduating class of my grammar school, their parents and friends. This was followed by the class's spirited rendition of "Ol' Man River." At the time, I was lamentably uninformed of the epideictic

FOREWORD

rules of Menander Rhetor, but I instinctively grasped the principle of *ap'archēs achri telous*, which I later found enunciated by Hermogenes. My career as an epideictic orator probably reached its apogee years later in a *logos prosphōnētikos* to the Chief Justice of the United States Supreme Court in the presence of the associate justices, members of Congress, and a governor or two. Students of epideictic may be interested to know that both my grammar school and the Supreme Court required me to submit the text of my intended remarks for approval in advance of delivery, an experience doubtless shared by some of the panegyrists of later antiquity.

As an undergraduate at Princeton I heard better sermons than I had in our country town, and I heard at first hand addresses by statesmen or would-be statesmen. I also learned to read Plato and Demosthenes in Greek with the encouragement of A. E. Raubitschek. As a graduate student at Harvard I studied with Werner Jaeger, taking courses in Aristotle and Hellenistic Literature and a seminar on "Longinus." Jaeger did not share the general prejudice against rhetoric, encouraged my interest in it, and on the last occasion on which I saw him, laid his hand apostolically upon my shoulder and said, "I have written *Paideia*; you must write *Peitho*." As my interests in rhetoric became better known, encouragement came from others, including Harry Caplan, Friedrich Solmsen, and G.M.A. Grube. I also discovered that west of the Appalachians universities included whole departments of speech which took rhetoric seriously and were interested in what I was trying to do. Fred Haberman at Wisconsin was the first to seek me out, followed by Jack Matthews at Pittsburgh and Donald Bryant at Iowa. As the latter's guest in Iowa City, I found, to my astonishment, I could engage in a serious discussion of *stasis* theory which might well have taken place in the

FOREWORD

second century before Christ. To all of these mentors I here record my gratitude.

Even as a graduate student I began to develop a plan for a series of studies of the history of rhetoric. This plan has been revised from time to time, and the volumes in it, published by Princeton University Press, have been interspersed with other works, but the plan still advances. Fourth in the sequence should probably be a study of Latin Rhetoric under Christian Rulers, which might then be followed by a volume on the coming of the renaissance of rhetoric.

In working on this volume I have had the assistance of a Kenan Research Leave from the University of North Carolina, a fellowship from the National Endowment for the Humanities, and a fellowship from the Center for Byzantine Studies at Dumbarton Oaks. I am greatly indebted for information and advice to H. Kenneth Snipes, my colleague in Chapel Hill, and to Nigel Wilson of Lincoln College, Oxford. My student Edwin Carawan gave much valuable help in assembling the final manuscript. I am also indebted to Robert Brown, who has copyedited the manuscript for Princeton University Press.

Chapel Hill
January, 1982

GREEK RHETORIC UNDER
CHRISTIAN EMPERORS

CHAPTER ONE

Introduction: Forms and Functions
of Secular Speech
in Later Antiquity

The classical world regarded logical and eloquent speech, effectively delivered, as the most characteristic feature of civilized life. The orations of Isocrates are the fundamental statement of the view. Plato's criticisms of rhetoric were well known among intellectuals and in some periods, such as the second century before Christ, created considerable tension between the values of wisdom and eloquence in educational circles, but public opinion consistently favored the more pragmatic ideal of the orator over the philosopher in daily life. It was the orator who was able to defend himself, his family, and his property; to participate in the civic life of his city; to express the values of his civilization. The strongest evidence is the strength of the formal study of rhetoric, beginning with the sophists in a few Greek cities in the fifth century, and by the first century before Christ spreading to every municipality in the Greek and Roman world. In the early centuries of the Christian era public policy reinforced private sentiment. From the time of Antoninus Pius to that of Justinian all municipalities of the empire were encouraged to appoint and pay, from public funds, official teachers of grammar and rhetoric.

Writers on rhetoric in later antiquity generally speak of their subject as a civic art, represent themselves as training public speakers for the law courts and deliberative assemblies, and take Demosthenes and the Attic orators as models for their students. With rare exceptions, they make no notice of changes in political, legal, social, and religious in-

3

stitutions which altered the conditions of public address. We are dealing, of course, with an age which put a nervous emphasis on tradition and authority as it sought to stave off those forces which it regarded as destroying society from inside and outside. It is characteristic of it to define its institutions in anachronistic forms, to call its philosophers Platonists, its poets Homeric bards, its emperors the successors of Augustus, and its orators the followers of Demosthenes. As we shall see, however, a rhetorical education came to perform other functions in addition to training in public address: it taught literary composition; it offered training for future bureaucrats in the civil service; it served as an introduction to dialectic and thus to philosophy; ultimately it provided training for preachers and controversialists in the Christian Church. But it is proper to begin with a consideration of the traditional forms and functions of speech in late antique society and of how public opinion was manipulated. In all periods and all societies this is the primary function of rhetoric from which other forms, such as literary composition, are derived.

The rhetoricians of late antiquity, like others in the classical tradition, regarded the genus of rhetoric as falling into three species: judicial, deliberative, and epideictic, or as it came more often to be called, panegyric. These are universal and exhaustive categories in the sense that they represent judgment of past actions, consideration of future action, and discourse fitted to a particular present occasion which calls for a belief or attitude but not necessarily an action. The three species furnish a structure for the classification of speech in later antiquity as in other periods. A second set of rhetorical categories, enunciated by Aristotle and known to, though not widely discussed by, rhetoricians of later antiquity will also be useful in a somewhat extended form. This is the distinction between external or

JUDICIAL ORATORY

nonartistic and internal or artistic modes of persuasion. Both are utilized in all societies, but classical rhetoric was largely concerned with internal modes, with *ethos, logos,* and *pathos* as manifested in an artistic speech. Aristotle (*Rhetoric* 1.1375a22-1377b12) limits external modes of persuasion to five forms of evidence introduced into judicial speeches: laws, witnesses, contracts, evidence taken under torture, and oaths. Many modern rhetoricians would go far beyond this and extend the concept of external means of persuasion beyond the evidence on which an argument is built and even beyond verbal communication itself. If rhetoric is the art of persuasion, it can find effective techniques in all manner of threats and promises, gestures and actions, and the uses of power and authority. In later antiquity and the Middle Ages such extended modes of persuasion were a powerful influence and clearly constitute a rhetoric in themselves. An Athenian jury or assembly of the classical period might on occasion be strongly influenced by the authority of a speaker apart from the character presented in his speech, or by bribery, or by the intimidation of a mob, but there was a general atmosphere of orderly procedure, rational deliberation, and calm decision making. In later antiquity and the Middle Ages external rhetoric appears to be a much more powerful influence. In the law courts and assemblies, as well as in other confrontations, the arbitrary imposition of power, the use of intimidation, the application of torture, and other barbaric methods are often the real basis of a decision. Conversely, much could be gained by flattery, which is a prevailing feature of speech in an autocratic age. Some of the most interesting situations in later Greek and Byzantine rhetoric are those in which we can see the clash of rational and external forms of rhetoric as practiced both by civil and ecclesiastical authorities.

SECULAR SPEECH IN LATER ANTIQUITY

Judicial Oratory

The theory taught and the exercises practiced in rhetorical schools, both in classical and postclassical times, to a large extent are devoted to the skill of composing a speech to be delivered in prosecution or defense, either by a litigant or an advocate, in a court of law. In late antiquity this skill retained some practical application. Orderly legal procedures represented one of the highest and noblest traditional values of the Roman state, and in late antiquity Roman law and procedure were given a theoretical basis and a systematic codification which represent one of the greatest achievements of the age. But it is clear to even a casual student of Roman history that there were many occasions on which this must have been more an ideal than a reality. When barbaric hoards were roaming Greece and Asia Minor, or a usurper was marching on the throne, the courts did not meet as usual. Famine, plague, and earthquake were endemic to these centuries and took their toll of lives and of principles. The provincial administration and the civil service were remarkable institutions; they attracted some good servants, but some who were lazy, ignorant, corrupt, and incompetent. Influential friends and money were essential for effective use of the system; a poor litigant had little chance of success and a poor defendant awaiting trial on a criminal charge had an excellent chance of dying in prison of starvation or disease.[1]

Even when times were normal and officials reasonably conscientious, the law courts of late antiquity were not the scene of the greatest oratorical triumphs of the period. As Tacitus' *Dialogus* already makes clear, the imperial courts were no longer practical forums for the great political clashes

---

[1] For a general account of legal procedure see A.H.M. Jones, *The Later Roman Empire, 284-602*, 3 vols., Oxford: Blackwell, 1964, I, pp. 470-522.

in which Demosthenes and Cicero had won their fame. Political clashes existed in the later empire, but they took the form of court intrigue or armed revolt. Trials usually evoked little public interest; the chief exception occurred when some prominent individual was brought to trial for treason or heresy and sought to defend himself. Although there exist descriptions of trials (and in one case to be discussed below versions of the speeches given as composed later by an historian), of the hundreds of speeches surviving from late antiquity not one was delivered in a court of law. From the Byzantine period there are a few speeches which seem actually to have been spoken in court.

Certain procedural changes reduced the importance of extended discourse in lawcourts. The law was professionalized to a greater degree than had been true in the early empire when Pliny the Younger gained his fame, not to say in the time of Cicero or earlier. Technical knowledge of legal language, formulae, precedent, and theory required professional study. The law school in Beirut dates from the Third Century and the "university" of Constantinople in the Fifth Century provided chairs of law side by side with rhetoric. Libanius, a lover of old traditions, often laments the eagerness of students to study law, or even shorthand, rather than rhetoric. Worst of all, law had to be studied in Latin.

A second, not unrelated, development was the greater reliance on written documents in legal procedure. In the Fourth and Fifth Centuries what had been extraordinary civil procedure *a libello* gradually became ordinary.[2] It gave a central place to the preparation and submission of a written indictment which was then examined in court by questions of the judge to the lawyers representing the litigants.

---

[2] See Paul Collinet, *La Procédure par libelle* (Etudes historiques sur le droit de Justinien IV), Paris: Recueil Sirey, 1932, esp. pp. 285 and 345.

A third and parallel factor is the greater authority given to judges. In criminal procedure in the late empire the judge often acts as both prosecutor and judge. The Justinian Codex (3.1.9) orders the judge to examine the matter before him and interrogate the parties involved.[3]

The ordinary courts of first instance were those of the governors (*praeses*) of provinces or the urban prefects of Rome and Constantinople.[4] Since governors no longer had military powers and since many aspects of administration were in other hands, their functions were primarily judicial. Some had legal training and experience in the civil service, but others had a rhetorical education and came to their offices through personal influence. From accounts of trials it seems clear that the amount of oratory tolerated in a court was very much determined by the inclinations and patience of the judge.

From the courts of provincial governors appeal was possible, first to designated higher officials in the various parts of the empire: prefects, proconsuls, vicars, and comites; and from them, except in theory from the praetorian prefects, to the emperor. The emperor heard appeals with his consistory or with the senate of Constantinople, but sometimes he did not personally attend and relied on the advice of his ministers. The daily routine of an emperor consisted in large part of holding court: of making administrative, military, and judicial decisions on the basis of information

---

[3] For the text see *Corpus Juris Civilis*, ed. Paul Krueger, Berlin: Weidmann, 1954, II, p. 120. On the extended authority of the judge see H. F. Jolowicz, *Historical Introduction to the Study of Roman Law*, Cambridge Univ. Pr., 1952, esp. pp. 461-63.

[4] See Jones, *Later Roman Empire* (supra, n. 1), I, pp. 479-84. There also existed special courts such as that which dealt with treasury matters, military courts, and courts which had jurisdiction over civil servants; see ibid., pp. 484-94. After 318, Christian bishops were given jurisdiction in minor matters and dispensed justice on a regular basis, see ibid., p. 480.

JUDICIAL ORATORY

and recommendations of his staff. In this process those who could speak effectively certainly had some advantage over those who could not, but again the procedure was more apt to be one of brief statements and questions rather than extended oratory. The imperial court was surrounded with an elaborate ceremonial and protocol. It constituted a form of rhetoric in itself designed to create a mystique of authority and to intimidate opposition. Detailed knowledge of the proper forms was as essential as cogency of thought or brilliance of expression.

Eunapius, whose *Lives of the Philosophers* is the most important work for an understanding of rhetorical education and sophistry in Fourth-Century Greece, describes a trial before the governor of Achaea in Corinth around 330.[5] After a brawl in Athens between the students of two rhetoricians, Julian and Apsines, Julian and his students have been arrested. Apsines tries to speak against them but is prevented by the governor, who says that the person who made the complaint at the first hearing must speak. This is Apsines' student Themistocles, who has, however, made no preparations. Julian also asks to speak and is refused permission. The governor says that he does not want to hear prepared speeches by the teachers and he will not tolerate any applause. He wants to hear the accuser and then to hear a reply by one of the accused students. Themistocles does the best he can, but it is poor. Julian points out how bad it is and asks the judge to let his student Prohaeresius, later one of the most famous of the Athenian sophists, speak. The point of Eunapius' story is the great extemporaneous ability of Prohaeresius. After a short proemium, Prohaeresius moves into a narrative of the sufferings of the students while held for trial and then, in what

[5] Eunapius, pp. 483-85 Kayser. For text and English translation see Wilmer Cave Wright, *Philostratus and Eunapius, The Lives of the Sophists* (LCL), Cambridge: Harvard Univ. Pr., 1952, pp. 468-77.

Eunapius calls a second proemium, declares "If it is permitted to do all kinds of wrong and to bring charges and for an accuser to be believed without any chance of defense, so be it. Let this be the city of Themistocles!" This is a play on the names of the complainant and the great fifth-century statesman Themistocles. The *gnōmē*, or clever utterance, has such a remarkable effect that everyone, even Apsines, cheers, and the governor lets them all go after a stern warning to Themistocles and his friends. Eunapius says that the governor, though Roman, was not uneducated—he clearly means in rhetoric. In fact, the governors of Achaea often seem to have sought their post because of cultural interests in the country, and it is likely that trials in Greece and in certain other places like Antioch preserved somewhat more of the old rhetorical tradition than elsewhere. The story indicates how much procedures depended on the inclination of the judge.

The historian Zosimus, writing about A.D. 500, describes three trials which may illustrate conditions in the courts.[6] In one case (4.14) the prefect of the treasury in Constantinople tried a soldier under his command who was accused of sorcery. Under torture the soldier implicated others not under his jurisdiction and the trial was transferred to the praetorian prefect. The emperor Valens allowed a large number of people to be arrested, but the prisons were not adequate to hold them and those accused were sentenced to death without due process of law. The result was that the treasury gained their property. Oratory had little opportunity in such cases.

In another case (4.52) Rufinus, as praetorian prefect, was trying a former official named Proculus whom he personally hated. The charge seems to be treason. Proculus went into hiding, but Rufinus deceived his father into lur-

[6] See Zosimus, *Historia Nova, The Decline of Rome* trans. James J. Buchanan and Harold T. Davis, San Antonio: Trinity Univ. Pr., 1967.

ing him back, having persuaded the emperor Theodosius to pretend that he intended them both for high office. Proculus appeared, was arrested and imprisoned; his father was immediately exiled. There were a series of hearings, of which no details are given; speeches may have been made against Proculus and he may have been given a chance to reply or at least to answer questions, but he was convicted and led off to execution. The emperor apparently disapproved of the procedures and forbade the execution, but Rufinus arranged for the emperor's messenger to dawdle and arrive too late.

In a third trial described by Zosimus (5.9) speech apparently played a greater role. Eutropius, intent on destroying Timasius, secured an infamous sausage-seller as an informant and the latter accused Timasius of coveting the throne:

> The emperor presided as judge for the case; at his side was Eutropius who, since he was, among other things, head chamberlain, held the power of pronouncing sentence. When everyone bore it ill that a sausage-seller was pressing charges against a man distinguished by so many offices and honors, the emperor withdrew from the case and turned it over to Saturninus and Procopius. Of these two men the former was of quite advanced age and had been decorated with great honors; still he was not above flattery, having grown accustomed in lawsuits to subserve the interests and intentions of those who had the emperor's ear. On the other hand, Procopius had been related by marriage to the emperor Valens and was a gauche and indomitable man who seemed in some matters to speak the truth frankly. Consequently, when the time came to pronounce sentence, Procopius objected to Saturninus that it was not fitting for Timasius, a man distinguished by so many offices and honors, to

be prosecuted by the calumnies of a cheap lewd fellow or (what was even more absurd) for a benefactor to suffer at the hands of the recipient of his benefits. Nonetheless, Procopius' boldness of speech availed nothing, the judgment of Saturninus, praised to excess, prevailing: Timasius was condemned to exile in the Great Oasis, whither a public convoy escorted him.[7]

Zosimus was a pagan who disliked the Christian court. His evidence is not entirely reliable, especially about motivations, and he wrote a century after the events he describes, but his accounts of procedure may be accepted. What debate there was seems to have occurred between the judges, one of whom functioned as prosecutor, the other as advocate. The influence of flattery, here presumably laid on by Eutropius, is evident.

Synesius of Cyrene mentions (*Dio* 11) a North African trial in the late Fourth Century in which pleaders were allotted time by a judge. This probably was a common procedure, as it had been since classical Greek times. In this case the judge dozed through the speeches.

The little work *On the Magistrates* by John Lydus supplies some observations of the law courts in Sixth-Century Constantinople.[8] John was for many years a civil servant, but became discouraged with the bureaucracy and turned to literature. He delivered a panegyric of Justinian before the court, was invited by the emperor to write an encomiastic history of his Persian wars, and was finally appointed to a professorship in the "university," probably that of Latin grammar (*De Magistratibus* 3.26-29). According to John, the reforms of Justinian made justice clearer, re-

---

[7] Ibid., pp. 201-2.
[8] For the text see Joannis Lydi *De Magistratibus Populi Romani*, ed. Richard Wuensch, Leipzig: Teubner, 1903. Translations cited in text are those of T. F. Carney, in John the Lydian, *On the Magistrates of the Roman Constitution* (Bureaucracy in Traditional Society III), Lawrence, Kans.: Coronado Pr., 1971.

duced opportunity for controversy in the courts, and curtailed the work of lawyers (3.1.3). He greatly disliked the praetorian prefect John the Cappadocian who, he says (3.66.1-3), gave up hearing cases himself and appointed unable men as judges. As a result, "the advocates felt no enthusiasm for embellishing their advocacy with rhetoric capable of persuading a magistrate of the highest competence." "Consequently then, none of the speakers who formerly were accustomed to be highly esteemed for their speeches on such matters spent their time on them for anyone." In contrast, in the Fifth Century, Anastasius had appointed as prefect the sophist Sergius, who had been a professor of rhetoric (2.21.1). But after the time of the Cappadocian, things improved again. Phocas, a senator well educated in both languages (3.73.7), rose to power:

> The prefect's staff took fire, just as though someone were pouring oil with a lavish hand on to a fire that was on the point of dying out. There was a bustle that came as a joy to those doing business; gains that were modest and welcome in the eyes of the law accrued to those serving the prefecture, and the Precincts of Justice were opened up. Orators began to be famous for their speeches; publishing of books and keen rivalry about them began recurring as part of the whole life style of the state; the . . . (3.76.10; p. 124 Carney)

and here his work abruptly breaks off.

Aside from some ecclesiastical trials to be considered in Chapter Four, the only extended account of a judicial procedure in late antiquity, including versions of the speeches delivered on either side, is to be found in the Fourth Book of Agathias' *History* of the years 552-559, which was written about twenty years later.[9] The case is extremely unu-

---

[9] For the text see Agathiae Myrinae *Historiarum Libri Quinque*, ed. Rudolf Keydell (Corpus Fontium Historiae Byzantinae [CFHB] II), Ber-

sual, and Agathias' description of it, as of other events in his *History*, is so strongly influenced by classical models and traditional rhetorical composition as to undermine complete confidence in its historical veracity, but it is an instructive example of how rhetoric was viewed in the time of Justinian and a review of it will serve as an introduction to *stasis* theory as taught in the schools, a subject which will be of importance in Chapter Two.

Gubazes was the king of the Lazi at the east end of the Black Sea. Agathias insists on calling them by their classical name, Colchians. The king was an enthusiastic supporter of the Romans, but made accusations to Justinian about the incompetence of the Roman commander, Martinus, and the imperial fiscal agent, Rusticus. The latter two, together with Rusticus' brother John, laid a plot against Gubazes. John was sent to Justinian to report secretly that Gubazes was betraying the Romans to the Persians, and he succeeded in extracting a letter from the emperor summoning Gubazes to court. This letter, through John's machinations, included a provision that force could be used against Gubazes if he refused to come, and in the final instance of resistance he could be killed. The confederates then met with Gubazes and said nothing about the letter, but asked his help in attacking the Persians. He refused help unless they corrected their past negligence in matters relating to him. John then drew a dagger and killed him (3.2-4). The Lazi, as a result, refused to have anything to do with the Romans.

Justinian ordered a full public trial of the confederates in Lazian territory, complete with Roman judicial forms

---

lin: de Gruyter, 1967. Translation by Joseph D. Frendo, in Agathias, *The Histories* (CFHB IIA), Berlin and New York: de Gruyter, 1975. See also Averil Cameron, *Agathias* Oxford: Clarendon Pr., 1970. Cameron's book is a valuable historiographic study, but unsympathetic to the attitude toward rhetoric in late antiquity.

and eloquence in the grand style (*megalēgoria*) (4.1.7). According to Agathias, the emperor wanted the barbarians to see the workings of Roman law at its best, and the ensuing scene describes "a Roman court, or rather, an Attic one" (4.1.8). Shorthand writers took down what was said (4.1.2), but it is not clear that Agathias had or even tried to get access to the records. A leading senator named Athanasius was appointed to be judge and a preliminary hearing held (3.14.4-5). This is not described, but apparently Agathias envisioned the defendants as being interrogated and as revealing the nature of their defense, which the prosecutor is thus able to anticipate in his speech.

The actual trial is conducted by Athanasius with the help of a retinue of legal advisers (4.1.2). In the later empire there are no true juries. The prosecutors are Lazi, "thoroughly conversant with the Greek language." Rusticus is the spokesman for the defendants. He demands that the emperor's letter authorizing the arrest be read, and this is done, but Agathias did not have the text and composed his own version (4.2.2). In the letter, Justinian expresses his surprise at the charges and his reluctance to believe them, but he summons Gubazes to Constantinople. If he refuses, he is to be arrested; if he fights back he may be killed as an enemy and whoever kills him will be given immunity.

Rhetoricians of the empire devoted much of their attention to teaching stasis theory, to identifying the basic issue of a case which a speaker must determine before he can develop his argument. Any Greek judicial speech has stasis, and the theory has application also to some deliberative speeches and to theological disputation. The first possible form of stasis is *stochasmos*, or stasis of fact. In this case, could the defendants successfully deny that they had killed Gubazes? Clearly they could not, and this form of stasis is not utilized. The second form of stasis is definition, *horos*.

Could they legally justify their action on the basis of Justinian's order? This certainly represented a possible defense, but it is not that which is utilized. The defendants, or Agathias if the speech is entirely his creation, apparently thought that a third form of stasis, *poiotēs* or quality, furnished a stronger defense. Stasis of quality seeks to justify an admitted action by demonstration of its justice, good intentions, beneficial results, or necessity. It is of two sorts, either legal or rational. The defendants here primarily employ a type of rational stasis of quality in which they argue that the killing of Gubazes was beneficial to the Romans, elaborating his vicious character to give the claim probability. The prosecutor, anticipating this defense, seeks to show the excellence of Gubazes' character, the disastrous results of his murder, the vicious character of the defendants, and the beneficial results which their punishment will bring. There is no *diēgēsis*, or narrative of the circumstances, as commonly found in the Attic orators; judicial rhetorical exercises in late antiquity commonly omit a narrative, though handbooks provided rules for composing one. The prosecutor also postpones almost to the end (4.5.7-9) his denial that the defendants acted in accordance with the specific requirements of Justinian's letter.

According to Agathias, the Lazi in the audience were amazed that the defendants were not immediately executed and that Rusticus was then allowed to speak for the defense as Roman law required (4.7-10). Rusticus' position is that he and his associates have brought about the downfall of a tyrant and rebel and have upheld the interest of the emperor. He does not deny the fact of the execution, as he says he would have had to do in a Persian court, and he does not seek to justify it in law, which would have been stasis of definition (4.7.6). From Gubazes' refusal to give military assistance at the final interview he argues that the king's treason was clear. There was, he claims, no point in

JUDICIAL ORATORY

waiting for more proof and Gubazes clearly had no intention of answering the summons to Constantinople. There was no practical way of sending him there against his will, and he might have gotten help from the Persians (4.9.9-11).

At this point, however, near the end of his speech, Rusticus seeks to transfer the stasis to letter and intent, which is one form of legal stasis of quality. He accuses the prosecution of too literal an interpretation and maintains that the details in Justinian's order were merely to test Gubazes' intentions. The defendants undertook this test and took the appropriate action (4.10.1-4). He then concludes with a protestation of loyalty and the claim that the execution was honorable, just, and timely. The speaker's argument from intent is basically weak, but its postponement to this place in the speech allows it to be viewed in terms of the treacherous character which he has sought to give Gubazes.

The judge then undertook a careful examination of the evidence. Presumably he interrogated the parties involved, as Roman law in this period required him to do. His finding was for the prosecution in the cases of Rusticus and John, and they were ordered to be beheaded. The question of Martin's complicity was referred to the emperor, who subsequently dismissed the case against him, but relieved him of his military rank (4.21.3).

The occurrence of the trial need not be doubted, and it is not unlikely that Justinian might have sought to demonstrate to the Lazi the workings of Roman justice. In the absence of other accounts it is possible that Agathias' version is a rhetorical composition drawing on exercises in the schools, but nevertheless it does reflect a contemporary view of what an ideal trial should be like. That ideal could clearly be approximated if Roman officials were determined to be thorough, patient, and fair.

Forms of speech in many periods and in many cultures

experience the phenomenon of *letteraturizzazione*, or adaptation to literary forms.[10] The tendency of the teaching of rhetoric itself to slip from exposition of an art of public address to techniques of literary composition is part of the same phenomenon, as is the incorporation of speeches into historical works as seen in Agathias. The orations of Isocrates, actually elaborate literary pamphlets, are the classical models for literary rhetoric. In the *Antidosis* Isocrates had used the form of judicial oratory for a personal apology, in partial imitation of the *Apology* of Socrates as published by Plato. Isocrates is an important influence on the sophists of later antiquity, and in their works can be found some judicial forms of composition. Good examples are Libanius' first oration, which is an apology for his career, or his fourteenth oration, which is a defense of his disgraced friend Aristophanes of Corinth, written out and sent to the emperor Julian. Like other such speeches it has panegyrical qualities, praising both Aristophanes and Julian, in this case with some delicacy, but the form easily succumbs to flattery under the influence of autocratic government and the complimentary etiquette fostered by the court.

Another aspect of the application of rhetoric to written forms is what may be called the rhetoric of the law.[11] The law codes of later antiquity, and the individual decrees and edicts of the emperors, are regularly set out in elaborate language which is designed to render the material impressive and persuasive. Striking examples include the preface to Diocletian's Edict on Prices of 296, which parades the emperor's titles, attacks those responsible for inflation, and amplifies the emperor's humanitarian concerns.[12] The Code

[10] See *CR & CST*, pp. 108-19.
[11] See Richard Honig, *Humanitas und Rhetorik im spätrömischen Kaisergesetzen*, Göttingen: Schwartz, 1960, esp. pp. 39-61.
[12] For translation see Naphtali Lewis and Meyer Reinhold, *Roman Civilization* (Records of Civilization XLV), New York: Columbia Univ. Pr., 1955, II, pp. 464-66.

of Justinian similarly contains elaborate prefatory material. To a modern reader the justifications common in the law of later antiquity may seem indicative of the insecurity of the age, and the polarization of loving emperor and vicious criminals produces a shrillness of tone which somewhat undercuts the dignity of the law while intending to reinforce it. Christians imitated this development in the anathemas issued by the Councils of the Church, as will be shown in Chapter Four.

Deliberative Oratory

Some opportunity for deliberative oratory continued to exist in later antiquity. The senates of both Rome and Constantinople enjoyed great prestige.[13] They were in theory consultative bodies, advising the emperor, but they also served as local councils for their cities. Their most consistent political function was to lend support to decisions the emperor or his staff had already made, and thus the oratory heard in the senate tended to be panegyrical. Our best Greek examples are the speeches of Themistius to the Constantinopolitan senate. Occasionally the senate was called upon to make actual decisions: examples include the Roman senate during Alaric's siege of Rome in 410 and the senate of Constantinople under the weak successors of Justinian at the close of the Sixth Century. The emperors sent written orations to the senates and occasionally addressed them in person. Theodosius II once tried to convert the Roman senate to Christianity by a speech from the throne (Zosimus 4.59). The emperors also addressed synods of the Church on matters of discipline. The earliest example is Constantine's address to the Council of Nicaea.

Literary adaptations of imperial rhetoric can be found in the historians, often in the form of addresses to the troops. All of the speeches in the extant portions of the Latin his-

[13] On the senates see Jones, *Later Roman Empire* (supra, n. 1), II, pp. 523-62.

tory of Ammianus Marcellinus are speeches of emperors to the troops. Generals' speeches are given scant notice by the rhetoricians, though Theon (II, p. 115 Spengel) and Hermogenes (II, p. 15 Spengel) list them as one of the types of personification practiced in schools of grammar and rhetoric.[14] The literary form had a long history from Homer, Herodotus, and Thucydides, through the Byzantine period and later, but it was recognized from an early time that addresses to the troops on the approach of battle as found in historians were a literary convention, remote from the actual conditions of the battlefield (see Polybius 12.25; Plutarch, *Moralia* 803B). If battles were not imminent, the general perhaps had more opportunity for oratory. An example which may have some historical veracity occurred in 350 and is splendidly set out by Gibbon in the eighteenth chapter of *The Decline and Fall* on the basis of the account in Zosimus (2.44).[15] Constantius addressed his troops in the presence of Vetranio, whose own troops had recently proclaimed him emperor. Constantius was anxious to eliminate Vetranio as a threat and to move against Maxentius, a greater rival. Much use was made of external means of persuasion: the stage was carefully set; key soldiers were bribed. Constantius then spoke and reminded the soldiers of what they owed to his father and of their oaths, and he inveighed against Maxentius. The soldiers, who had been primed to do so, cried out that the power should not go to illegitimate claimants and turned on Vetranio, who was given no chance to speak and was led away to enforced retirement.

Another deliberative form seen regularly in the historians is the ambassador's speech (*presbeutikos logos*). Ambas-

[14] See Theodore C. Burgess, *Epideictic Literature* (Chicago Studies in Classical Philology III), Univ. of Chicago Pr., 1902, pp. 209-14.

[15] See the edition by J. B. Bury, London: Methuen, 1896, II, pp. 236-38.

sadors sometimes were haughty and demanding, as was Titianus when sent by Constantius to Magnentius (Zosimus 2.49), sometimes conciliatory, as those sent by Julian to Constantine (Ammianus 20.8.2-19). As in the latter case they often carried letters expounding the views of their superiors, and thus ambassadorial rhetoric is closely associated with epistolography. It also has ties with epideictic. This is especially true of congratulatory embassies. In 357 Themistius was chosen by the senate of Constantinople to go to Rome and congratulate Constantius on his military victories. He was prevented from going by poor health, but delivered his intended speech (Or. 4) to the senate at home as a panegyric of the emperor. The following spring he did go to Rome and delivered his *Embassy Speech* (Or. 3), congratulating the emperor on twenty years of rule. He himself (Or. 34.13) dates his successful political career from this point, for Constantius made him proconsul in Constantinople for 358-359. Menander Rhetor devotes a short chapter to the *presbeutikos logos* in his handbook of epideictic forms (III, pp. 423-24 Spengel), but discusses only the situation in which an ambassador is seeking compassion for a city and recommends use of the *topos* of the fickleness of fortune, as seen in the case of Troy. Conventions of the form were largely learned from imitation of literary models. Collections of ambassadorial speeches were made for imitation as early as the Hellenistic period. *On the Embassies of the Romans* is a collection of ambassadorial speeches from historians of antiquity, edited in its present form in the Tenth Century.[16]

Some of the more bizarre embassies were to barbarian rulers. Constantius sent the sophist Eustathius to address

[16] See *Excerpta de Legationibus*, ed. C. de Boor, Berlin: Weidmann, 1903. On earlier embassy speeches see Cecil W. Wooten, "The Ambassador's Speech: a Particularly Hellenistic Genre of Oratory," *Quarterly Journal of Speech* 59 (1973), 209-12.

the Persian king Sapor. It must have been a novel experience for that monarch. According to Eunapius (*Lives of the Philosophers*, pp. 456-66 Kayser) the magi had to prevent the king from abandoning his throne and becoming a Greek philosopher. But Eunapius was partisan and in fact the embassy accomplished nothing. Valentinian III sent the grandfather of Cassiodorus on an embassy to Attila the Hun. According to Cassiodorus, the terror of the age was pacified by his eloquence and "condescended to seek favor."[17] Such accounts reflect the traditionally high value put on speech and a certain amount of wishful thinking in this pragmatic age.

A great deal of speech went on in municipal councils, usually on local matters. Some picture of this can be gained from the letters of Libanius in Antioch. The *Second Katastasis* of Synesius of Cyrene is possibly a speech delivered in the council in his native city around 410 urging that the province request a continuation of the appointment of the Roman commander Anysius and the sending of additional troops for defense against barbarian incursion. We cannot, however, be certain that it is a speech and not a letter. In either case it is an extremely poignant document, almost a monody for the fall of Cyrene, the coming destruction of the Pentapolis, and the death of Synesius himself, which followed in a year or two. The speech, if delivered, must have had an exceedingly depressing effect on the audience; it ends with the following words, which powerfully convey the experience of living in the provinces in later antiquity:

> How many times shall I call upon God and turn to him? How often shall I press my hands upon the rail-

---

[17] See Thomas Hodgkin, *The Letters of Cassiodorus*, London: Henry Frowde, 1886, p. 146. The story is rendered unlikely by the Hun's presumed ignorance of Latin.

ings? But necessity is a mighty thing and all-powerful. I long to give my eyes a sleep uninterrupted by the sound of the trumpet of alarm. How much longer shall I guard the intervals between the turrets? I am weary of picketing the night patrols, guarding others and guarded myself in turn, I who used to hold many a vigil, waiting for the omens from the stars, am now worn out watching for the onset from the enemy. We sleep for a span measured by the water clock, and the alarm bell often breaks in upon the position allotted me for a slumber. And if I close my eyes for a moment, oh, what sombre dreams![18]

Some opportunity for deliberative oratory existed in the Councils and synods of the Church and some forms of preaching may be classified as deliberative as well. This subject can be best left for discussion in Chapter Four.

Epideictic Oratory

Epideictic oratory, regarded by Aristotle as the oratory of praise and blame and by modern rhetoricians as occasional oratory, existed in classical Greece, for example, in Athenian funeral orations (*epitaphioi logoi*) and in speeches delivered at festivals (*panēgyrikoi logoi*), but its great development came in the Hellenistic, imperial, and Byzantine periods. To those who highly valued speech but lived under autocratic government it offered the chief opportunity for eloquent public address. At the same time it performed important cultural, social, and even political functions and should not be dismissed as a quaint artificiality. The Renaissance found it useful in much the same ways.

Some of these functions may be briefly summarized here.[19] Epideictic oratory offered, first, an opportunity for

---

[18] Translation by Augustine FitzGerald, *The Essays and Hymns of Synesius of Cyrene*, London: Oxford Univ. Pr., 1930, II, p. 367.

[19] See Lellia Cracco Ruggini, "Sofisti Greci nell'impero Romano," *Athenaeum* 49 (1971), 402-5, and Herbert Hunger, "Aspekte der grie-

public participation in official occasions such as the victories, birthdays, and deaths of the rulers and the various holidays celebrated by the cities of the empire—speeches at festivals honoring the return of spring, for example, or of the Church year. Large crowds sometimes came together; civic and national unity was demonstrated; the best products of the local schools vied with one another to exhibit their art. In the orations of Himerius one can see how epideictic was also applied to private occasions, such as birthdays, weddings, and the arrival and departure of friends. Second, such speeches offered a vehicle for the transmission of cultural values, particularly the heritage of Hellenism. They were important for the survival of paganism, as seen for example in the speeches of Libanius; they were used by Themistius for the presentation in popular form of Platonic and Aristotelian philosophical views and by him and others for the development of the political theory of the monarchy. Epideictic forms were, furthermore, adapted by the Church in the course of the Fourth Century. Gregory of Nazianzus in particular achieved an eloquent synthesis of Hellenic culture and Christian values in his great funeral orations, such as that for Basil.

The most obvious political function of epideictic is in expression of loyalty to the state by an individual, sometimes a suspect individual, or on the part of a city, but the speeches were conversely used to express to the public the values or ideals of the rulers themselves through the mouths of those who praised them. It must have been difficult for many people in the empire to know what was going on, what they were supposed to believe. Epideictic oratory thus performed some of the functions of a state-controlled press in a society which lacked newspapers. Finally, in the mouth

---

chischen Rhetorik von Gorgias bis zum Untergang von Byzanz," Oesterreichische Akademie der Wissenschaften, Wien, Philosophisch-historische Klasse, *Sitzungsberichte* 277, 3 (1972), 1-27.

EPIDEICTIC ORATORY

of a courageous or subtle orator, epideictic could, while keeping within established traditions of decorum, convey to a ruler some of the qualities which he lacked and could also convey to a perceptive audience a criticism of the addressee. If the great fault of epideictic is to indulge in flattery or to gloss over realities, a fault into which even Christian epideictic easily slipped, the tone of adulation can also be ironically manipulated. Excessive praise of the mildness of a tyrant can be used as indictment of his brutality. It is, however, exceedingly difficult to judge when this level of meaning is intended. We rarely know enough about the personalities involved, their predictable reactions, the circumstances governing the occasion, or the tone of delivery. In making such judgments, Greek rhetorical handbooks offer no help.

Instruction in the forms of epideictic oratory was not a major feature of the work in schools of rhetoric in later antiquity, but some provision for it was made. Preliminary exercises in composition, called *progymnasmata*, were regularly practiced by students in the more advanced stage of grammatical study and the more elementary stage of rhetoric. These will be discussed in Chapter Two. Among these exercises, the *enkōmion* afforded students practice in praising a god, a man, a city, or other subjects, but the exercise was not tied to a specific occasion such as an arrival, a departure, a wedding, a funeral, a festival, an embassy, or the like. The *psogos*, or invective, was also a progymnasmatic form. Bitter personal attack, already common in the speeches of Demosthenes and Aeschines, remains common in late antiquity and is borrowed by Christians in their opposition to Jews, pagans, and heretics. The *synkrisis*, or comparison, is another standard exercise, and epideictic orations regularly included *synkriseis*, comparing the subject of the discourse to other great examples of the past. Two incomplete treatises bearing the name of Menander Rhetor, probably written by two different authors in the late Third Century, outline the structure and topics proper to many of the encomiastic occasions as then observed and provide valuable tests for commonplaces in the analysis of extant epideictic speeches.[20] These treatises are, however, unusual, being paralleled only by a discussion falsely attributed to Dionysius of Halicarnassus. They represent an extension of progymnasmata in the form of handbooks which might be useful to one called upon to deliver such speeches. In later antiquity, as in the classical period, epideictic was largely learned by imitation. Sophists like Himerius in Athens and Libanius in Antioch delivered a variety of epideictic speeches before their schools on appropriate occasions and thus furnished models for their students. They often prefixed their speeches with *protheōriai*, or introductory remarks on the treatment they would follow. A number of these introductions survive. In addition, since epideictic is a very self-conscious art form, it is not unusual for an orator in his proemium or elsewhere to comment on the problems he faces or the treatment he has adopted.

Many epideictic orations are preserved from later antiquity. The term "panegyric," originally a variety of epideictic delivered at a festival, became the common word for public epideictic, though other words such as *enkōmion* are occasionally used as well. Epideictic in the sophistic schools will be discussed in Chapter Three. Christian adaptations of the forms will be discussed in Chapter Four. The chapter on Byzantine rhetoric will note some later examples of public epideictic. Here it is perhaps enough to examine public address by three of the greatest epideictic orators of the Fourth Century, Julian, Themistius, and Synesius of Cyrene. Their works represent a variety of reactions to

[20] See D. A. Russell and N. G. Wilson, *Menander Rhetor*, Oxford: Clarendon Pr., 1981.

rhetoric, philosophy, the political situation, and Christianity.

Julian the Apostate

The first oration of Julian was ostensibly delivered before Constantius and his court at Milan in 355, shortly before Julian went off to take command of the army in Gaul.[21] It was from victories there that he eventually returned for a brief reign as emperor from 361 to 363. With great hesitation and only after the elimination of all other candidates and at the urging of the empress Eusebia had Constantius recognized Julian as his heir. The function of this speech is a public declaration of loyalty and admiration for Constantius on the part of Julian. It is possible that the text represents a published version of the original remarks, sent to the emperor at a later date to reassure him again of Julian's loyalty. Actually we know from his subsequent writings (e.g., *Letter to the Athenians* 274c-277d) that he feared and loathed Constantius, but he played the role fate had assigned him and addressed to Constantius a nearly perfect example of a *basilikos logos*, a fulsome eulogy of a king. Its structure accords in almost every respect with the rules of Menander Rhetor. There is no reason to believe that Julian had ever read Menander, and his desire to study with the sophist Libanius had been frustrated by the court, but he had studied rhetoric and philosophy in Constantinople, Nicomedia, Pergamum, and Athens, and the use of a highly conventionalized form filled the needs of the occasion without involving him in complete commitment to the contents.[22]

[21] For the text and translation see Wilmer Cave Wright, *The Works of the Emperor Julian* (LCL), Cambridge: Harvard Univ. Pr., 1913, I, pp. 2-127. Valuable discussion in the Budé text, ed. J. Bidez: L'empereur Julien, *Oeuvres complètes*, 2 vols. Paris: Les Belles Lettres, 1932.

[22] See Burgess, *Epideictic Literature* (supra, n. 14), pp. 132-33, and F. Boulenger, "L'empereur Julien et la rhétorique," *Mémoires*, Univ.

The proemium of Julian's encomium of Constantius is a good introduction to several features of the rhetoric of the Fourth Century. Julian claims he has long wished "to hymn" Constantius' virtue, deeds, wars, and suppression of tyrants. Oratory in this period performs many of the functions earlier performed by poetry, and many epideictic orations, including encomia, epithalamia, and celebrations of the gods, are hymns in poetic prose. Among Julian's orations are prose hymns to the Sun (Or. 4) and to the Mother of the Gods (Or. 5). Constantius, Julian says, has drawn away the bodyguard of one of his rivals "by speech and persuasion"; this is probably a hendiadys for "persuasive speech," but Julian must have been aware that Constantius used forms of persuasion other than rational speech. Julian, like almost every encomiast, expresses the fear that he will be inadequate for his theme, for which he uses the word *hypothesis*. This is the word used in the rhetorical schools for a subject which involves specific persons and events in contrast to a philosophical *thesis*. He goes on to say that those trained in political contests or poetry would not find the task so difficult; the former have had practice in *meletē*, the judicial and deliberative exercises of the schools, and are also accustomed to *epideixis*. Julian has primarily studied philosophy, which "does not dare to show its nakedness in the theatre." Naked, that is, because philosophy is not adorned with rhetorical colors. Sophistry is often referred to as performed in the theatre and filled some of the cultural functions of Greek drama

---

de Lille, 32, 3 (1927). The speech shows the influence of earlier panegyrics of Constantius by Libanius and Themistius, see C. Gladiis, *De Themistii, Libanii, Juliani in Constantium Orationibus*, Breslau: Societas Typographorum Vratislaviensium, 1907. It has recently been argued that Julian's slavish observance of rhetorical convention was a way to avoid responsibility for the contents; see Polymnia Athanassiadi-Fowden, *Julian and Hellenism: An Intellectual Biography*, Oxford: Clarendon Pr., 1981, p. 61.

of earlier times. The poets have a license to invent their subjects, which is lacking to orators, but the latter have a license to flatter: "It is not a disgrace for a speaker to praise those who are unworthy of praise." This rather dangerous sentiment is, however, sophistically converted into a tribute to Constantius: so great, so patent are Constantius' achievements, Julian need give only a plain narrative (*diēgēsis*) of them. Many have sought to praise him and fallen short of their goal. Julian will take his philosophical belief in virtue as his starting point and speak no word that cannot be tested against virtue and philosophy. He may be accused by others of currying favor with the emperor, but will put his faith in the real virtues of the man he celebrates. He then gives a brief summary of the topics and structure of the speech which is to follow. It is in this approach that his observance of the conventions of the *basilikos logos* becomes most clear:

> Assuredly I must begin with the virtues of your ancestors through which it was possible for you to come to be what you are. Next I think it will be proper to describe your upbringing and your education, since these contributed very much to the noble qualities that you possess, and when I have dealt with all these, I must recount your achievements, the signs and tokens, as it were, of the nobility of your soul, and finally, as the crown and consummation of my discourse, I shall set forth those personal qualities from which was evolved all that was noble in your projects and their execution.[23]

If Julian had a salve for his conscience in his eulogy of Constantius it had to take the form of an awareness that the speech was necessary for his survival and a feeling that the virtues he celebrated were philosophically good in

[23] See Wright, *Julian* (supra, n. 21), pp. 11-13.

themselves. They were the qualities which a great king should have, and there was perhaps some slight hope that in holding them up as the virtues of Constantius he might inspire the emperor to seek in some small way to be worthy of praise. The panegyrics of Trajan by Pliny and by Dio Chrysostom had a worthier subject, but they, too, sought to hold up to the emperor a model for his imitation and education.

The second speech of Julian is also an encomium of Constantius,[24] but composed in Gaul (see section 56b and 76b), which perhaps gave Julian a feeling of greater independence. The speech may have been recited to the troops and sent in writing to the court. It appears to have two different audiences: the emperor himself, whom Julian apparently still wished to assure of his loyalty, and Julian's intelligent friends, who might have appreciated his cleverness in praising the unpraiseworthy and to whom he wished to present his ideas on legitimate succession and on philosophical kingship.[25] The speech begins with an account of the quarrel between Achilles and Agamemnon in the *Iliad*; these heroic figures are clearly to be taken as images for Julian the general and Constantius the king, respectively. Use of mythological allegory is relatively common in epideictic as we shall see in Chapter Three. Agamemnon is not, however, the noblest model for Constantius which Julian might have found, and the speech thus has from the start the possibility of subtle interpretation or even irony. Such a technique was practiced in the rhetorical schools in the form of "figured problems," to be discussed

[24] Ibid., pp. 131-269.

[25] Older scholarship treats the speech as a straight encomium; recent writers have been more doubtful. See G. W. Bowersock, *Julian the Apostate*, Cambridge: Harvard Univ. Pr., 1978, p. 43, "not without visible signs of strain"; Athanassiadi-Fowden, *Julian and Hellenism* (supra, n. 22), pp. 63-66, regards the speech as deliberately confrontational.

in Chapter Two. The moral of the quarrel, as drawn by Julian (50b), is that kings should not be insolent and generals should not resent insolence. It is not, of course, expressly said that the emperor has been insolent; far from it. Constantius, Julian claims, has revealed his Homeric education in his noble deeds (50c), and the basic conceit of the speech is a *synkrisis*, which it will be recalled is a progymnasmatic form commonly adapted to epideictic, of the Homeric heroes and Constantius, ostensibly to the latter's advantage. The trouble with this is that Constantius had been insolent, had abused his power and been carried away by anger at members of his family, and that Julian had resented the insolence. According to Ammianus (21.16.4) Constantius affected learning, but because of innate dullness he was a failure at both rhetoric and poetry. Julian may have hoped the emperor's dullness was such that he would not get the irony of his treatment, but there were those at court ready to explain it to him.

Of the literary forms practiced in late antiquity, the two most influenced by classical rhetoric are historiography and epistolography. The use of artificial oratory in historical writing has already been noted, though prologues, narratives, descriptions, and comparisons in the historians also show the influence of the schools. Elaborate epistles are sometimes difficult to distinguish from speeches, since often it is not known whether an oration was orally delivered, sent privately to the addressee, or widely published in written form. The most elaborate of Julian's extant letters is a written address to the Athenians, defending his acceptance of the empire and his revolt against Constantius. It is the first of his works in which his true feelings against Constantius are openly revealed. His most famous letter is the official rescript (*Ep.* 36) in which he prohibited Christians from teaching pagan literature and thus effectively debarred them from official positions in state-supported schools.

The letter sets forth his reasoning in some detail. Its direct effectiveness was brief, owing to the shortness of Julian's reign, but it had the indirect effect of awakening in some Christians, like Gregory of Nazianzus, the desire to defend the rights of Christians to share in the heritage of Hellenic culture and eloquence.

Themistius

Julian aspired to be a philosophical orator, but his time was brief and his efforts were disappointed. The major philosophical orator of the Fourth Century was Themistius. Though a pagan, he shows the influence of the Christian Eusebius and he couched his thought in terms which many Christians could share; his political theory was permanently influential in the Greek world. This may be summarized as the belief that a philosophical ruler must be born to his task; he will learn from professional philosophers, but lives in a world of action; he understands government and protects his subjects; he shares many moral qualities with others, but is distinguished by *philanthrōpia*, a godlike love of mankind. The ideal king is the personification of the law (e.g., Or. 5.64).[26]

Themistius was born in Paphlagonia in 317 and became

---

[26] See Vladimir Valenberg, "Discours politiques de Thémistius dans leurs rapport avec l'antiquité," *Byzantion* 1 (1924), 557-80; Kenneth M. Setton, *Christian Attitude towards the Emperor in the Fourth Century Especially as Seen in Addresses to the Emperor*, New York: Columbia Univ. Pr., 1941, esp. pp. 25-28; Glanville Downey, "Philanthropia in Religion and Statecraft in the Fourth Century after Christ," *Historia* 4 (1955), 199-208; idem, "Education and Public Problems as Seen by Themistius," *TAPhA* 86 (1955), 291-307; Norman H. Baynes, "Eusebius and the Christian Empire," *Byzantine Studies and Other Essays*, London: Athlone Pr., 1960, pp. 168-72; G. Dagron, *L'empire romain d'orient au IVᵉ siècle et les traditions politiques de l'hellenisme. Le témoinage de Thémistius* (Travaux et Mémoires III), Paris: de Boccard, 1967.

a professor of philosophy in Constantinople in 345.[27] In the following years he wrote most of his extant paraphrases of works of Aristotle and composed diatribes which defended moral theses, for example (Or. 30), *Should one work the soil?* The question has some practical application. Themistius was indeed a practical philosopher, seeking to make the political and ethical views of Plato and Aristotle understood in his own age. The mystical side of Platonism, so strong in his time, had little appeal to him. Although he consistently took the side of philosophy in its dispute with rhetoric (e.g., Or. 23, 27, and 28), he also argues that the philosopher should use the methods of the sophists (Or. 21).

Themistius' first oration is an encomium of Constantius, delivered before him in Ancyra in 350. It does not observe the conventions of classical panegyric as seen in Julian's encomium. At the outset the orator tells Constantius that he admires his soul, not his possessions, and though he affects to believe that Constantius has the virtues which he admires, he also lectures him. A Greek philosopher with adequate credentials, like a Christian bishop, could venture to take a firm moral stance: "There is no advantage of having your crown on straight, but your character dragging in the mud, and your scepter of gold, but your soul more worthless than lead, and to clothe your body in fine and

[27] See Schmid-Stählin, pp. 1004-14; *R-E* VA, 1642-80; for text, Themistii *Orationes Quae Supersunt*, ed. H. Schenkl, G. Downey, and A. F. Norman, 3 vols., Leipzig: Teubner, 1965; 1970. Only a few portions of Themistius are available in translation: see Glanville Downey, "Themistius' First Oration," *GRBS* 1 (1958), 49-69; Carl Wendel, "Die erste Kaiserliche Bibliothek in Konstantinopel," *Zentralblatt für Bibliothekswesen* 59 (1942), 194-96 (portions of Or. 4); Ernest Barker, *From Alexander to Constantine*, Oxford: Clarendon Pr., 1956, pp. 377-80 (portions of Or. 5); Hubert Kesters, *Discours XXVIe, Plaidoyer d'un Socratique contre le Phèdre de Platon*, Louvain and Paris: Nauwelaerts, 1959, pp. 225-79; Hugo Schneider, *Die 34. Rede des Themistius*, Winterthur: Keller, 1966.

colorful raiment, while exhibiting a mind bare of virtue, and to hit birds when you shoot them, but to miss wisdom when you take counsel, accustomed to sit easily on a horse, but more easily to fall from justice." (Or. 1.12).[28]

In 355 Constantius appointed Themistius to the senate of Constantinople. He continued active there until his death around 388. Orations one through nineteen are all encomia of the emperors Constantius, Jovian, Valentinian, Valens, and Theodosius, delivered in the senate or elsewhere, usually on imperial commission. Theodosius made him tutor to the future emperor Arcadius. He also had close relations with Julian, indeed had been his teacher in philosophy, and on Julian's accession had written him a letter of advice. It does not survive, but we have Julian's reply, which stresses the dangers of Christianity for classical culture and rejects Themistius' doctrine of the divine right of kings.[29]

Toward the end of his life Themistius suffered from the feeling that he was not understood. His contemporary Libanius went through a similar phase, which has its model in the circumstances which caused Isocrates to compose the *Antidosis*. Themistius' views of what he had been trying to do are summed up in a passage from one of his later speeches:

> Following the most famous of ancient philosophers, who think there are two roads of philosophy, one more divine, one more commonly useful, I followed that which

[28] As translated by Downey, "Themistius' First Oration" (supra, n. 27), p. 62.
[29] For Julian's reply see Wright, *Julian* (supra, n. 21), II, pp. 203-37. See further Glanville Downey, "Themistius and the Defense of Hellenism," *Harvard Theological Review* 50 (1957), 259-74, and Francis Dvornik, "The Emperor Julian's Reactionary Ideas on Kingship," *Late Classical and Medieval Studies in Honor of A. M. Friend, Jr.*, ed. Kurt Weitzmann, Princeton Univ. Pr., 1955, pp. 71-81.

is useful to you [members of the senate] rather than that involving myself alone, and I chose philosophy within the state, following Socrates and Aristotle and before them the celebrated Seven Wise Men. By mixing deeds with words they preached a philosophy which was neither ineffectual nor unprofitable. Following all these men, I have for nearly forty years passed my life serving you with speeches and going on embassies one after another, numerous as you know, neither with dishonor nor disgrace nor in a way unworthy of your election of me, either alone or jointly with the best among you. (31. 352b-d)

Synesius of Cyrene

A deliberative speech by Synesius has been mentioned above. More characteristic of him are epideictic forms. Synesius was born around 370 in Cyrene, studied Platonic philosophy with Hypatia in Alexandria, visited Athens and Constantinople, and married a Christian woman in Alexandria. In 410 he was elected Christian bishop of Cyrene, a position which he accepted reluctantly and on the condition that he would not renounce Platonic philosophical beliefs, such as the preexistence of the soul, and would not divorce his wife so as to live celibately. Cyrene, seriously threatened by barbarians as we have seen, needed his spiritual leadership. He died around 412.[30] Synesius is an impressive figure: learned, cultured, courageous. Three of his works require attention here, the *Encomium of Baldness*, the *Discourse on Kingship*, and the apologetic work called *Dio*.

Since the fifth century, Greek sophists had cultivated

[30] On Synesius' life and works see Christian Lacombrade, *Synésius de Cyrène, Hellène et Chrétien*, Paris: Les Belles Lettres, 1951. For text of the orations see Synesii Cyrenensis, *Opuscula*, ed. Nicolaus Terzaghi, Rome: Regia Officinia Polygraphica, 1944.

paignia, or playful verbal exercises on some unexpected subject which allowed an opportunity for logical conceit and verbal wit. The genre has been called adoxography.[31] One of the most famous examples was the *Encomium of Hair* by the late First-Century sophist-philosopher Dio Chrysostom. Dio is an important influence on Synesius' thought and writing, and the latter's *Encomium of Baldness* is a reply to Dio's praise of hair.[32] Since the subject is essentially trivial, the more tongue-in-cheek the praise the more charming the result. In this respect Synesius' work far surpasses Dio's. He describes his own premature baldness in mock tragic tones and musters entertaining examples of the advantages of baldness from mythology, history, and nature, with numerous references to Homer, Plato, and other classical writers. Among his arguments is the following epicheireme:

> It was necessary, I think, that the cosmos should be a living thing, should be composed of living creatures. To the simpler souls it is a matter of indifference that they must take up their abode in a hairy head, far removed from the clearly defined pattern, but each wise soul according to its own deserts has received as its portion— one a star to dwell in, another a bald head. For if nature here below is weak at producing perfect precision, nevertheless she does not tolerate the part of us which looks upward and towards heaven to be formed otherwise than as a universe in its shape. Baldness, then, appears plainly

[31] See Arthur Stanley Pease, "Things Without Honor," *CPh* 21 (1926), 27-42.

[32] See J. R. Asmus, "Synesius und Dio Chrysostomus," *BZ* 9 (1900), 85-151. Translation by Augustine FitzGerald, *Essays* (supra, n. 18), II, pp. 243-74. For a reply to Synesius see B.E.C. Miller, *Elogue de la chevelure. Discours inédit d'un auteur grec anonyme en réfutation du discours de Synésius intitulé Elogue de la Calvitie*, Paris: Brockhaus et Avenarius, 1840; see Lacombrade, *Synésius* (supra, n. 30), p. 44.

to us as also a heaven, and as many praises as one might sing of a sphere, so many does one relate to baldness also.(8)[33]

Synesius thus spoofs both philosophy and sophistry in an epideictic form whose intention is primarily to entertain an audience of readers.

In 399 Synesius was sent by his native province to Constantinople to negotiate a tax remission needed because of the depredations of the barbarians. Here he composed and recited two impressive works, the *Discourse on Kingship* and the *Egyptian Tale*, which show perhaps better than anything else the possibilities for serious criticism still open to rhetoric in later antiquity. On the eastern throne sat Arcadius, the twenty-one year old son of Theodosius, completely overshadowed by the leaders of opposing factions in his court. Synesius was given an audience with the puppet emperor, presented him with a gold crown, and addressed to him a royal discourse modeled to some extent on Dio Chrysostom's addresses to Trajan.[34] The weak Arcadius was a very different king from the great Trajan, and Synesius does not hesitate to lecture him sternly on his duties. The philosophy expounded is Platonism and there are no direct Christian allusions, but the moral thought is not inconsistent with Christianity. It seems possible that Synesius, appalled at the court and political conditions as his letters show, hoped that the young king would be encouraged to assert himself as a virtuous ruler, acquiring wisdom from philosophy, but it is equally difficult to believe that his

[33] From FitzGerald, *Essays* (supra, n. 18), II, p. 254.
[34] For historical background see *Cambridge Medieval History*, I, ed. H. M. Gwatkin and J. P. Whitney, Cambridge Univ. Pr., 1911, pp. 456-60, and A.H.M. Jones, "Collegiate Prefectures," *Journal of Roman Studies* 54 (1964), 81. For translation see FitzGerald, *Essays* (supra, n. 18), II, pp. 108-47. See also Setton, *Christian Attitude* (supra, n. 26), pp. 152-62.

remarks were entirely unacceptable to the faction then in control, the empress Eudoxia and the prefect Aurelian. They may not have been eager for the emperor to assert himself, but they were probably anxious to increase his prestige and their security, and they disliked his inclination to leave military leadership to their enemy, the Goth Gaïnas.

Synesius encourages the emperor to look beyond his corrupt court, to beware of flattery, to avoid the influence of barbarians, to lead his army in person, and to make direct contact with his people:

> This majesty and the fear of being brought to the level of man by becoming an accustomed sight, causes you to be cloistered and besieged by your very self, seeing very little, hearing very little of those things by which the wisdom of action is accumulated. You rejoice only in the pleasures of the body, and the most material of these, even as many as touch and taste offer you; and so you live the life of a polyp of the sea. As long as you deem man unworthy of you, you will not attain man's perfection. . . . those on whom you bestow your royal approval are rather men with small heads and petty minds whom nature by some error stamps amiss, even as dishonest bankers falsify coins.(10)[35]

At one point (3) Synesius notes, or affects to note, the discomfiture of some in his audience, but claims they had been forewarned of his intentions.

He later describes himself as more bold than any Greek in his approach to the emperor (*On Dreams* 9). We know that Synesius thought well of the prefect Aurelian (*Ep.* 31 and 61), and those attacked are doubtless Aurelian's opponents, but he may have gone beyond what was expected. He has much to say which reflects his own view as a phi-

---

[35] From FitzGerald, *Essays* (supra, n. 18), I, pp. 124-25.

losopher and as a provincial, including a plea for tax abatement (19). He accomplished his specific mission for Cyrene (*Hymns* 3.469-93) and obtained exemption for himself from curial responsibilities (*Epistle* 100), but was unsuccessful, as far as one can see, in having any impact on Arcadius.

While in Constantinople Synesius also wrote and recited, in part, a work *On Providence*, also known as the *Egyptian Tale*.[36] It is an example of *letteraturizzazione*, the application of rhetoric to written composition. The work is an allegorical *mythos*, the legend of Osiris and Typho, who represent, as the brief preface hints, Aurelian and an opponent, probably Eutychian. We have already seen in Julian's First Oration that myth was used by orators as allegorical description of contemporary individuals, but there is nothing in the sophists to equal the detailed working out of the equation here attempted and nothing that deals with such controversial and dangerous material. Synesius does not identify the audience he addresses; it is likely to have been something less public than the court.

In the spring of 402 Synesius left Constantinople suddenly after an earthquake and sailed to Alexandria. Although he visited Cyrene to report on his embassy, it was in Alexandria that he lived for the next few years, married a Christian woman, and composed the treatise called *Dio*, although it was not published until his final return to Cyrene in 405.[37] The work is of great importance for understanding how rhetoric was viewed by a leading intellectual of this period who had been trained in Greek philosophy and who was yet sympathetic to Christianity. Understanding of it is facilitated by a letter from Synesius to Hypatia

[36] For translation see ibid., II, pp. 275-325.
[37] See Georg Misch, *Geschichte der Autobiographie*, I, 2, Bern: Francke, 1950, pp. 607-11, and Lacombrade, *Synésius* (supra, n. 30), pp. 139-49. For translation see FitzGerald, *Essays* (supra, n. 18), I, pp. 148-82.

(*Epistle* 154), consulting her about its publication.[38] He says here that he has written it "because of the slander of men. Some of those who wear the white or dark mantle have maintained that I am faithless to philosophy, apparently because I profess grace and harmony of style, and because I venture to say something concerning Homer and the figures of the rhetoricians. In the eyes of such persons one must hate literature in order to be a philosopher and must occupy himself with divine matters only." Those in the white mantle are Neoplatonic philosophers in the tradition of Iamblichus; those in the dark mantle are the monks of Egypt. Synesius had by this time moved into a close, if uneasy, contact with Christian preachers, but makes no sharp distinction between Christian theology and neoplatonic theurgy. Of the philosophers he has the following to say:

> There are certain men among my critics whose effrontery is only surpassed by their ignorance, and these are the readiest of all to spin out discussions concerning God. Whenever you meet them, you have to listen to their babble about inconclusive syllogisms. They pour a torrent of phrases over those who stand in need of them, in which I suppose they find their own profit. The public teachers that one sees in our cities come from this class. . . . They wish me to become their pupil; they say that in a short time they will make me all-daring in questions of divinity and that I shall be able to speak day and night without stopping.

As to the monks,

> They would like to be famous in the same way, but fortunately for them they are incapable even of this. . . .

[38] Translations that follow are from Augustine FitzGerald, *The Letters of Synesius of Cyrene*, London: Oxford Univ. Pr., 1926, pp. 250-54.

Their philosophy consists in a very simple formula, that of calling God to witness, as Plato did, whenever they deny anything or whenever they assert anything.

Synesius does not mean that the monks are Platonists; the comparison of their appeal to God to Socrates' love of oaths is ironic. The monks' philosophy is based on revelation and is proclaimed or asserted, not argued and proved. Synesius says that his *Dio* deals with the "loquacity" of the philosophers and the "silence" of the monks, actually mostly with the latter, "none the less, it has found means of dragging in those other men also, and it aims at being no less an *epideixis* than an encomium of *polymatheia*, or great learning." The letter continues with a comparison of Synesius' method in the treatise to the passage in Plato's *Phaedrus*, the classic text on philosophical rhetoric, in which various kinds of beauty are analyzed. Synesius claims that he has sought to use the gifts of nature and art to make one thing follow logically from another. In other words, he is using the method of definition and division as taught in the rhetorical and dialectical schools of the time. We will explore this procedure in Chapter Two.

The *Dio* is thus an encomium of classical learning and an apology for Synesius' position, which puts the highest value on philosophical truth, but insists that it can only be effectively and properly expounded in a humanistic and literate way, both in terms of rational argument and stylistic ornament. It is an example of and a plea for philosophical rhetoric in the Platonic tradition. "Dio" is of course Dio Chrysostom, who is taken as a partial model of what Synesius has in mind. He begins (1-3) with Philostratus' account of Dio, goes on to a *synkrisis* of Dio and Aristocles, who moved from philosophy to sophistry, and concludes that there were two distinct phases in Dio's career: only after his exile did he emerge as an eloquent philosopher. He then introduces a personal note (4): he is planning the education of his unborn son and wants to show him the educational and recreational value of the Muses. The true philosopher harmonizes all things; he communes with God and with himself, but through speech also with men. Polarization of the contemplative and active life should be rejected (5): "If our human nature is a variable quality also, it will certainly weary of a life of contemplation, to the point of foregoing its greatness and of descending; for we are not mind undefiled, but mind in the soul of a living creature; and for our own sakes therefore we must seek after the more human forms of literature, providing a home for our nature when it descends" (6)[39]

The solitary philosophers, that is, the monks, fail to understand that they are men: "Now I should wish it to be a property of our nature to be always lifted up toward contemplation; but as this is obviously impracticable, I should like in turn to cling to the best and again in turn to descend to nature, there to cleave to merriment and annoint life with cheerfulness" (7).[40] Merriment was hardly a characteristic of Egyptian monastic life, whatever it became at times in Western Europe. Nor was rational argument, and that also Synesius desires: "Now what could be more allied to mind than argument, or what ferry is more suited to conduct us to mind? For whenever there is argument, there also, I assume, is mind, and if not, at all events some knowledge of inferior subjects which implies intellectual perceptions" (7).[41] Here Synesius is engaged in the *ergasia*, or working out, of epicheiremes and enthymemes, a procedure taught in the rhetorical schools, as we shall see in Chapter Two.

Synesius denies the Christian claim to a superior wis-

[39] From FitzGerald, *Essays* (supra, n. 18), I, p. 160.
[40] Ibid., p. 162.
[41] Ibid., pp. 162-63.

dom-not-of-this-world not learned by argument. Instead, he thinks, there is a path of progression leading from reason to revelation, much as seen in Plato: "To exercise the critical faculty, to compose a prose or poetical work, is not outside the province of mind. Again, to purify one's style, to find the main argument, to arrange it in order, and to recognize it when arranged by another, how can all these things be matters devoid of interest and mere toys? . . . How is a path possible where there is no gradual progress apparent; where there is no first and second stage or any order of going?" (7).[42] Those who seize upon revelation fall as rapidly as they rise, "for reason did not speed them on their way, neither did it receive them on their return." Loss of faith among the uneducated monks seems usually to have resulted from temptations of the flesh. Synesius' argument is that this is less likely to happen if reason has supported them in their search for the philosophical life: "They say of a truth that the sowing of Cadmus produced in one and the same day a crop of heavy armed men; but a crop of theologians—no legend ever recounted such an awful portent as this! For truth is not a commodity lying on the ground, or deposited by the wayside, or a quarry to be captured in a hunt. What then? Let philosophy be summoned here as an ally, and let those who are to endure all that outward journey, prodigious in length, be prepared for it by education both early and late" (9).[43]

This constitutes the main argument of the *Dio*. Brief attention is, however, given to empty sophists, with a vivid description of one of their performances:

> He has come bringing a delightful and sweet recitation to his haughty favorites, on account of whom he is in bad case, though he pretends to be in good health. He

[42] Ibid., p. 163.
[43] Ibid., p. 169.

also has bathed himself before the appointment and has gone to meet it with brilliant dress and appearance in order that he too may be a noble spectacle. He salutes the auditorium with a smile, and rejoices, but his soul is on the rack; and further he has been biting gum in order to speak clearly and tunefully. Not even the most worthy of these men would pretend that this is a matter of complete indifference to him, and that he has taken no trouble about his voice, since right in the midst of the declamation he turns and asks for his flask, which the attendant, who has long had it ready, hands over to him. Then he swallows and gargles some of it, that he may put a youthful note into his melodies. Not even after all this trouble does the unlucky fellow happen upon sympathetic auditors; rather would they like him to sing himself out, for then they would have their laugh. (11)[44]

Synesius denies that he is a teacher, for a teacher tends to become jealous of his knowledge; far better is the model of Socrates, who listened to a banal discourse by Phaedrus and entertained him with another (13). He describes how he gives readings from tragedy, comedy, and philosophy, but goes beyond the text to invent something new and add an explanation of it, to the applause of the audience. There is no "idea" of poetry in which he is not expert. "And as many 'characters' of style as exist, and however divine, in every one of my imitations of these my own personal note must be added. It is thus that the highest string, itself awaiting the rhythm, reechoes it to the melody that is being played" (16). So ends the *Dio*. It is not a literary masterpiece, like a Platonic dialogue, but it has lightness of touch and energy. Synesius is as determined in his opposition to the anti-intellectualism of the monks as he had been to the corruption of the imperial court. Nor does the work have

[44] Ibid., p. 173.

great originality of content: the philosophical and educational views are similar to those of Porphyry or Themistius. What is unusual is the insistence on applying those views to Christian preaching as it was developing in Synesius' time.

All the traditional forms of Greek oratory were practiced in later antiquity. Well aware from their education of the speeches and political activities of Demosthenes and other Attic orators, public speakers occasionally found opportunities to rise above flattery or subtly to invert it into criticism which would be understood by those with ears to hear. Effective, artistic speech continued to be regarded as the characteristic function of human beings. What is missing, in contrast to the classical period, is not oratory, sometimes powerful oratory, but open debate. The clashes which emerge are conflicts between a single orator and external means of persuasion: impressive and intimidating ceremony, threats of arrest, imprisonment, torture, or death; bribery and favoritism. Against such opponents reason and eloquence had little defence in the short run. What is remarkable, however, is that orators continued to cherish ancient Hellenic ideals and that the human spirit continued to assert some right to freedom of speech. That this claim was just, even some autocrats knew in their hearts, for it was the principle that Justinian held out to the Lazi as a symbol of Roman civilization.

Before proceeding to examine rhetorical theory and the activities of sophists and preachers in late antiquity it is important for the reader to be aware of the development in the Greek language of separate registers or levels. The phenomenon of Atticism is central to this process.

Atticism

Atticism, in its strictest form, is the principle that the only acceptable model for diction and composition in literary prose is to be found in Athenian writers of the fifth and fourth centuries.[45] This principle emerged in the first century in the works of Caecilius of Calacte, Dionysius of Halicarnassus, and others. In the writings of the critics it represented primarily a reaction against Asianism, or the lack of discipline in Hellenistic oratory, but it also reflects the view that *koinē* Greek, the lingua franca of the Hellenistic age, lacked grace and subtlety. Thus not only the bombast of Hegesias, but the simpler Greek of the Septuagint or later the New Testament fell outside the limits of literature. Atticism is a form of classicism and was motivated by a deep feeling that literary standards had declined since the classical period and that literary excellence could only be achieved by imitation of classical models.

Atticism reached an acme in the Second Century of the Christian era in the works of the Second Sophistic, including writings of Lucian and Aelius Aristides, and was perpetuated throughout later antiquity and the Byzantine period by the teaching of grammarians and rhetoricians. Standards were, however, somewhat modified. In the Fourth Century, when the Church became a public institution, many of its leaders sought to create a prose style which would be both literary and Christian, and though the fundamental touchstone remained the Attic orators, Atticism

---

[45] See Robert Browning, "The Language of Byzantine Literature," *Byzantina kai Metabyzantina I. The Past in Medieval and Modern Greek Culture*, ed. Speros Vryonis, Malibu, Calif.: Undina, 1978, pp. 103-33. Basic works include Wilhelm Schmid, *Der Atticismus in seinen Hauptvertretern von Dionysius von Halicarnass bis auf den zweiten Philostratus*, 5 vols., Stuttgart, 1887-96, reprinted Hildesheim: Olms, 1964; Eduard Norden, *Die antike Kunstprosa vom VI. Jahrhunderts vor Christus bis in die Zeit der Renaissance*, Leipzig: Teubner, 1909, esp. pp. 357-67; L. D. Reynolds and N. G. Wilson, *Scribes and Scholars. A Guide to the Transmission of Greek and Latin Literature*, Oxford: Clarendon Pr., 1974, pp. 39-47; Jaakko Frösén, "Prolegomena to a Study of the Greek Language in the First Centuries A.D.," Helsinki Dissertation, 1974.

in works on religious subjects accepted the Septuagint and the New Testament as models, as well as admitting some words from Homer and the classical poets, as did pagan writers of the period. Meanwhile, *koinē* continued its development as a spoken language with simplified syntax and new vocabulary, sometimes borrowed from Latin or other languages. To some extent in later antiquity, to a greater extent in the Byzantine period, the levels of language open to a speaker or writer constituted a form of rhetoric. He could choose among them on the basis of what he thought most appropriate to the occasion and the subject, within conventions of genre and conditioned by his own education or that of his audience. His choice was not limited to two extremes, Attic or illiterate *koinē*, but covered a spectrum ranging from the most classicizing to the most conversational. The three major stages are, first, what is called standard late Greek[46] or in the Byzantine period the *Hochstil*, the language for example of most panegyric; second, written *koinē*, the language of public administration and technical writing; and third, contemporary *koinē*, seen in some private papyri and in local saints' lives.

To assist the person seeking to speak or write the highest literary level, lexica were compiled and survive from several different periods, for example those by Pollux and Phrynicus in the Second Century, by Photius in the Ninth, and by Thomas Magister in the Fourteenth. All of the orators and writers discussed in this book are Atticists, though in varying degrees. Later Greek and Byzantine rhetoric is couched in an artificial language, deliberately and artifi-

---

[46] See Cyril Mango, *Byzantium. The Empire of New Rome*, London: Weidenfeld and Nicolson, 1980, pp. 233-55, and Ihor Ševčenko, "Levels of Style in Byzantine Prose," *Jahrbuch des oesterreichischen Byzantistik* 31, 1 (1981), 289-312. For the development of standard late Greek see M. J. Higgins, "The Renaissance of the First Century and the Origin of Standard Late Greek," *Traditio* 3 (1945), 49-100.

cially preserved, and its use was primarily restricted to an intellectual and social elite in aristocratic society and in the Church. Grammatical and rhetorical education survived in part, sometimes with official sponsorship, to preserve and transmit knowledge of this idiom.

Could a Greek audience of the Fourth, or the Fourteenth, Century understand a speech in Attic? The general answer seems to be yes, though the degree of understanding varied with the locale and the education of the audience. In Athens or Constantinople general standards of education and even of popular speech were higher than in villages of Syria or North Africa. In late antiquity and in some Byzantine periods elementary literary education was available in major cities. It was, among other things, an avenue for advancement in the Church and in the civil service. Furthermore, although vocabulary and syntax adhered to Attic models, pronunciation was allowed to develop naturally. An oration of Lysias, if read slowly to a modern Greek audience with the vowels and consonants given their modern values, would be partly comprehensible. But Lysias wrote a simple, clear Greek. The problems of comprehending Attic Greek, especially in the Byzantine period, began with the diction and were greatly compounded by a fondness for deliberate obscurity of thought, regarded as somehow achieving a higher level of reality, and a feeling that literature consisted in composing in a way that only the few could understand.

Not only did the pronunciation of the vowels and consonants follow the natural development of the language, but the accent of the syllables tended to do so as well.[47]

---

[47] The basic principle is that an even number of unaccented syllables, usually two, should intervene between the last two accented syllables of a clausula. See Paul Maas, *Greek Metre*, trans. Hugh Lloyd-Jones, Oxford: Clarendon Pr., 1962, pp. 17-18, and for more detail S. Skimina, *Etat actuel des études sur le rhythme de la prose grecque, II* (Eos Supplement xi), Paris: Les Belles Lettres, 1930.

ATTICISM

Understanding of the rules of classical quantitative prose rhythm fades in later antiquity and is replaced by a system of stress accent which resembles the *cursus* of the Latin West. Libanius is one of the last to use the quantitative *clausulae* as practiced by Demosthenes and the other Attic orators; his contemporary Himerius, no less classicizing in many other ways, shows a preference for stress accent.

The corpus of classical and imperial Greek literature survived in large part through the Sixth Century, but it must not be assumed that it was all well known or widely read. What was probably best known was the curriculum of reading in the grammar schools: all or parts of the major poets such as Homer, Hesiod, Pindar, the tragedians, Aristophanes, Apollonius, and Theocritus, plus the historians Herodotus and Thucydides. Universal histories, such as that by Diodorus Siculus, or historical compendia were more popular than some of the original sources and in more contemporary language. In the schools of rhetoric the Attic Orators were read, especially Demosthenes, Aeschines, and Isocrates. These are the poets and orators to whom scholia were composed, attesting their school use. Aelius Aristides and later Libanius and Themistius also achieved authority as school texts. The dialogues of Plato and some works of Aristotle were systematically studied in the philosophical schools. There are occasional signs of knowledge of the *Rhetoric* of Aristotle, but it was not widely studied. Dionysius of Halicarnassus and Hermogenes are the major authorities for rhetorical theory in later antiquity. Outside the schools, Plutarch, Lucian, and the Greek novelists continued to have readership. With the chaos of the later Sixth and early Seventh Centuries, including the closing of most schools and libraries, a great deal of classical literature was irretrievably lost, but some works made their way into monastic libraries where they were found in the classical renaissances of the Ninth, Tenth, and later centuries.

SECULAR SPEECH IN LATER ANTIQUITY

Scholars interested in other aspects of late antiquity often reveal considerable hostility to its rhetoric: they view epideictic oratory as empty and tiresome; they resent the tendency of historians, of whom Agathias is a good example, to cast everything into classical style at the expense of historical veracity; they are irritated by the habit of orators and writers in almost all genres of preferring the general to the specific. This convention, which begins in the empire and continues strong throughout the Byzantine period, prefers allusion to documentation, and masks contemporary life in classical vocabulary and nomenclature. It seems to reflect a distaste for the age in which the writers themselves lived and an attempt to view events in a more philosophical way which will identify them with conditions of the glorious past. The world was growing old and tired and both classicism and Christianity struggled to hold on to values which once were more fully experienced. But critics who view the rhetoric of later antiquity with distaste are doing themselves a disservice; they are refusing to accept the age on its own terms.

Viewed in its own terms, the rhetoric of later antiquity is a remarkable art form, demanding and subtle and offering opportunities for artistic creation. Gregory of Nazianzus and Synesius of Cyrene are the greatest Greek orators since Demosthenes and have not since been surpassed. Himerius practiced a type of literary composition which rivals that of Pindar and the lyric poets, however bizarre it may seem to a modern reader. The speeches of Eusebius and Themistius laid the foundation for the political theory of the next millennium; the preaching of the Cappadocian Fathers and John Chrysostom developed the philosophical basis of Christian doctrine to a high level of sophistication. The subject matter of the rhetoric of later antiquity is the public exposition of the three greatest causes of the age: the preservation, transmission, and survival of Hellenism; the reinforcement of the unity of the state around the person of the emperor and his loyal subordinates; the cause of Christianity, both against pagans and within Christian sects in their strife to establish orthodoxy. Finally, the clash between rational rhetoric and barbaric intimidation is an edifying if somber chapter in intellectual history.

CHAPTER TWO

Later Greek Rhetorical Theory

Later Greek rhetorical theory differs from that of the classical period, as seen in Aristotle or the *Rhetorica ad Alexandrum*, in several ways. Most evident is the great attention it gives to *stasis* theory, a concept originally formulated by Hermagoras in the second century though derived from Aristotelian roots (*Rhetoric* 1.1358b 29-33), and to the theory of the "ideas" of style, which represent a restatement of the Aristotelian and Theophrastan "virtues" of style in terms of different "characters" or kinds. Latin rhetoricians like Cicero and Quintilian largely assimilate stasis theory into invention, which remains the first of the five parts of rhetoric for most Western writers. Later Greek rhetoricians, however, characteristically set up stasis theory, sometimes under the rubric *noēsis*, or understanding, as the first of three *erga*, or acts of the orator.[1] This is then followed by *heurēsis* (invention) as the second of the *erga*, containing discussion of the parts of a judicial oration and of argumentation. Third comes style, or *hermēneia*, treated in terms of the "ideas." Figures of speech are a part of the theory of ideas, but were systematically treated in separate handbooks. Delivery is largely neglected and memory almost completely. This seems to reflect a change in the objectives of rhetorical study away from preparation for public address, though the practice of declamation remained vigorous in the schools.

What then was the primary objective of the study of

[1] In the Hermogenic corpus the three stages are represented by *On Staseis*, *On Invention*, and *On Ideas*. The term *noēsis* may have been first used by Minucianus, see Gloeckner, p. 28. The Latin equivalent is *intellectio*, found in Sulpicius Victor, *RLM*, p. 315. See Lausberg, section 97; Martin, p. 15.

Greek rhetoric in later antiquity? One answer is clearly skill in literary composition, but few things emerge more clearly than the role of the Neoplatonic philosophers, beginning with Porphyry, in reorganizing the discipline on a philosophical basis as an introduction to dialectic. The logical process of definition and division, fundamental for all philosophical understanding, is given a preliminary presentation to the student through stasis theory. Rhetoric thus became the teaching of clear, systematic thinking applied to judicial and deliberative issues, in which all citizens may be assumed to have some interest, and dealing with matters which can be discussed at the level of probability. The higher levels of philosophical study beckoned to the small number of students with the motivation and ability to subject themselves to its demanding and more scientific discipline; for most, education ended with rhetoric, if not with grammar.

Two other characteristics of later Greek rhetoric are its integration of the study of progymnasmata into a rhetorical education and its adoption of the commentary method. Progymnasmata are preliminary exercises in composition, undertaken before the student is ready for true *gymnasmata*, the *meletai*, or declamations of the sophist. In later antiquity progymnasmata were probably regularly begun with a grammarian, with an emphasis on simple exposition, but they were continued under a rhetorician as exercises in persuasive techniques. Even more than the theory of style, they become the bases of rhetorical composition in literature. Much of later Greek literature can be analyzed in terms of structural units such as the narrative, the *thesis*, the *synkrisis*, and the *ekphrasis*, which are used as building blocks for larger works. Use of the commentary method in teaching rhetoric is parallel to the commentaries on works of Plato and Aristotle, representing written versions of the lectures of the philosophers, and parallel also to exegesis of the Bible as practiced by Christian teachers and preachers. Works on progymnasmata by Aphthonius, and on stasis, invention, ideas, and figures by, or attributed to, Hermogenes of Tarsus became the authoritative texts for teaching rhetoric. Most writing on rhetoric after the Fourth Century takes the form of introductions (*prolegomena*) and commentary (*hypomnēmata, scholia*) to these texts.

The primary sources for what is known of later Greek rhetorical theory are manuscripts of the middle and later Byzantine period containing rhetorical *corpora*, compiled for the use of teachers and students, and made up of a treatise on progymnasmata, usually that of Aphthonius, plus all or part of the Hermogenic corpus, with prolegomena and extensive commentary material. Study of later Greek and Byzantine rhetoric requires sorting out the composition of these collections and seeking to identify the sources of the commentary material, some of which comes from the Fourth and Fifth Centuries, some from later times. Scholarship is greatly indebted to the labors of Hugo Rabe, who significantly advanced this study in the first three decades of the Twentieth Century.[2]

The following discussion will begin with the progymnasmata and then investigate the formation of the Hermogenic corpus, including the role of the Neoplatonists, turning finally to that part of the commentary material which seems to date from late antiquity and to various separate treatises on figures.

Progymnasmata

Exercises were a part of the formal study of rhetoric as early as the schools of the sophists in the fifth century.[3]

---

[2] On the manuscripts see Hugo Rabe, "Rhetoren-Corpora," *RhM* 67 (1912), 321-57.

[3] On the history of progymnasmata see Karl Barwick, "Die Gliederung der *Narratio* in der rhetorischen Theorie und ihre Bedeutung für

The first occurrence of the term *progymnasma* is in the *Rhetorica ad Alexandrum* (1436a26), but may be a later intrusion in that text. In the Christian era the term comes into regular use. It begins to occur in the text of Theon (II, p. 61 Spengel), though more frequently he uses the word *gymnasma* (e.g. II, pp. 59 and 64 Spengel). Quintilian, writing about A.D. 92, speaks of *primae exercitationes*. Priscian, adapting Hermogenes for Latin readers about A.D. 500, uses *praeexercitamina* which becomes the standard Latin term for the Middle Ages and Renaissance. Existence of at least some of the exercises can be documented from the first century. In *Rhetorica ad Herennium* (1.12) we are told that one meaning of *narratio* is an exercise intended to give ability to handle narration in speeches and that there are two forms, one based on facts, one on persons. The figure of thought *expolitio* as described in the same work (4.54-58) is reminiscent of the working out of a type of a *chria*. Paraphrase, which is a feature of grammatical progymnasmata, was one of the exercises practiced by Crassus according to Cicero in *De Oratore* (1.154).

Quintilian (2.4) describes twelve exercises. Two of these, narrative of myth and of the plot of a play, are based on material from the poets and thus, in his opinion, properly taught by grammarians, whereas historical narrative belongs to the rhetorician; refutation and confirmation may be practiced on either poetic or historical subjects and are presumably also to be shared. Quintilian says elsewhere (2.1.13) that it was common among Greeks in his time to begin studies with a rhetorician while still continuing work with a grammarian, a custom he would like to see imitated in Latin. The rest of the exercises described by Quintilian embody the distinction between subjects relating to persons and those relating to things seen in *Rhetorica ad Heren-*

die Geschichte der antiken Romans," *Hermes* 63 (1928), 283; W. Kroll in *R-E*, Suppl. VII, 1117-19; Hunger I, pp. 92-120.

nium: encomium of a person; denunciation of a person; comparison of persons; *loci communes*, which he says are denunciations of some action; *theses*, which involve a comparison of things (though he mentions also philosophical theses); chria or anecdotes about a person; and praise or blame of a law. The last is described in detail and includes a variety of treatments and subdivisions which move the student close to the arguments and techniques of actual oratory. Quintilian also notes (2.4.12) that a teacher sometimes dictates fair copies of exercises as models for his students to imitate; otherwise they are presumably assigned a problem, such as to write a comparison of two famous historical figures. Latin literature shows signs of progymnasmatic compositional blocks as early as the Augustan age. The *Heroides* of Ovid are versified *prosopopoeiae*, and the *Metamorphoses* is in a sense a stringing together of myths, *prosopopoeiae*, narratives, comparisons, and *ekphraseis*. Among Greek writers of the First Century, Dio Chrysostom probably best exemplifies the adaptation of progymnasmata to extended composition, but the *Parallel Lives* of Plutarch contain the most famous examples of *synkriseis*.

The later Greek commentators refer to many discussions of progymnasmata written in the first four or five centuries of the Christian era, but only four such works survive: those by or attributed to Theon, Hermogenes, Aphthonius, and Nicolaus. In addition there are fair copies of progymnasmata by teachers, especially ninety-six examples representing all fourteen common forms by the Fourth-Century sophist Libanius.

The treatise on progymnasmata by Theon is apparently the earliest.[4] Quintilian (3.6.48; 9.3.76) mentions a rhet-

---

[4] For the text see *Rhetores Graeci* I, pp. 137-257 Walz, and II, pp. 59-130 Spengel. On the author, composition, and history of the text see W. Stegemann in R-E VA, 2037-54, and Italo Lana, *I Progimnasmi di Elio Teone I. La storia del testo*, Turin: Università, 1959.

orician of that name who is probably to be identified with the sophist Aelius Theon, listed in the Byzantine encyclopedia *Suda* as the author of progymnasmata and works on rhetoric and grammar.[5] Similarities with Quintilian's account of the exercises tend to confirm the First-Century date.

Theon's treatise begins with a preface in which he criticizes students who undertake declamation without preliminary training and even without a liberal education. The exercises which he will describe are useful for all kinds of composition: rhetorical, historical, and poetic. For example (II, p. 60 Spengel), the writing of a history is the composition of a "system" of narrative. Each of the forms can be illustrated from literature of the classical period (II, pp. 65-66 Spengel). Thus the story told by Plato early in the *Republic* about what the aged Sophocles said when asked if he was still interested in sex is an example of a chria. Moreover (II, pp. 70-71 Spengel), progymnasmata are the foundation of every "idea" of speech; if they are properly introduced into the souls of the young, commensurate results will follow. Such statements are the basis of later Greek and Byzantine views that literary composition is an imitation of generic models of content, structure, and style. Theon claims to have added some exercises to those taught by others (II, p. 59), and his defense of the encomium as an exercise (II, p. 61), suggests that this may be a case in point, though the exercise is mentioned by Quintilian as commonly known. The preface ends by advising that all the exercises should involve reading aloud, listening to others read, and paraphrase of models, and that original composition and the argument of opposing views should come only after the student has attained facility. Quintilian notes (2.5.1-3) that assistant masters in Greek rhetorical schools

[5] The best edition of the *Suda* is by Ada Adler, Suidae *Lexicon*, 5 parts, Leipzig: Teubner, 1928-38.

of the First Century supervised students' reading of historians and orators, whereas in Latin schools students were rushed into declamation at an early stage.

In the preface (II, pp. 64-65 Spengel) Theon recommends that the exercises be undertaken in the order chria, myth, narrative, followed by ecphrasis, prosopopoeia, encomion, and synkrisis. In the preliminary stage, refutation (*anaskeuē*) and confirmation (*kataskeuē*) should be avoided in the treatment of the exercises, but later the student can be asked to attempt a refutation of a chria, a fable, or a narrative, as well as to argue or refute a thesis and to argue for or against a law. In the body of the text, however, this principle is not followed out, and Theon begins with the myth, including the Aesopic fable, followed by the narrative, as do later writers. The general sequence from the more simple to the more difficult remains, but it is possible that Theon took over much of his material from an earlier writer. The description of the earlier exercises is more extensive than that of the later, which may suggest that he has worked over this material more carefully. Unlike later teachers, Theon does not divide up the exercises among judicial, deliberative, and epideictic forms and does not identify an exercise with a particular part of the oration. Theon's work was not especially well known in later times: there appear to be only four manuscripts, with relatively little scholia, and his name is rarely mentioned by later writers.

The second surviving work on progymnasmata is that attributed to Hermogenes, who is known to have had a brief, meteoric career as a sophist in Asia Minor in the reign of Marcus Aurelius.[6] Its authenticity, however, is

[6] For the text see Hermogenis *Opera*, ed. Hugo Rabe, Leipzig: Teubner, 1913; for English translation Charles S. Baldwin, *Medieval Rhetoric and Poetic*, New York: Macmillan, 1928, pp. 23-38; for Priscian's Latin version see *RLM*, pp. 551-60; for English translation of the latter

doubtful, despite the attribution found in eleven or more Greek manuscripts.[7] A scholiast (VII, p. 511 Walz) says that it is by Libanius, not by Hermogenes, and the manuscripts of Priscian's Latin version of the work attribute it to Hermogenes "or Libanius." There are no cross-references to it in genuine works of Hermogenes, despite his habit of cross-reference, and there are some differences from his terminology and style elsewhere. The attribution to Libanius has no additional grounds for support. Possibly the work was at some time added, for the convenience of a teacher or his students, to a manuscript of Hermogenes and thus acquired his well known authority. The sole source of information about Hermogenes seems to have been the passage in Philostratus' *Lives of the Sophists* (2.7), which mentions none of his writings, for Philostratus had almost no interest in rhetorical theory.

The Hermogenic treatise lacks a preface and gives a very brief account, with little suggestion for treatment or illustration, of thirteen exercises. The order is approximately that found in our texts of Theon, but *gnōmē*, or saying, in Theon a variant of chria, is given separate treatment, as are refutation and confirmation, which in Theon are features of the treatment of other exercises; there is no discussion of invective; prosopopoeia is called ethopoeia. The work is apparently a handbook for teachers who found earlier accounts, such as Theon's, beyond the ability of their students or themselves.

The third and most important of the handbooks of progymnasmata is that by Aphthonius of Antioch, of which there are numerous manuscripts. Aphthonius is known to

---

by Joseph M. Miller see *Readings in Medieval Rhetoric*, ed. Miller, Michael H. Prosser, and Thomas W. Benson, Bloomington: Indiana Univ. Pr., 1973, pp. 52-68.

[7] See Rabe's edition (supra, n. 6), pp. iv-vi, and Radermacher in *R-E* VIII, 877.

have been a student of Libanius, and thus to have lived in the second half of the Fourth Century, and he also is said to have written a commentary on Hermogenes, but the latter was probably limited to the only commonly known work, *On Staseis*.[8] Aphthonius defines fourteen exercises, subdivides them into subordinate forms, and gives a complete example of each. The exercises are the same as in the Hermogenic work and in the same order, except that *psogos*, or invective, is reintroduced. The simplicity of the discussion, the clarity of the divisions, and the inclusion of examples, as is expressly noted in later prolegomena to the treatise, won for Aphthonius the authoritative place he had in Byzantine times.[9] An extensive body of commentary, some of it published in Walz's *Rhetores Graeci*, was built up over the next millenniuim, and the treatise was translated into Latin by Rudolph Agricola in the late Fifteenth Century, making it available for wide use in the schools of Western Europe.

Because progymnasmata are basic to rhetorical and literary composition in later Greek and will often be mentioned in the following chapters, it is desirable here to set out briefly the exercises as described by Aphthonius.

1. *Mythos*, or fable: "a composition which is false, but gives the semblance of truth" (II, p. 21 Spengel). There are Sybaritic, Cilician, and Cyprian types, but all are eclipsed by that associated with Aesop. Aphthonius distinguishes three forms: rational, involving a human being; ethical, involving an animal; mixed, involving both. A moral prefixed to a myth is a *promythion*; a moral affixed to the end

---

[8] See Libanius, *Epistle* 11 (p. 189 Foerster); *Suda* s.v. "Aphthonius"; Hugo Rabe, "De Aphthonii Vita et Scriptis," in Aphthonii *Progymnasmata*, Leipzig: Teubner, 1926, pp. xxii-xxv; *R-E* I, 2797-2800. The text of Aphthonius is also to be found in Walz I, pp. 55-120 and Spengel II, pp. 21-56.
[9] See *PS*, p. 79.

is an *epimythion*. The exercise took the form of assigning the student to write a simple fable in imitation of Aesop. (See Lausberg I, pp. 533-34.)

2. *Diēgēma*, or narrative: "a composition giving an account of an action which has happened or as though it had happened" (II, p. 22 Spengel). *Diēgēsis* is the narration of a speech and ordinarily sets forth a series of actions; a *diēgēma* describes only one. Its divisions are dramatic, or fictitious; historical, based on "ancient report"; and political, "which orators use in their contests." The constituent elements are six: agent, action, time, place, manner, and cause. These are derived from Aristotle's categories. The virtues of narrative are four: clarity, brevity, persuasiveness, and purity of language. These are probably ultimately derived from Isocrates (see Quintilian 4.2.31). (See Lausberg I, pp. 534-36.)

3. *Chreia*, or anecdote: "a brief reminiscence referring to some person in a pithy form" (II, pp. 23-25 Spengel). Called chria because it is *chreiōdēs*, useful. Divisions are *logikē*, reporting a saying; *praktikē*, reporting an edifying action; *miktē*, reporting a saying and an action. Students were not expected to invent a chria; they were given a saying or a description of an action by a famous person and expected to work it out (*ergasia*) by writing a paragraph expanding and developing the meaning with the following headings: praise of the chria; paraphrase; statement of the cause; example of the meaning; contrast and comparison; testimony of others; epilogue. The chria selected as an example by Aphthonis is "Isocrates said that the root of education is bitter, but its fruit is sweet." (See Lausberg I, pp. 536-40.)

4. *Gnōmē*, or saying: "a summary declarative statement, recommending or condemning something" (II, pp. 25-27 Spengel). The divisions are protreptic, apotreptic, declarative, simple, and compound; headings are the same as

those of the chria. The *gnōmē* worked out as an example is an adaptation of a couplet from Theognis (1.175-76): "The victim of poverty should throw himself into the yawning sea or, my Cyrnis, down from sheer cliffs." (See Lausberg I, p. 540.)

5. *Anaskeuē*: "the refutation of any matter at hand" (II, pp. 27-30 Spengel). Divisions are attack on those who hold the opposite view, followed by exposition using the following headings: unclear and improbable; impossible, illogical, and unsuitable; inexpedient. The exercise, as Theon had stressed, can be applied to myth, narrative, or chria. Aphthonius' example is a refutation of the story of Daphne and Apollo as improbable. (See Lausberg I, pp. 540-41.)

6. *Kataskeuē*, "the confirmation of any matter at hand" (II, pp. 30-32 Spengel). Again the subject must be neither self-evident nor impossible, but the treatment is exactly the opposite of *anaskeuē*. Aphthonius' example is "the story of Daphne is probable." It should be noted that refutation comes before confirmation in the progymnasmata; this is probably because it is easier for a student to attack something which has been argued by another than to undertake an independent proof.

7. *Koinos topos*, or commonplace: "a composition which amplifies inherent evils" (II, pp. 32-35 Spengel). So called because the statement fits types—for example, tyrants—rather than specific individuals, as does invective. In Theon and the Hermogenic treatise the exercise is defined as amplification of either vice or virtue, but in the latter work it is already clear that it is primarily applied to attacking vice, and this remains true in the later history of the exercise. Aphthonius says that it is like a second speech in a trial and has no proemium, except when one is added in the schools for practice. No divisions are specified. The headings for *ergasia* are: contradiction or exposition to sharpen opposition; synkrisis, comparing something better to what

is attacked; gnomic heading, attacking the motivation of the doer, followed by *parekbasis*, or digression, castigating his past life; rejection of pity; and what are called *telika kephalaia*, "final headings" or "headings of purpose." These are common to some other progymnasmata and are also the basis of argument in deliberative oratory. They include legality, justice, expediency, practicability, honor, and result. (See Lausberg I, p. 204 and pp. 541-42.)

8. *Enkōmion*, or praise: "a composition expository of attendant excellences" (II, pp. 35-40 Spengel). A hymn celebrates gods and is brief, an encomium celebrates mortals and is worked out in accordance with art. Subjects are persons, things (like justice), times (like spring), places, animals, and growing things (like olive trees); they may be common, for example the Athenians, or individuals. Headings are: proemium; *genos*, divided into nation, city, ancestors, and parents; upbringing, divided into habits, art, and laws; deeds, divided into those relating to soul, body, and fortune; synkrisis, or favorable comparison with another; epilogue, for example a prayer. Aphthonius supplies an encomium of Thucydides, comparing him to Herodotus, and an encomium of wisdom.[10] The progymnasmatic encomium is the basis of many epideictic forms practiced by the later sophists and described by Menander Rhetor in the treatises to be noted below. (See Lausberg I, p. 542.)

9. *Psogos*, or invective: "a composition expository of attendant evils" (II, pp. 40-42 Spengel). Aphthonius says that it differs from the *koinos topos* in that it does not seek punishment, but in fact it differs more significantly in attacking some person or thing specifically named, rather than a type. Headings are identical with those of encomium. The example given is an invective against Philip of Macedon.

[10] See Th. Payr, "Enkomion," in *Reallexikon für Antike und Christentum* V, Stuttgart: Hiersemann, 1960, 332-43.

10. *Synkrisis*, or comparison: "a comparative composition, setting something greater or equal side by side with the subject" (II, pp. 42-44 Spengel). In general, it may be viewed as a double encomium or an encomium coupled with an invective, and its subjects are similar to those of the two preceding exercises. Its effect is *deinos*, or forceful, a word borrowed from the theory of style. The subjects compared should not be dealt with separately, but the student should consider both, heading by heading. Aphthonius' example is a synkrisis of Achilles and Hector. (See Lausberg, I, pp. 542-43.)

11. *Ēthopoeia*, or personification: "an imitation of the ethos of a person chosen to be portrayed" (II, pp. 44-46 Spengel). Aphthonius uses ethos in the Aristotelian sense of the character of a speaker, including presentation of moral choice embodied in words and arguments. "Imitation" means that the exercise takes a dramatic form in which one or more characters is imagined as speaking. There are three forms: *eidolopoeia* is a speech attributed to the ghost of a known person; in *prosōpopoeia*, used by Theon for the exercise as a whole, the character of the speaker is a creation of the writer, for example a mythological figure; in *ēthopoeia* narrowly defined, the third form, the speaker has an historical or traditional character, but is imagined in some situation where the writer has freedom in imagining what he would say. Aphthonius' example is a speech for Heracles in reply to Eurystheus when the latter imposes the labors on him. The divisions of ethopoeia as a whole are pathetical, ethical, and mixed. The "characters" of style to be applied to ethopoeia are, according to Aphthonius, clarity, conciseness, floridity, lack of finish, and absence of figures; this terminology is not that of Hermogenes on style, indicating that his work was not yet the standard authority. Instead of headings there are to be divisions into past, present, and future time. (See Lausberg I, p. 543.)

12. *Ekphrasis*, or description: "a descriptive composition bringing the subject clearly before the eyes" (II, pp. 46-49 Spengel). The subjects, like those of encomium, may be persons, actions, times, places, animals, and growing things. The description should be complete, of a person for example from head to foot, of actions from before the start to the results. Divisions are simple and compound. The "character" of style should be *aneimenos*, relaxed, but ornamented with a variety of figures. Aphthonius' example is an ecphrasis of the acropolis of Alexandria.[11]

13. *Thesis*, or argument: "a logical examination of a subject under investigation (II pp. 49-53 Spengel). The forms are political and theoretical. Political theses include not only such matters as Should the city be walled? but also social questions, Should one marry? Theoretical theses are those which cannot be put into practice, but are debated: for example, Is the heaven spherical? Hypotheses add attendant circumstances of person, action, cause, "and the rest"; for example, "The Lacedaimonians deliberate whether to wall Sparta as the Persians approach." Aphthonius seems to assume that thesis is a progymnasma, hypothesis a *meletē*, or declamation. The divisions of thesis are *ephodos*, or approach, used instead of a proemium, followed by the "final" headings which were noted under *koinos topos*. His example is a treatment of the thesis Should one marry? It includes not only defense of the thesis, but an antithesis and a *lysis*, or solution. (See Lausberg I, pp. 544-46.)

14. *Nomou eisphora*, or introduction of a law (II, pp. 46-51 Spengel). This exercise Aphthonius calls a gymnasma rather than progymnasma, and it has many of the characteristics of an hypothesis, though the principals are not necessarily named. It takes two forms, *synēgoria*, or

[11] See Glanville Downey, "Ekphrasis," in *Reallexikon* (supra, n. 10), IV, 1959, 922-43; Lausberg I, p. 544; Henry Maguire, *Art and Eloquence in Byzantium*, Princeton Univ. Pr., 1981, pp. 22-52.

advocacy of a proposed law, and *katēgoria*, or opposition. The headings are constitutionality, justice, expediency, and practicability. The thesis for or against the law is to be stated, then the counterargument, then the headings are to be listed. The example furnished is a speech opposing a law requiring an adulterer, taken in the act, to be killed. From such an exercise it would be an easy step to those meletai on imaginary court cases involving husbands, wives, and adultery which are frequently cited in the Hermogenic corpus. (See Lausberg I, p. 546.)

The characteristics of Aphtonius' work as a whole may be summarized as rigorous attention to definition (*horos*) and division (*diaeresis*), some interest in etymology and in relating the exercises to characters of style. No attempt is made to coordinate the exercises with the theory of three species of rhetoric or the parts of the oration, as later rhetoricians like to do.

The fourth treatise on progymnasmata is by Nicolaus, who was born in Myra in Lycia in 410 or 412, studied in Athens with the Neoplatonists Plutarch and Proclus and the sophist Lachares, and taught rhetoric in Constantinople in the reign of Leo (457-474). He is said to have published declamations and an art of rhetoric as well as his handbook of progymnasmata.[12] In the latter treatise he seems to draw on Theon and the Hermogenic work, but not on Aphthonius.[13] References to Plato and Porphyry attest his interest in rhetoric as understood by the Neoplatonists. His work survives in at least eight manuscripts and is referred to by Byzantine rhetoricians including John of Sardis, John Doxapatres, and Maximus Planudes.

Nicolaus' treatise is the most thoughtful and mature of the four. Its preface relates the subject to the study of rhet-

---

[12] See Nicolai Sophistae, *Progymnasmata*, ed. Joseph Felten, Leipzig: Teubner, 1913, pp. xxi-xxvii, and W. Stegemann in R-E XVII, 424-57.
[13] See Felten (supra, n. 12), pp. xxvii-xxxiii.

oric as a whole; the exercises are fully described and well illustrated, even though complete examples are not supplied; definition and division are rigorous, as befits a student of the Neoplatonists, but alternative views are mentioned without the malice found in some academic rhetoric. As a leading rhetorician in the capital, Nicolaus doubtless attracted some of the best students and supplied them with a demanding course. He assumes in his students a good knowledge of Greek literature: they will understand references to passages in Demosthenes, Isocrates, Homer, Plato, and Aelius Aristides.

In the preface Nicolaus explains that his work is a synthesis of earlier views, sometimes taken over word for word. He then continues with an introduction to the study of rhetoric which is analogous to the prolegomena being composed by others in his time, though it does not use the common structure of four or ten questions. He says that man is by nature a reasoning and speaking animal, but that the historical process of conceptualization of rhetoric was slow and the subject remains difficult for the young. There is thus a need for simple introductory exercises which practice the student "in each of the parts separately" before declamation is undertaken.

Nicolaus claims that progymnasmata perform various functions for the student: some exercise us in judicial rhetoric, some in deliberative, some in panegyric; some teach the use of *prooemia*, some of *diēgēsis*, others of the *agōnes* in *antithesis* and *lysis*, some the use of the epilogue. This principle is applied in the discussion of the individual exercises. In each case, Nicolaus defines the exercise, gives its divisions, identifies the species of rhetoric and part of the oration to which it applies, and ends by commenting on the appropriate style. Myth, for example, is deliberative and contributes to teaching the composition of the narration; chria and *gnōmē* are also deliberative, but may be applied to any part of a speech. *Anaskeuē* and *kataskeuē* are of course judicial. Encomium and psogos as a whole are panegyrical, but may be inserted into judicial or deliberative speeches.

At the end of the preface Nicolaus asks what rhetoric is and adopts a definition which he attributes to Diodorus: "a faculty of invention and orderly expression of the available means of persuasion in every discourse."[14] The definition is very similar to that of Aristotle (*Rhetoric* 1.1355b25-26). The duty (*ergon*) of the orator is, on every subject, to consider (*noēsai*) what should be said, to arrange (*oikonomēsai*) the material, and to express it (*hermēneusai*) in the best way. The goal of rhetoric is not to persuade, but to speak persuasively. This too is Aristotelian.

Nicolaus' discussion of encomium (pp. 47-53 Felten) is especially interesting because it reveals how the various kinds of panegyric were brought into the systematic teaching of rhetoric. From the works of the fourth-century sophist Himerius and others we know that these forms were an important activity in the sophistic schools, but the Hermogenic corpus fails to discuss them. They are discussed in detail in the two treatises attributed to Menander of Laodicea.[15]

At the beginning of his account of encomium Nicolaus says that the subject is complex, "for *epibatērioi*, *prosphōnētikoi*, *epithalamioi*, *epitaphioi*, prose hymns to the gods, and all speeches of good omen fall under this species. It is necessary, therefore, to say at this point as much as is appropriate for beginners" (p. 47 Felten). *Epibatērioi* are

[14] Felten altered the Diodorus of the MS to Theodorus on the basis of Quintilian 2.15.16, but modern editors (Winterbottom; Cousin) prefer Eudorus there. The definition cannot be that of Theodorus of Gadara, for which see Quintilian 2.15.21.

[15] See *Menander Rhetor*, ed. with translation and commentary by D. A. Russell and N. G. Wilson, Oxford: Clarendon Pr., 1981, and J. Soffel, *Die Regeln für die Leichenrede*, Meisenheim: Hain, 1974.

speeches to or by one who is disembarking; *prosphōnētikoi* are speeches of welcome, but include occasional addresses to important persons; *epithalamioi* are speeches at weddings; *epitaphioi* at funerals or memorial services. Both *epithalamioi* and hymns were of course originally poetic forms, but in the empire have made the transition to poetic prose. Subsequently (p. 49 Felten), Nicolaus mentions additional subspecies including the *sminthiakos*, or speech at a festival of Apollo, the *panathēnaikos*, and other speeches at festivals. Menander discusses about thirty different forms, to most of which he gives technical titles, but many are very similar to each other. Among the more important which he mentions and Nicolaus does not are encomia of places, *laliai*, which may deal with almost any subject but celebrate it in a personal, sometimes conversational style lacking the structure of other forms, and monodies, which are laments for the death of a person or the destruction of a city. Menander's account is chiefly concerned with listing the commonplaces appropriate for each form and indicating the order in which they should be arranged. There appears to be only one reference to the work in late antiquity, and that is in a private letter (Papyrus Berolinensis 21849); it is somewhat better known in the Byzantine period. At least eleven manuscripts contain all or part of the work, with the material arranged in varying sequences, and there are occasional references to it as an authority on the part of Byzantine rhetoricians.[16]

In the Hellenistic and early imperial period occasions for epideictic oratory gradually increased and sophists were often asked to speak. Some of them used the progymnasmatic exercises as an opportunity to give their students instructions in the technique. An early stage in the process can be seen in Theon. In his preface (II, p. 61 Spengel)

[16] See Russell and Wilson (supra, n. 15), pp. xxxiv-xxxvi.

he draws attention to the fact that he has included the encomium among the forms of progymnasmata, as though earlier discussions had not done so; previously (p. 59) he has claimed that he will add some new forms. In the chapter on encomia (pp. 109-12) he mentions *epitaphioi* and hymns, and he outlines the basic system of treating the goods of mind, body, and estate and the deeds of the subject throughout his career, which are the structural features of most panegyric. In the chapter on prosopopoeia (pp. 115-18) he treats some additional epideictic forms, including the protreptic and the speech of consolation. A handbook wrongly attributed to Aelius Aristides, but probably later than Theon and anterior to Menander,[17] gives a more detailed account of epideictic forms such as might have developed out of the progymnasmata. No canonical list of the forms, such as we find in the case of progymnasmata, was developed in late antiquity; sophists continually experimented with new adaptations, some of which were taken over into Christian preaching. In contrast to judicial oratory, the various epideictic forms remained rather on the fringe of formal rhetorical study. They never were given the attention accorded to declamation, and advanced students practiced them chiefly on extracurricular occasions as will become clear when we consider the school of Himerius.

A second subject on the fringe of formal education in later antiquity is letter writing.[18] The Aphthonian-Hermogenic corpus did not discuss it, but Theon (II, p. 115 Spen-

[17] Translation in ibid., pp. 362-81.

[18] The texts discussed below are translated and discussed by Abraham J. Malherbe, "Ancient Epistolary Theory," *Ohio Journal of Religious Studies* 5, 2 (1977), 3-77. See also R-E Suppl. v, 185-220; Heikki Koskenniemi, *Studien zur Idee und Phraseologie des griechischen Briefs bis 400 n. Chr.*, Helsinki: Akateeminen Kirjahauppa, 1956; Klaus Thraede, *Grundzüge griechisch-römischer Brieftopik* (Zetemata XXVIII) Munich: Beck, 1970; Hunger I, pp. 199-213.

gel) and Nicolaus (pp. 66-67 Felten) refer to it briefly. The latter notes that ethopoeia is a useful exercise for all three species of oratory and for "the epistulary character," since letters should portray the mind of the sender and the recipient. The writing of letters, of course, represents a major application of rhetoric in later antiquity. We have numerous collections, often showing great art,[19] and insofar as grammar and rhetoric were studies preparatory for careers in the civil service, study of letter writing had great utility, for the writing of letters was the major activity of the bureaucracy, as is clear from the descriptions in John Lydus.

The only rhetorical treatise to give serious attention to letters is the Hellenistic work *On Style* (sections 223-25) attributed to Demetrius, but references in Cicero (e.g., *Ad Familiares* 2.4.1) imply the existence of a theory of letters which included the identification of a variety of species. A short treatise entitled *Typoi Epistolikoi*, perhaps of Hellenistic date, classifies fourteen kinds of letters: friendly, commendatory, blaming, reproachful, etc. Collections of model letters were made, of which fragments are preserved in papyrus, and it is likely that the technique was largely learned by imitation.

From the later empire there survives a short treatise on *Epistulary Characters* which gives some insight into what Nicolaus meant by that term.[20] It is attributed by some manuscripts to Proclus, by others to Libanius, suggesting that it was regarded as a probable product of a rhetorical school. Forty-one types of letters are defined, followed by some general remarks. The style of a letter should be appropriate and aim at clarity, but it should be moderately concise and may employ archaism. References to history,

---

[19] See *Epistolographi Graeci*, ed. R. Hercher, Paris, 1873; reprinted Amsterdam: Hakkert, 1965.

[20] For the text see Libani *Opera*, ed. R. Foerster, Leipzig: Teubner, 1927, IX, pp. 27-44; Malherbe (supra, n. 18), pp. 62-77.

fable, and the classics will lend charm. Philosophy is acceptable, but should not be dialectically argued. Then follow examples of the forty-one forms, each limited to a few sentences. These are thus not really models of the different types, but germs of thought which could be developed by amplification. The examples often constitute an enthymeme: for example, in the letter of blame (53), "You did not act well when you wronged those who did good to you. For by insulting your benefactors you provided an example of evil to others."

Two passages in important writers of the empire comment briefly on letter writing and show the influence of rhetorical theory. The first letter of Philostratus (II, pp. 257-58 Kayser), author of the *Lives of the Sophists*, praises the style of letters by Dio Chrysostom, Herodes Atticus, and certain other Greeks and notes that the "idea" of a letter, the Hermogenic term for style, should be more Attic than conversation, but more colloquial than the literary language. The writing should be graceful and clear. Periodic sentences are acceptable in a short letter, but in a longer one a series of periods becomes "agonistic," that is, rhetorically contentious, and a period should only be used at the end. Epistle 51 of Gregory of Nazianzus says that letters should be concise, clear, and charming. The style should be *lalikon*, that is, in the easy, conversational manner of the lalia. *Gnōmai*, proverbs, and sayings are appropriate and a few tropes, but antithesis, parisosis, or isocolon are not. Gregory excuses himself from going into more detail; Nicoboulos, to whom he writes, can learn about letters from "those skilled in such things." Apparently Nicoboulos' formal education had not included instruction in writing letters; we may guess that those skilled in such things are persons with experience in the civil service who offered "business" courses including such matters as letter writing and stenography for those seeking positions or advancement. As in the case of the epideictic forms, the standard rhetorical curriculum, represented for us by the Aphthonian-Hermogenic corpus, did not devote time to letter writing. The tradition continues throughout the Byzatine period: we find collections of letters, which might be used as models, and comments in letters on appropriate treatment, but only occasional references to letters on the part of rhetoricians.[21]

Stasis

Progymnasmata introduced the student to simple argumentation, primarily in deliberative or epideictic contexts, as well as providing him with compositional skills in the arrangement of topics and in style. In order to succeed in judicial declamation, the major exercise of the rhetorical schools, it was regarded as essential that the student understand stasis theory. The theory had practical application in the courts of state and Church, but it also came to be regarded by the Neoplatonists as a useful introduction to dialectic and philosophical method. Except for Plotinus, the Neoplatonists characteristically taught by commenting on authoritative texts. For dialectic the authorities were the logical works of Aristotle, canonized as the *Organon*. Although the *Rhetoric* came to be regarded as a part of the *Organon* and was read to some extent by the philosophers, no commentaries to it appear to have been written in late antiquity. The primary reason for this is that it does not discuss stasis theory and thus did not provide for basic instruction in the part of rhetoric which had emerged as central to the discipline. The need for an authoritative text on which teachers could base their instruction and on which commentaries could be written was ultimately filled by the treatise of Hermogenes *On Staseis*, composed in the Sec-

---

[21] See Krumbacher, pp. 452-53, and Hunger I, pp. 201-39.

ond Century of the Christian era. It becomes the fundamental rhetorical textbook from the Fifth to the Fifteenth Century. Rabe's edition cites over a hundred manuscripts, and there are doubtless more. The choice of Hermogenes, over many possible alternatives, seems to have resulted from the dialectical qualities of his work: the formal validity, systematic method, and clarity of his treatment.

An extensive survey of the earlier history of stasis theory is probably not necessary here, though certain features of it may be briefly noted.[22] Stasis is the basic issue of a dispute and results from the stance taken by the antagonists. It may be most clearly illustrated in a case at law. A prosecutor makes an allegation of wrongdoing. The defendant may be able to deny that he committed the act alleged. If so, he is employing stasis of fact, known as *stochasmos*. Or he may admit performing the act but deny that it is illegal, stasis of definition or *horos*. Or he may admit both act and illegality and claim that he was justified in the circumstances or should at least be forgiven, *poiotēs* or stasis of quality. A different kind of defense can be offered by claiming that the tribunal or assembly has no authority over the issue, *metalēpsis* or stasis of transference. The situation is complicated by the fact that in many cases the law is not entirely clear: a theory of stasis needs somehow to integrate questions of letter and intent, ambiguity, or conflict of laws into its system.

Hermagoras of Temnos, writing about 150 B.C., is credited with the first statement of stasis theory.[23] His work has not survived, but can be reconstructed in some detail from later references, especially the presentation of the subject

---

[22] See APG, pp. 303-19; O.A.L. Dieter, "Stasis," *Speech Monographs* 17 (1950), 345-69; Ray Nadeau, "Classical Systems of Stases in Greek: Hermagoras to Hermogenes," GRBS (1959), 51-73; Martin, pp. 28-52.

[23] See Dieter Matthes, "Hermagoras von Temnos, 1904-1955," *Lustrum* 3 (1958), 58-214.

in Cicero's *De Inventione* and the *Rhetorica ad Herennium*, composed two generations later. Hermagoras was probably disqualified from becoming the permanent authority on the subject because of his crabbed style and because his successors found so many aspects of his treatment confusing or unsatisfactory. Although he seems to have constructed his system in part out of Aristotle's categories and topics and aspects of Stoic dialectic, his work may be regarded as part of the effort in his time to assert the claims of rhetoric over philosophy as the core of the liberal arts.

It is clear that by the first century, teachers of rhetoric regarded the exposition of stasis theory as an essential part of their task. Since the determination of the issue was fundamental to the whole treatment of the case, they generally placed it at the beginning of their course, anticipating the later Greek tradition of separating stasis theory out as a part of rhetoric prior to invention. The first step in this direction can be seen in Cicero, whose teacher had divided *inventio* into two subjects, *materia* which includes stasis, and *partes*, or the parts of the oration (*De Inventione* 1.9).

The history of the later Greek treatment of stasis theory may be said to begin in the mid-Second Century with P. Hordeonius Lollianus, the first holder of the public chair of rhetoric in Athens.[24] According to Philostratus (*Lives of the Sophists* 1.23, p. 527 Kayser) he both declaimed and taught rhetorical theory, something which the more flamboyant representatives of the Second Sophistic seem to have avoided. His published works apparently consisted of separate treatises on stasis and the parts of the oration. He distinguished five separate kinds of stasis, but we do not know what ones: perhaps fact, definition, quality, transference, and the legal headings. His subheadings were not so numerous as in later Greek writers (Sopatros v, p. 174

[24] See Gloeckner, pp. 52-53.

Walz). His contemporary Hermagoras, at least the third rhetorician to bear that name, added two more categories, *pragmatikē* and *dikaiologia*, which result from dividing subjects for declamation between deliberative and judicial problems, respectively.[25]

More influential was the work of Minucianus.[26] He was a political orator in Athens in the time of Antoninus Pius and left a collection of speeches. He was not regarded as a sophist, for he is not discussed by Philostratus, but he may have taught rhetoric privately, since he wrote a work on progymnasmata, a commentary on Demosthenes, and an *Art of Rhetoric* in two books, perhaps limited to the subjects of stasis and invention. There are many later references to his discussion of stasis. Hermogenes, living a generation later, never mentions him by name, but is clearly opposing his views on many subjects as confused and irrelevant. Although their differences may reflect some antagonism on the part of a young sophist of Asia Minor toward a practicing politician of the previous generation in Athens whose family continued to be influential and whose writings perhaps seemed overvalued as a result, it would be a mistake to think of Hermogenes and Minucianus as the leaders of two opposed schools of thought.[27] There were many rival writers on stasis and many complex interrelationships, and the differences between Minucianus and Hermogenes are not great philosophical differences about the nature and functions of rhetoric, but matters of detail. Hermogenes' major headings of stasis were basically the same as Minucianus'. Although Hermogenes separates *paragraphē* and *metalēpsis* into two headings, whereas Minucianus had combined them in one, it seems clear

[25] Ibid., pp. 55-56.
[26] Ibid., pp. 22-50, and W. Stegemann in *R-E* xv, 1975-76.
[27] See Kustas, pp. 5-10. For specific differences between the theories of Minucianus and Hermogenes see Gloeckner, pp. 26-44.

that Minucianus had in practice treated the two separately (Syrianus II, p. 55 Rabe). Hermogenes begins his discussion of several staseis with *probolē*, which Minucianus did not do. Minucianus, in common with other rhetoricians, thought that stasis was determined by the defendant; Hermogenes, like Quintilian (3.6.15-16), thinks it is sometimes the defendant, sometimes the plaintiff, depending on who first challenges the claim of the other. Hermogenes thought that a problem involved both persons and actions, Minucianus that there could be problems involving only one of these. Minucianus identified six categories of persons, Hermogenes seven. Perhaps more important, Minucianus identified stasis as the first *erga* of the orator. Hermogenes does not disagree, but refrains from any discussion of divisions of rhetoric prior to the headings of stasis. His silence offered the Neoplatonists an opportunity to write their own prolegomena to the subject.

Hermogenes' treatise seems to have been little appreciated in the two centuries following its publication, at least outside of Asia Minor. It was the work of Minucianus which the Neoplatonists first sought to use as the authority to link rhetoric with dialectic in an educational system. The key figure is Porphyry (c. 232–c. 305), the biographer of Plotinus and author of grammatical, literary, and historical works, commentaries on Plato and Aristotle, and the *Eisagōgē* or introduction to logic which became the basic textbook of dialectic in both Latin and Greek for over a millennium.[28] Porphyry was born in Palestine and went to Athens as a young man to study with the famous rhetorician Casius Longinus. Eunapius (*Lives of the Philosophers* p. 456) calls Longinus a "living library" and "walking mu-

---

[28] See Porphyry the Phoenician, *Isagoge*, translation, introduction, and notes by Edward W. Warren, Toronto: Pontifical Institute of Medieval Studies, 1975, and L. G. Westerink, *Lectures on Porphyry's Isagoge*, Amsterdam: North-Holland, 1967.

seum" and says that Porphyry studied grammar and rhetoric with him before moving on to Rome in 263, where he met Plotinus. An *Art of Rhetoric* by Longinus is partially preserved:[29] what survives begins in the middle of a discussion of argumentation in the proof of a speech and continues with discussion of the epilogue, arrangement, style, and delivery. There is no discussion of stasis. Longinus is not cited as an authority on stasis by later writers, and he may well have taught that subject out of Minucianus' handbook. In any event, Porphyry composed a commentary to Minucianus on stasis, which was frequently used by Neoplatonists down until at least the Fifth Century.[30] It was perhaps also Porphyry who began the custom of writing prolegomena to the study of rhetoric which fit the discipline into a philosophical scheme and deal with the delicate question of why rhetoric should be taken seriously, given Plato's objections to it in the *Gorgias*.[31] His interests in a comprehensive educational system are also seen in his composition of the *Eisagōgē*, and it may have been he who assembled the logical works of Aristotle into the *Organon*. Plotinus' works show no particular interest in rhetoric, though he developed an aesthetic theory. Iamblichus, the next major Neoplatonist, wrote a lost work *On the Choice of the Best Speech*, which favored the middle style and recommended Homer, Plato, and Demosthenes as models (Maximus Planudes v, p. 443 Walz), and his writings show a familiarity with technical terms of style.

Two other figures who wrote on rhetoric from a Platonic

---

[29] Text in Walz ix, pp. 552-79 (pp. 543-51 are part of a different work); Spengel I, pp. 299-320; *Libellus De Sublimitate Dionysio Longino fere Adscriptus Accedunt Excerpta Quaedam e Casii Longini Operibus*, ed. Arthur O. Prickard, Oxford: Clarendon Pr., 1906.

[30] The most important references are in Sopatros, e.g., v, p. 9 Walz. See Gloeckner, pp. 76-77; *R-E* IIIA, 1002-6.

[31] See *PS*, p. v.

point of view are Evagoras and Aquila.[32] Unfortunately they cannot be dated securely before or after Porphyry. According to the *Suda* (s.v.), Evagoras wrote an *Art of Rhetoric* in five books. These possibly represent progymnasmata, stasis, invention, ideas, and method, the five parts of the later canon. Syrianus says (II, pp. 128-29 Rabe) that Evagoras and Aquila combined knowledge (*epistēmē*) of divine philosophy with theories of staseis and created more accurate definitions and divisions of problems. A specific example of what he has in mind may be their justification for putting stasis of fact first in the sequence on the Aristotelian ground that the question Does a thing exist? is logically prior to the question What is it? (Syrianus II, p. 60 Rabe). These questions become a part of the Neoplatonic prolegomena.

For later Neoplatonists the authority on stasis is not Minucianus, Evagoras, or Aquila, but Hermogenes. We have, for example, commentaries to Hermogenes' *On Staseis* and *On Ideas* by Syrianus, who was head of the Neoplatonic School in Athens in the Fifth Century. Before considering these it seems necessary to describe as succinctly as possible the rhetorical theory set forth in the four treatises attributed to Hermogenes. Of Hermogenes himself we only know what Philostratus says (*Lives of the Sophists* 2.7, pp. 577-78), that he was a famous declaimer by the age of fifteen, that Marcus Aurelius (reigned A.D. 161-180) came to hear him, that his oratorical powers deserted him when he became an adult, and that he lived to a ripe old age.[33] Maximus Planudes (V, p. 222 Walz) writing in the Fourteenth Century, says that *On Staseis* was written when

[32] See Gloeckner, pp. 64-71, and Hugo Rabe, "Aus Rhetoren-Handschriften. Nachrichten über das Leben des Hermogenes," *RhM* 62 (1907), 260-62.

[33] See Rabe, ibid., pp. 247-62 and Radermacher in *R-E* VIII, 865-77.

Hermogenes was seventeen years old, *On Ideas* when he was twenty-two. This may be a misunderstanding of Philostratus through a series of intermediate commentators, and Hermogenes may have turned to teaching rhetorical theory when he abandoned sophistic display. If it has any basis in truth, it has a striking analog in the West, where Cicero's *De Inventione*, written when the author was under twenty, became the major authority on its subject until the Renaissance.

On Staseis is a treatise of about sixty printed pages, in Attic Greek save that it utilizes the technical terms developed in the three centuries before its composition.[34] It consists of an introduction, a chapter on method, and an extended account of the *diaeresis*, or division of stasis into *kephalaia*, or headings. The term "heading" had first been used by Theodorus of Gadara in the first century (Quintilian 3.6.2; 3.11.26). Theodorus was an important influence on subsequent rhetoric and Hermogenes also follows him (see Quintilian 3.11.21-27) in avoiding the complicated stages of formulating stasis, each with a technical term, which was an inheritance from Hermagoras of Temnos.

Hermogenes begins (p. 28 Rabe) with the claim that the most important part of rhetoric is diaeresis and apodeixis, or division and demonstration, of political questions. The subject overlaps with invention, but does not include some parts of the latter. A political question is a logical disputation dealing with particular instances arising under the laws or customs of each state on the matter of what is deemed just or honorable or expedient or all of these together or some of them. It is, however, the function of philosophy, not of rhetoric, to examine honor or expe-

[34] Text in Rabe's edition (supra, n. 6), pp. 28-92. See also Hermogenis *De Statibus*, ed. Jerzy Kowalski, Warsaw: Prace Wrocławski, 1947; Ray Nadeau, "Hermogenes *On Stases*: A Translation with an Introduction and Notes," *Speech Monographs* 31 (1964), 361-424.

diency or the like in absolute or general terms. We have already met these virtues as the "final" headings in some of the progymnasmata. They had, of course, been identified by Aristotle as the final cause of the three species of rhetoric. Most of Hermogenes' account deals with judicial situations, some with deliberative; passing reference is giving to epideictic. The laws and customs which he cites are not those of the Roman empire; the student did not learn law by studying rhetoric. A few are derived from classical Greek city states, but most are imaginary laws devised by earlier rhetoricians in setting themes for their students to practice. For example, "If an alien should mount the wall, let him be put to death"; "Let a woman who has been raped have the choice of marriage to her assailant or his execution." To the law posited, a situation is then added: "an alien mounts the wall and saves the city"; "a man rapes two women and one demands his death, the other marriage." This gives the student a problem to tax his rhetorical ingenuity. We can see how such problems were treated in later Greek schools in the numerous surviving declamations by Libanius. Declamations (*meletai*) on judicial themes such as these were called *dikaiologiai* (Latin *controversiae*). There are also deliberative exercises or *pragmatikai* (Latin *suasoriae*) on mythological or historical themes, for example "The Athenians deliberate whether to honor with burial the barbarians who fell at Marathon." Such themes were often inspired by incidents in the Greek historians or speeches of the Attic orators, but no attempt was made to preserve historicity. Declamation not only did not teach law, it did not teach history either.[35]

Both persons and deeds, according to Hermogenes (p. 29 Rabe), supply subjects for disputation. Persons fall into

[35] See George Kennedy, "The Sophists as Declaimers," *Approaches to the Second Sophistic*, ed. G. W. Bowersock, University Park, Pa.: American Philological Association, 1974, pp. 17-22.

seven divisions (the process of diaeresis begins here): specific and proper, like Pericles; related, like a father; discreditable, like a profligate; ethical, like a farmer; combined, like a rich youth; combined including quality and act (e.g., effeminate youth accused of prostitution); and descriptive (e.g., a soldier). Deeds are those of the accused, those of others which connect the accused and a crime (e.g., a man is charged with treason when the enemy erect a statue of him), and intermediate, when the evidence is more circumstantial, as when Archidamus was accused of accepting bribes because Pericles recorded an unidentified "necessary" expense of fifty talents. Questions are capable of stasis if there are persons and acts to be judged, or at least one of these, if plausible arguments are available, and if the decision is uncertain (p. 32 Rabe). Otherwise the case is as *asystaton*, not capable of stasis. Of this, Hermogenes lists eight headings. They are not found in earlier rhetoricians and may be his contribution. The introduction ends with a reference to the fact that different kinds of speeches will have different styles, but stasis should be studied before style. This is indicative of the view of rhetoric as a logical discipline which recommended it to the Greek Neoplatonists. In the Latin tradition there is a tendency to view style as easier than logic and thus to be studied by students at an earlier stage.

The discussion of method (pp. 36-43 Rabe) is a brief statement of Hermogenes' entire system of headings of stasis. Its unusual feature is that it links the various headings in a progression of alternatives, rather than separating them into parallel categories. In the chart, Hermogenes' Headings of Stasis, the order followed is that in this chapter on method. Numerals indicate the order in which the headings are subsequently discussed in detail in the treatise.

A subject for decision (*to krinomenon*) is unclear if it is not agreed by the disputants whether an action was per-

CHART 1. HERMOGENES' HEADINGS OF STASIS

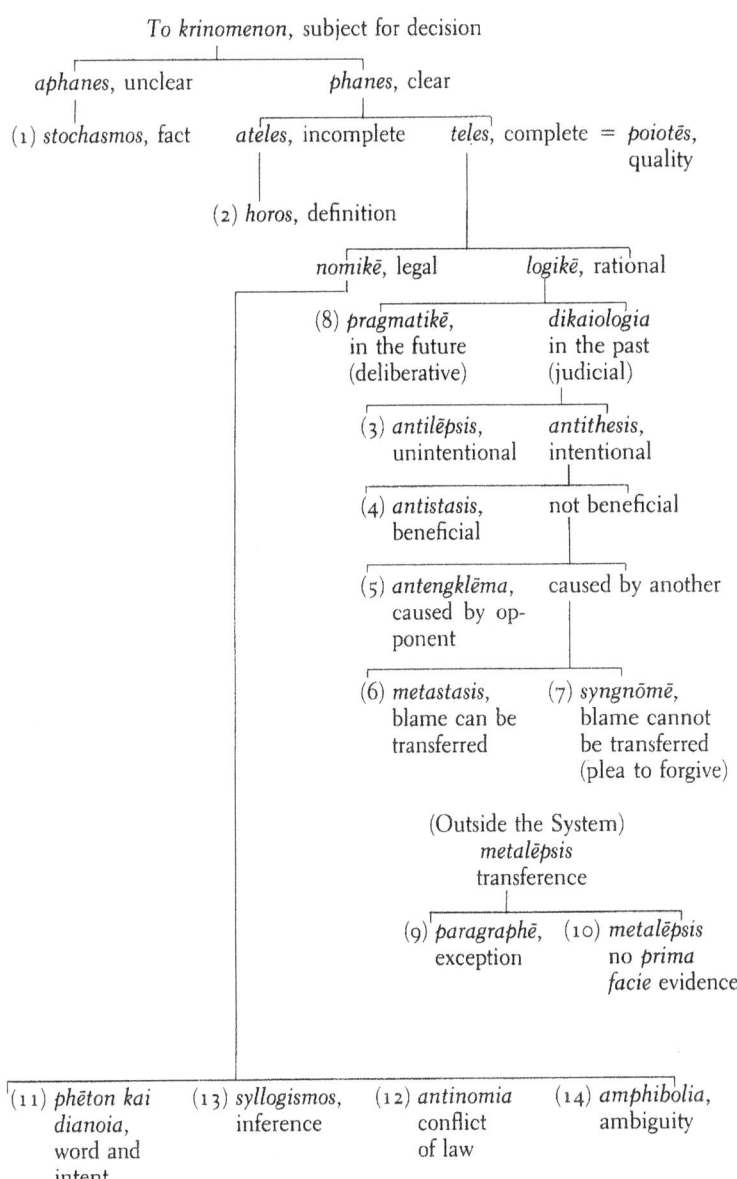

formed at all, for example, whether the accused killed someone. The issue then becomes *stochasmos*, stasis of fact. If the action is admitted, however, the subject is said to be *phanes*, clear, but it may be imperfect (*ateles*) if there are questions about the definition of terms in the law. For example, it is legal to kill a tyrant, but what is a "tyrant"? If both fact and definition of terms are admitted, the subject is said to be complete (*teles*) and dispute must be about the quality (*poiotēs*) of the act or its doer. This can be treated either from a legal standpoint (*nomikē*)—for example, by arguing that an action was justified by another law, or by the intent as opposed to the actual wording of the law cited under definition—or it may be justified logically (*logikē*) without further consideration of the law. This applies both to deliberation about future actions (*pragmatikē*) and judgment of past actions (*dikaiologia*). In the latter case the action may have been unintentional (*antilēpsis*), or if intentional, may have been beneficial in some way (*antistasis*), as the slayers of Gubazes claim in Agathias' account, or may have been caused by another person, either the prosecutor (*antengklēma*), as when a subordinate claims that the superior bringing charges against him was himself responsible for the action, or another person (*metastasis*). Failing any of this sequence of arguments, a defendant must plead to be forgiven (*syngnōmē*). At each stage in this system there is a bifurcation and a division to the right. Each stage represents a heading, but only those headings which are not in turn bifurcated are forms of stasis. There are twelve forms of stasis resulting from working out the system. Two additional ones result from the claim that the court has no right to decide. *Metalēpsis* is used as a general heading for such stasis of transference, but it is broken down, becoming *paragraphē* if the plea is a formal one, that the court lacks jurisdiction, or *metalēpsis* in a narrower sense if the defendant denies there is *prima facie* basis for indictment. Most commentators say (e.g., Syrianus II p. 55 Rabe) that Hermogenes taught a system of fourteen staseis, but Marcellinus (PS, p. 288 Rabe) counts thirteen because of the double meaning of *metalēpsis*.

In the rest of the work Hermogenes takes up the headings of stasis one by one, but postpones *pragmatikē* until he has discussed all forms of *dikaiologia*, and *nomikē* until he has discussed all forms of *logikē*. The discussion of *stochasmos* is the longest because, as he says (p. 43 Rabe), much of the material there relates also to the following headings. There are in fact ten subdivisions of *stochasmos*, several of which are similar to forms of stasis discussed later, for example *metalēpsis* and *antilēpsis* (pp. 48-49 Rabe). The theoretical difference is that here the fact is in question (pp. 58-59 Rabe), but it is hard to see a distinction in some cases.[36] Some subheadings are actually techniques or topics which can be used in a variety of kinds of stasis. What Hermogenes calls *ap' archēs achri telous*, or "from beginning to end," is an example (p. 47 Rabe). It consists of the particulars of Who? What? Where? How? When? Why?—interrogative forms of Aristotelian categories—and is used in laying out a narrative account from the point of view of prosecutor or defendant. As used in *stochasmos* it brings out the performance or nonperformance of the act, but it can be used also to show motivation or the gravity or triviality of the offense. All of the headings are illustrated from themes for declamation current in Hermogenes' time, but the references are often stated in rather cursory form and assume that the reader will be familiar with the theme.

Rhetoricians often claimed that stasis theory was applicable to all kinds of oratory. In Hermogenes' system the division between *pragmatikē* and *dikaiologia* is the basis of

[36] E.g., how *antilēpsis* as a part of *stochasmos* (p. 48 Rabe) differs from *antilēpsis* as a separate heading (pp. 65-71 Rabe).

inclusion of deliberative and judicial oratory, respectively, and of their *meletai*. *Pragmatikē* is divided (p. 76 Rabe) into the lawful, the just, the expedient, the possible, the honorable, and the anticipated result. Each of these headings draws on subdivisions of other kinds of stasis for its arguments, on *nomikē*, for example, to demonstrate legality. The emphasis of stasis theory was certainly judicial, but rhetorical education did thus provide some training for deliberative oratory, as it did for epideictic in the progymnasmatic exercise of encomium. In practice, reliance on a single stasis in a lawcourt is rare and often unwise. Although this is not a feature of Hermogenes' teaching, Greek rhetoricians were well aware of it and discussed the combinations when they lectured on the texts of the Attic orators. These lectures are the basis of our scholia to Aeschines and Demosthenes, where such points are repeatedly made.

The strength of Hermogenes' stasis system was its logical clarity; it could be memorized and reproduced by a student and then practiced in declamation. The Neoplatonists found Hermogenes' definitions formally superior to Minucianus', though sometimes not complete enough. This is clear, for example, from Syrianus' commentary.

Invention

The third work in the standard rhetorical corpus, after *Progymnasmata* and *Staseis*, is a treatise in four books *On Invention*.[37] The first two books are brief, rather unsatisfactory treatments of the proemium and the narration. They lack any dedication or introductory explanation, omit a number of concepts commonly found in earlier discussions, contain some material not found elsewhere, and may constitute an excerpt of the unusual parts from an original

---

[37] Text in Rabe's edition (supra, n. 6), pp. 93-212. There is no English translation. See Radermacher in *R-E* VIII, 873-77.

INVENTION

longer treatise. Byzantine rhetoricians found the discussion somewhat unsatisfactory and turned to the third-century handbooks of Apsines and Longinus to supplement it. As the epitomizer of Longinus puts it (OCT Longinus, p. "A"), "Great is the rhetoric of Hermogenes of Tarsus, for it is (as a whole) the most inclusive of all parts of the art, but not inferior to it is the *Rhetoric* of Longinus, which is easier for a student to learn and starting with the proemium makes clear the virtues of each method of the art." Books Three and Four discuss the proof and its stylistic amplification in greater detail. There is no discussion of the epilogue, and for this reason later rhetoricians again had to turn to another source. A good choice was Apsines, whose account is quite full and includes an extended discussion of how to arouse pity.[38]

Books Three and Four of the Hermogenic *On Invention* demand examination here, since they lay out in considerable detail a theory of rhetorical composition which differs in a number of ways from earlier Greek accounts, as well as from what is found in the later Latin rhetoricians, and which may prove useful in understanding composition as practiced by Greek orators and writers beginning in the Fourth Century. They deserve study by all interested in the literature of late antiquity. A brief introduction to Book Three (p. 126 Rabe) addresses a certain Julius Marcus in terms suggesting that the work as a whole once had a dedication to him. This personal tone reappears (p. 128 Rabe) and is a sign either of a different authorship from that of Books One and Two, or of the absence of editing which reduced those books to their present compass.

We are told in the introduction that this book will deal with the most important part of rhetoric: the introduction of the headings (= stasis), their kinds and sources; *lyseis*, or

[38] For the text see Spengel I, pp. 384-406.

solutions of logical difficulties and their sources; epicheiremes and the topics from which they are derived; and *ergasiai*, or the working out of epicheiremes and enthymemes. First, however, the author says he must discuss *prokataskeuē*, or preface to the proof, which takes the form of a proposition and partition of the argument. The term does not seem to occur in any earlier extant rhetorical writer, although the rhetorician Troilus, perhaps working in the Fifth Century, alleges (*PS*, p. 52 Rabe) that it was a part of the theory of Corax, the inventor of rhetoric, and was used after the proemium to help dispel prejudice. The authority of Hermogenes seems to have established a standard order of the parts of the oration: proemium, *prokatastasis* (or introductory statement of the case, discussed in Book Two and also to be found in Apsines), *diēgēsis* (sometimes called *katastasis*), *prokataskeuē*, *kataskeuē* (or proof), and *epilogos*. It is noted, however (p. 128 Rabe), that the order can be varied: the *prokataskeuē* can sometimes be found after the proemium, as it is in Demosthenes' *On the False Embassy*, sometimes after the *diēgēsis*, as in Demosthenes' *Against Aristocrates*. Our scholia to Demosthenes show familiarity with these terms.

The discussion of *prokataskeuē* is followed in the manuscripts by a discussion of *biaion*, but Rabe, relying on the order of discussion in one of the commentators, postpones that to a more logical place later in the work and continues at this point with a chapter on headings. A heading, according to the author of *On Invention*, will need either confirmation or rebuttal and this is accomplished by epicheiremes. Many writers have discussed them, but not clearly. He will describe as exactly as possible "the invention of an epicheireme, which confirms the heading or the lysis (solution), and the invention of ergasia (working out), which confirms the epicheireme, and the invention of the enthymeme, which confirms the ergasia" (p. 133 Rabe).

If the heading is introduced, that is, if the stasis is determined, by the speaker, simple statement and proof is enough, but a fuller form is required if he responds to an opponent's heading. The parts of this fuller statement are: (1) the opponent's *protasis*, or premise; (2) his *hypophora*, or reason; (3) the speaker's *antiprotasis*, or response; (4) his lysis or *anthypophora*, supporting reason. For example, (1) "perhaps some such statement as this will come from my opponents, (2) that it is difficult to dig a canal through the Chersonese; (3) it is not difficult to refute their view, (4) for it is an easy thing to dig a canal" (p. 134 Rabe). There will then be need of epicheiremes to prove the point. The author is aware that nothing is really proved by this argument; "it is an ornament of discourse and often nothing more" (p. 134 Rabe). He also notes that each of the four parts can sometimes be omitted.

The manuscripts continue at this point with a chapter on epicheiremes, which is also postponed by Rabe to a later point. The result is that the next topic discussed is *enstasis*. *Enstasis* is the point in the argument where the heading emerges. If a speaker declares, "It was permitted for me to kill a son," he is declaring the stasis on which he hopes to rely. If the opponent says, "It was not permitted," he is employing *enstasis*. If he adds a second line of defense, "And even if it were permitted, it was not right to do it in the presence of his mother," he is employing *antiparastasis* (p. 136-37 Rabe). Since debate was not a part of declamation, this exchange will not literally take place, but *enstasis* and *antiparastasis* will still be found in such expressions as "my opponent claims that . . . but I say . . ." and sometimes declaimers inserted dramatic dialogue. A third form of response is *biaion* (pp. 138-40 Rabe), which occurs when it is possible to take some statement of the opponent and convert it to the speaker's purposes, as when Demosthenes cried (19.134), "But (Aeschines says)

Philip will be distressed if we vote down the peace treaty of the ambassadors." His distress will be an argument in favor of the action as viewed by Athenians. The terminology of this discussion is not found in earlier Greek rhetorical treatises. *Enstasis* is an Aristotelian word for an objection to an argument, but it is not found in the rhetoricians. *Antiparastasis* occurs in Apsines (I, p. 366 Spengel) as one of several forms of *anatropē*, which is a kind of lysis, but it is found in approximately its Hermogenic meaning in a context with the participle *enstans* in the early Third-Century philosopher Alexander of Aphrodisias (*In Metaphysica* 518.28). The development of the terminology is thus probably after the time of Hermogenes of Tarsus.

The ensuing discussion of argumentation also differs considerably in concept and terminology from earlier accounts. To understand what is meant by proof and enthymeme in the later Greek and Byzantine periods a reader must consciously reject what is found not only in Aristotle but also in Boethius and the Latin tradition. Rhetoricians of the Second and Third Centuries (Minucian the Younger, the Anonymous Seguerianus, and Apsines) follow Aristotle in laying out a system of external and artistic proof, the latter divided into ethical, pathetical, and logical. They call the instrument of logical proof by the name epicheireme and subdivide it into the example and the enthymeme, but their definition of the enthymeme varies considerably (see esp. I, p. 447 Spengel). Topics are the source of enthymemes. In contrast, the Hermogenic *On Invention* does not discuss modes of proof but seeks to relate argumentation to stasis theory. Beginning with the heading, the author describes (pp. 140-54 Rabe) a series of parts which he calls respectively lysis, epicheireme, ergasia, and enthymeme. For example, in *pragmatikē*, or deliberative declamation, "it will be difficult to dig through the Chersonese"; lysis from *enstasis*: "it will not be difficult," epi-

INVENTION

cheireme: "for we shall dig earth and digging is child's play"; ergasia: "even the king of the Persians, when forced, once dug through Athos"; enthymeme: "yet he dug through a mountain and we shall dig through earth." Epicheireme is thus a supporting statement to a lysis, which is the speaker's answer to whatever an opponent claims. Epicheiremes, we are told (p. 140 Rabe), are drawn from the circumstances of the speakers, the speeches, the facts, the courts, the case, and "life" and are divided into place, time, manner, person, cause, and act. These are topics, though not here so called. An ergasia, which supports an epicheireme, is derived from comparison, example, the lesser, the greater, the equal, and the opposite, which are also topics. An enthymeme is then the supporting statement to an ergasia and, as it were, clinches the argument. It is characterized by *drimytēs*, or sharpness (p. 150 Rabe), one of the "ideas" of style. Enthymemes are derived from the same source as epicheiremes and assume the same form as ergasiai. It is possible to add an epenthymeme, or additional supporting statement: "and yet he (the king) did so in order to conquer, we in order that we not suffer by being conquered" (p. 152 Rabe).

Instead of arguing by the system of enthymemes just outlined, it is possible to use the technique of *ap' archēs achri telous*, from beginning to end, which we also met in Hermogenes' *On Staseis*. This (pp. 154-58 Rabe) has its own "topic" of proof, called *hypodiairesis*, which amplifies one or more significant words. For example, "Then he killed three sons," subjected to *hypodiairesis* "from beginning to end," might become "Then, not in a moment of passion, but after a time of thought, he did not inform on, but killed, not one son, but three, not someone else's, but his own." Another form of proof "from beginning to end" is *to plaston epicheirema* (pp. 158-61 Rabe), a hypothetical argument, often *a fortiori*, for example, "If he had promised to do a favor, you would have rewarded him; now that he has done it, will you deny him a reward?" "From beginning to end" is difficult to counter; the author suggests (pp. 161-62 Rabe) a "method" which is to utilize the antithetical forms of stasis. As to the arrangement of epicheiremes within the speech, the author recommends putting the more strictly logical ones first and moving toward "the more panegyrical" (pp. 161-62 Rabe), but even better is to arrange them into a logical sequence so that the speech becomes "a single fabric and body" (p. 163 Rabe). The remaining chapters of Book Three comment on how to counter arguments in the stasis of *horos* and *syllogismos* with *diaskeuē*, or elaboration, which the author equates with *diatypōsis*, or vivid description. Its sources are what has gone before, what is present, and what is going to come (p. 168 Rabe).

In Book Four aspects of style are treated as part of invention. That is, their study helps the student of rhetoric discover what to say. Chapters are devoted to figures (no distinction is made between figures of thought and figures of speech, but most of the devices fall under the former category), tropes, levels of style, and the treatment of figured and comparative problems for declamation. Two general categories of style are described, determined by the nature of the epicheiremes and ergasiai. If they are "political," the style should be *strongylos*, compact or tense, containing the "idea" of *drimytēs*, or sharpness, and the figures to be used to achieve this are antithesis and the period. If the epicheiremes are panegyrical, the style should be *pneumatikos*, characterized by longer sentences which can, nevertheless, be delivered in a single breath (*pneuma*) (p. 171 Rabe). Antithesis is viewed as a compositional device by which a thought can be amplified: "Since it is day, it is necessary to do this" by antithesis becomes "If it were not day, but night, probably it would not be necessary to

INVENTION

act, but since it is day it is fitting to act." The similarity to what was called *hypodiaeresis* above is apparent. Just as an epicheireme is worked out through a series of stages, so an antithesis, by multiplication of its cola, can be worked out into a *pneuma*, which is the author's term for a long, complex sentence. A *pneuma* may be periodic if grammatical completion is postponed until the end, but a period in itself is shorter, with from one to four cola. The author shows how to construct a period in which the "turning" or key word for suspending the grammar is in each of the Greek cases (pp. 177-78 Rabe). In the following example the "turning" word is "this," which in Greek is in the accusative: "Are you not ashamed, if that which you would suffer, had he the power to do it, this though having the opportunity, you dare not do?" The units of delivery which make up a *pneuma* or a period are three: a unit of up to six syllables is a comma; a longer unit up to the length of a line of hexameter is a colon; a still longer unit is called *schoinotēs*, which the author says is useful in proemia (p. 184 Rabe). If a *pneuma* exceeds the ability of a speaker to deliver it in one breath, it becomes a *tasis*; *tasis* in a passage of invective is called *kataphora* (p. 192 Rabe). Additional figures, here meaning devices for amplifying the composition, are discussed, but the technical nature of the work is perhaps clear from this sampling. These compositional forms, learned in the rhetorical schools out of the Hermogenic corpus, can be found commonly in elaborate Greek of late antiquity, just as can the larger compositional units, the progymnasmata.

That the primary goal of instruction was to prepare students for declamation is evident throughout, but nowhere more clearly than in the discussion of "figured problems" which concludes *On Invention*. We also know about these problems from a handbook falsely attributed to Dionysius of Halicarnassus (VI, pp. 295-358 Radermacher) and from discussion in Apsines (I, pp. 407-14 Spengel). Figured problems are part of the declaimers' search for novelty. In the simplest form (*enantion*) as described in *On Invention* (pp. 205-6 Rabe), the speaker argues against his personal interest, as when he takes the role of Pericles imagined as arguing in favor of the Athenians' handing him over to the Spartans as a hostage. The author of *On Invention* claims (p. 208 Rabe) to have invented a new kind of figured problem in which a speaker speaks in his own self-interest without appearing to do so. For example, there is a rumor that a father-in-law has seduced his daughter-in-law, who becomes pregnant. An oracle declares that the child who is to be born will be the murderer of his father. The true father, not wanting to be killed, favors having the child exposed, though of course he pretends to be acting in the interests of his son. The son opposes this: he pretends that it is because he loves his child, but actually it is his desire that it grow up and fulfill the oracle. Since it is unseemly for a son to accuse a father of adultery, the son must use "emphasis," that is, he must carefully choose his words so that they mean more than he says. "Imagine, O father," he can say, "that the child is your own. You are killing that which you begot. . . ." The audience for the declamation would of course know the full hypothesis. Another refinement for the jaded audiences of declamation was the comparative problem in which the speaker not only rebuts charges against himself, but seeks to prove that they apply to another, especially to his opponent as in stasis of *antengklēma*. *On Invention* concludes with discussion of such problems.

Although the definitions and divisions set forth in *On Invention* are not particularly good, the treatise is unusually specific in how to work out the composition of declamations and rich in examples, especially from Demosthenes, whose works have clearly become the student's bible.

INVENTION

This is consistent with authorship by Hermogenes, but the weight of critical opinion is against the treatise's being a genuine product of the Second-Century rhetorician. Hugo Rabe succinctly states the evidence.[39] The manuscripts attribute the treatise to Hermogenes, but that could easily arise from its place in the corpus, framed by two undoubtedly genuine works. Hermogenes definitely wrote a work on invention, which he mentions in *On Staseis* (p. 53 Rabe) and in *On Ideas* (p. 378 Rabe), but the references do not fit our texts of *On Invention*. The author of *On Invention* claims to have composed a work on stasis, which he calls *Diaeretikē Technē* (p. 132 Rabe), but the reference does not well describe the contents of Hermogenes' *On Staseis*. Syrianus (II, pp. 2-3 Rabe), writing in the Fifth Century, apparently knew of Hermogenes' treatise on invention only from the reference in the genuine works. On the other hand, he seems to refer (I, p. 36 Rabe) to the text of *On Invention* and attribute it to Apsines, and still another passage is attributed to Apsines in a comment which originated with the Fifth-Century sophist Lachares. It is possible that the treatise was thus commonly attributed to Apsines in the Fifth Century, but that attribution poses as many questions as it answers, since the contents are not consistent with discussions in the extant work of Apsines. The style of *On Invention* differs both from that of Hermogenes and that of Apsines. The thought of the treatise, however, is generally consistent with that of Hermogenes elsewhere, and we may well be dealing with a work by an unidentified teacher of declamation who made some use of Hermogenes' works, even including a lost treatise on invention. This teacher would probably have lived in the Third or Fourth Century, more likely the latter when declamation equalled or surpassed its popularity in Hermo-

[39] Edition of Hermogenes (supra, n. 6), pp. vi-ix.

genes' own times. As has been said before, the first two books seem to be an edited version of an original longer text.

Ideas

The fourth work in the rhetorical corpus is Hermogenes' *On Ideas*, whose authorship by the Second-Century rhetorician is unquestioned. The concept of ideas of style has some similarity to the characters of style, for example, the four characters of the plain, the elevated, the elegant, and the forcible as discussed in the treatise of Demetrius, probably dating from the early Peripatetic School, but it specifically developed out of the "virtues" of style as discussed by Dionysius of Halicarnassus. The ideas are not original concepts of Hermogenes; they had been discussed before his time by Dionysius of Miletus, Basilicus, and Zeno, and are also to be found in a treatise falsely attributed to Aelius Aristides, but Hermogenes' account is worked out in greater detail. It had great influence throughout the Byzantine period and significant use in the Renaissance, when it was translated into Latin and influenced composition in major Western European literature. *On Ideas* can be briefly treated here since it is the best known of the Hermogenic treatises.[40]

On Ideas begins with a rather diffuse introduction (pp. 213-26 Rabe) in which the following points emerge. Understanding ideas of style is both necessary for an orator and the basis of criticism of ancient and later works. Natural ability is desirable in a student, but without critical

[40] For the text see Rabe's edition (supra, n. 6), pp. 213-413. Partial English translation by D. A. Russell in *Ancient Literary Criticism*, ed. D. A. Russell and M. Winterbottom, Oxford: Clarendon Pr., 1972, pp. 561-79. See Dieter Hagedorn, *Zur Ideenlehre des Hermogenes* (Hypomnemata VIII), Göttingen: Vandenhoeck and Ruprecht, 1964; Annabel M. Patterson, *Hermogenes and the Renaissance: Seven Ideas of Style*, Princeton Univ. Pr., 1970.

guidelines it can lead to disaster in practice, whereas an average student can achieve success, even preeminence, by study and practice. The discussion utilizes the nature-theory-practice commonplace found in rhetorical writers since the early sophists and refers to the traditional concept of *logos* as the distinctive activity of man. Ideas, Hermogenes continues, are general qualities found in composition and are not characteristics of an individual author, but an understanding of them leads to an understanding of authors. In most writers some one idea predominates and gives his writings their peculiar flavor. The ideas are combined in a variety of ways to make style poetical, panegyrical, deliberative, judicial, or something else. The great master of these combinations was Demosthenes, even of the panegyrical style. It is desirable to discuss the ideas with exactness, but previous accounts—none are identified—are called confused. Criticism of Demosthenes in particular has suffered from lack of attention to the ideas.

The seven basic ideas, all found in Demosthenes, are then identified (pp. 217-18 Rabe) as *saphēneia* (clarity), *megethos* (grandeur), *kallos* (beauty), *gorgotēs* (rapidity), *ēthos* (character), *alētheia* (sincerity), and *deinotēs* (forcefulness). Some are individual entities, others exist only in combination; *megethos* consists of six subordinate ideas, *ēthos* of four, and other ideas are also broken down into constituent parts. As it happens, they are treated in groups which could be identified with the plain, the grand, the middle, and a mixture of styles, but Hermogenes does not make this point and apparently thought that such categories, which remain basic in the Latin tradition, were of little use in teaching composition. He regards the ideas as having their origin—embodiment might have been a better word—in what he calls the elements of speech, which are listed (p. 218 Rabe) as *ennoia* (thought), *methodos* (approach, but subsequently especially identified with figures of thought), *lexis* (initially conceived as style, but subsequently treated as diction), *schēmata* (figures of speech), *kōla* (clauses), *synthesis* (word order), *anapauseis* (cadence), and rhythm, which results from the arrangement of words and pauses.

The preface leaves some questions unasked and unanswered. Idea is described, but not defined. Hermogenes, characteristically, shows no interest in the philosophical dimension of the ideas, in whether they are real or nominal. Nor does he attempt a logical division of the whole subject, as he does in the case of stasis theory. These omissions do not seem to have bothered the later Neoplatonists. Syrianus calls the treatise "the most philosophical" (II, p. 3 Rabe). Despite its lack of definition and division, it is extremely systematic, and the whole spectrum of style, like the system of stasis, is worked out with almost mathematical beauty. Furthermore, the literary art and some of the philosophical views of Plato are given sympathetic treatment, though Hermogenes regards Demosthenes as the greater artist. Despite the pedagogical goal set forth in the preface, *On Ideas* is chiefly a work of criticism which attempts to isolate the stylistic qualities of great writers. In contrast to *On Staseis* and *On Invention*, it does not specifically apply these concepts to contemporary declamation.

The first idea discussed by Hermogenes is *saphēneia*, or clarity, which is a product of two qualities, *katharotēs*, or correctness, and *eukrineia*, or good judgment. Correctness results from the correct use of all the elements of speech as listed in the second paragraph above. *Eukrineia*, on the other hand, emerges when an orator gives clarity to a complicated or confused subject by an orderly treatment of it. In *saphēneia* the thought should be clear and familiar; the method is an orderly presentation of the "bare subject"; thus figures of thought are avoided; the diction employs common words; the figure is *orthotēs*, that of narration in the nominative without figures of speech; *kōla* should be kept short and divided into *kommata*; the composition will be simple, the pauses appropriate, the rhythm iambic or trochaic. *Saphēneia* thus constitutes the standard of the simplest and most natural form of expression; all other ideas are in a sense departures from it.

In contrast to clarity are the ideas which make up a quality which Hermogenes describes by the three terms *megethos*, *ongkos*, and *axiōma*: grandeur, bulk, and dignity. This quality is produced by six ideas: *semnotēs* or solemnity, *peribolē* or abundance, *trachytēs* or asperity, *lamprotēs* or brilliance, *akmē* or florescence, and *sphodrotēs* or vehemence. The first two of these six "exist on their own," the others appear only in combination with other ideas. Hermogenes' arrangement is to discuss *semnotēs* first, then the four combining qualities, and then *peribolē*, "because Demosthenes excels in it, and the reason why he employs it to achieve bulk cannot be understood until we have learned about asperity, brilliance, florescence, and vehemence."[41]

Although Hermogenes does not apply Platonic definition and diaeresis in the initial identification of ideas, the treatment of individual ideas is often characterized by divisions which appealed to the Neoplatonists. In discussing *ennoia* of *semnotēs*, for example, he distinguishes (pp. 243-46 Rabe) four types of solemn thoughts which are suggestive of levels of being: things said of the gods as divine, for example, in the *Timaeus* (29e-30a): thoughts about divine things, such as the nature of the universe; thoughts about things divine by nature, but manifested in human affairs, like justice; and great and glorious human events, such as the Battle of Marathon. Plato is cited as an example of the method of *semnotēs* and also (p. 247 Rabe) for his use of long vowels to secure solemn diction.

After treating the six ideas of *megethos*, Hermogenes turns

[41] See Russell (supra, n. 40), p. 567.

(p. 296 Rabe) to *epimeleia* and *kallos*, elegance and beauty, treated as a single idea. This corresponds roughly to the middle style in some ways, but it can also accompany *megethos*. Reference is made to Plato's *Phaedrus* and to Isocrates as well as to Demosthenes.

The ideas discussed in Book Two are all either mixtures of ideas or ideas which mix with others. *Gorgotēs*, or rapidity, can accompany *megethos* and *kallos*. It is not a matter of *ennoia*, but of securing momentum through method, diction, and composition (p. 312 Rabe). Ethos, which follows, derives from four ideas: *apheleia* or simplicity, *glykytēs*, or sweetness, *drimytēs*, or sharpness, and *epieikeia*, or moderation. These make up a spectrum of qualities in the portrayal of character. *Alētheia*, or sincerity, though specifically associated with ethos (pp. 321 and 352 Rabe), is then associated with *barytēs*, or sternness, and treated as a separate idea. Finally, we are ready for the greatest of the ideas, *deinotēs*, or forcefulness, which Hermogenes says (pp. 368-69 Rabe) is "the correct mixture of all the aforesaid forms of speech and their opposites." It is here that the greatness of Demosthenes is most evident. Three levels of *deinotēs* are distinguished (p. 372 Rabe): speech which is both *deinos* and seems to be, as in the *Philippics*; that which is, but does not seem to be, for the art escapes notice, as in private orations of Demosthenes; and that which appears to be, but is not, for example the style of Gorgias and Polus as characters in Plato's *Gorgias*. The sophists' fault was that they had no knowledge of how to use the ideas appropriately (p. 378 Rabe).

On Ideas concludes with a long chapter on civic oratory, defined in the traditional terms of deliberative, judicial, and panegyrical. For successful public speaking the most important idea is clarity, plus ethos, sincerity, and rapidity, and among ideas giving *megethos* abundance, correctness, and correct judgment (p. 381 Rabe), but other ideas ought to be found as well. Deliberative especially seeks *megethos* and *deinotēs*, judicial seeks the ideas associated with ethos. The best panegyric is Platonic and employs the ideas of *megethos*, except for asperity and vehemence, and *glykytēs*. All poetry is regarded as a part of panegyric, and Homer and Hesiod are discussed in terms of *ennoia*, *methodos*, and the other elements (pp. 389-95 Rabe). Plato in the *Gorgias* (502d2) had called poetry a form of rhetoric, and Hellenistic critics had applied rhetorical theory to the analysis of poetry, but the general decline of poetry in later antiquity, seen for example in the prose hymns of the sophists, gave practical meaning to the concept.

Hermogenes then turns to what he calls the purely political writers. Lysias, Isaeus, Hyperides, Isocrates, Dinarchus, Aeschines, the two Antiphons, Lycurgus, and Andocides are briefly discussed (pp. 395-403 Rabe). Hermogenes shows familiarity with the canon of the Ten Attic Orators, to which he adds Critias (p. 403 Rabe). *On Ideas* then concludes with a critical examination of what are called the purely panegyrical writers: Xenophon, Aeschines the Socratic, Nicostratus, Herodotus, Thucydides, Hecataeus. Historiography and the dialogue are thus embraced within the concept of panegyric. These are classical writers with the exception of Nicostratus, who lived in the Second Century; elsewhere Hermogenes occasionally cites Aelius Aristides as a classical model. Theopompus, Ephorus, and Hellanicus are dismissed as not classics. At the very end Hermogenes returns to the greatest models, Homer, Plato, and above all Demosthenes.

Method

Hermogenes clearly thought of his separate treatises on stasis, invention, and ideas as together constituting an Art of Rhetoric (p. 378 Rabe), thus foreshadowing the later rhetorical corpus. *On Ideas* contains references to a projected addition *On the Method of Deinotēs* (e.g., pp. 238, 380), and the epilogue (p. 413 Rabe) indicates that this is to follow immediately. The fifth place in the rhetorical corpus of the manuscripts is indeed filled by a treatise *On the Method of Deinotēs*, but it seems unlikely this is the work by Hermogenes. It consists of thirty-seven short chapters, in no very clear order, discussing miscellaneous devices of style. It is probably largely a work of the Second Century, and may reflect an attempt by editors to fill a void caused by the loss of Hermogenes' work or by his failure ever to complete it. Syrianus in the Fifth Century knows (I, p. 1 Rabe) of Hermogenes' *On the Method of Deinotēs*, but may mean the work we have.[42]

Of the five works in the traditional rhetorical corpus, two are thus genuine writings of Hermogenes, *On Staseis* and *On Ideas*. A third, *On Method*, is probably not by him, but may have been written in his time. The first work in the corpus, the *Progymnasmata*, was composed in the Fourth Century by Aphthonius. The remaining work in the series, *On Invention*, is perhaps also a composition of the Fourth Century. We do not know when or by whom the corpus of these five works was put together and given its later authority, though something of the process can be observed. As noted above, Hermogenes himself regarded his treatises as forming a sequence, but they were perhaps not widely used as such for some time. In the Third Century, Philostratus does not treat Hermogenes with much respect and Porphyry chose the works of Minucianus for his rhetorical commentary. But Metrophanes of Eucaria, who probably

[42] For the text see Rabe's edition (supra, n. 6), pp. 414-56. See *R-E* VIII, 872-73; E. Bürgi, "Ist die dem Hermogenes zugeschriebene Schrift *Peri methodou deinotes* echt?" *Wiener Studien* 48 (1930), 187-97, and 49 (1931), 40-69. Some of the material may come from Telephos of Pergamum, see Hermann Schrader, "Telephos der Pergamer," *Hermes* 37 (1902), 551-54.

lived in the Third Century, is described by Syrianus (II, p. 55 Rabe) as a Platonist and an interpreter of Hermogenes. This is confirmed by the *Suda*, which also attributes commentaries on both Minucianus and Hermogenes to Menander, the author of the handbook on epideictic, who was probably working at the end of the Third Century. Evagoras and Aquila, whose work on stasis has been mentioned earlier, are mentioned in contexts which may imply some knowledge of Hermogenes. In the Fourth Century, Libanius and Eunapius are silent about Hermogenes, but *On Invention* perhaps shows his influence, and the first of the extant commentaries to *On Staseis* was composed then, that by Sopatros. In the Fifth Century the influence of Hermogenes can be seen to grow with the lectures of George of Alexandria and the important commentaries to *On Staseis* and *On Ideas* by Syrianus, head of the Neoplatonic School in Athens. Syrianus, however, knows only some individual works of Hermogenes, and not a corpus of four works, or of five with Aphthonius. References to all four Hermogenic works are to be found in the scholia to Demosthenes, which largely derive from a commentary on the orator, perhaps the work of Zosimus of Ascalon, composed around A.D. 500.[43] John of Sardis in the Ninth Century wrote commentaries to Aphthonius, *On Staseis*, and *On Invention*. The development of minuscule script in the Ninth Century perhaps facilitated a corpus of rhetorical texts and commentaries in one codex, though uncial could be written small if necessary. The actual existence of such a codex cannot be documented before the Eleventh Century, as seen, for example, in *Parisinus Graecus* 1983, and even some eleventh-century *corpora* do not include *On Method*.

[43] See Rabe, "Rhetoren-Corpora" (supra, n. 2). I expect to publish shortly a study of the Demosthenic scholia and its relation to the Hermogenic corpus.

Sopatros

From the late Fourth to the Fourteenth Century we have a series of commentaries on parts or all of the rhetorical corpus. The earliest such commentary is probably that by Sopatros to *On Staseis* (V, pp. 1-211 Walz). There is additional material credited to Sopatros in a composite commentary which also includes notes by Syrianus and Marcellinus (IV, pp. 37-846 Walz). In addition, under the name of Sopatros we have fragments of a work on *metapoiēsis*,[44] fragmentary progymnasmata,[45] a prolegomenon to Aelius Aristides,[46] and a treatise entitled *Diairesis Zētēmatōn* or *Division of Questions* (VIII, pp. 1-385 Walz), which contains examples, with pedagogical instruction, of eighty-one themes for declamation arranged by stasis. Hermogenes is not mentioned in this work and the terminology is not exactly his, but the exercises could be coordinated with his treatise. It was one of the best known collections of declamation available for study by later students and, despite its wearisome length and often trivial contents, would probably repay more careful study than it has received. The author of the prolegomenon to Aristides says that he studied and taught at Athens; the author of the *Diairesis* seems to refer (VIII, p. 318 Walz) to himself as a student of Himerius, and thus as having lived in the second half of the Fourth Century. The commentary was used by George of Alexandria in the Fifth Century.[47] It seems probable that these are all writings of one late Fourth Century Athenian rhetorician working in Neoplatonic circles, and it is possible that he is the grandson of the philosopher of the same

---

[44] See Stephan Gloeckner, "Aus Sopatros Metapoiesis," *RhM* 65 (1910), 504-14; Hunger I, p. 90.

[45] Text in Rabe's edition of Aphthonius (supra, n. 8), pp. 57-70.

[46] Text in Aristidis *Opera* III, ed. W. Dindorf, Leipzig, 1829, pp. 737-57.

[47] See *R-E* IIIA, 1002-6.

name, described by Eunapius (pp. 458 and 462-63 Kayser) as a student of Iamblichus with some ability at rhetoric who held a public post under Constantine, but was put to death.

Sopatros' *Hypomnēma*, or commentary, to Hermogenes' *On Staseis* (v, pp. 1-211 Walz) begins with a prolegomenon, or introduction, which well illustrates how Neoplatonic philosophy reached out to embrace rhetoric as an introductory logical discipline. The contents of this prolegomenon partially overlap with material found in the prolegomena to be discussed later in this chapter, but the organization is different and the tone more philosophical than in most prolegomena. Sopatros begins by describing his subject as a logical art and then proceeds to define and divide *logos* and *technē*. Two species of *logos* are identified, *prosphorikos* or expository, which produces discourse and reasoning, and *endiathetos* or internal, by which we are rational when silent or asleep. Expository logos is in turn divided into grammatical and rhetorical and rhetorical again into two arts, that which produces beauty, which is the art of the ideas of style and the figures, and that which teaches, which is accomplished either through the emotions or through demonstration. The *erga* of the orator are three: *noēsis, heurēsis*, and *diathesis* (v, p. 3 Walz). *Noēsis* is the consideration of the proposed treatment of the case and is of three sorts: medical, philosophical, and political. The first two occur if a case involves medical or philosophical questions; political *noēsis* is rhetorical stasis.

Sopatros then turns (v, p. 3 Walz) to the question of art: "In as much as there are three things by means of which an activity takes place, I mean *technē* (art), *epistēmē* (knowledge), and *empeiria* (acquired experience), it is necessary to ask which rhetoric is. There are three questions about every activity: What is it? Who is the doer? and How do we accomplish the deed? In the first question we must ask whether it is an art, knowledge, or result of experience, how it came into existence, and what is its utility." The concepts of *technē, epistēmē,* and *empeiria* derive ultimately from Plato's *Gorgias,* the questions of what, who, and how from logical works of Aristotle. These were authoritative texts to the Neoplatonists. Both sets of concepts were applied to the definition of a variety of disciplines, and Sopatros, in common with some subsequent rhetoricians, employs an analogy between rhetoric and medicine in the ensuing discussion. Rhetoric is not knowledge, he says, because it deals not with universals, but with particulars: It is not acquired experience, as Plato "slanderously" said (v, p. 4), because it involves an understanding of cause and of forms rather than being simple imitation. Sopatros follows a view he attributes to the Stoics, that there are three kinds of art: theoretical, practical, and mixed. An art is theoretical if it does not aim at producing an action, for example, grammar. It is practical if it does aim at action, for example, music. Rhetoric and medicine are mixed, but panegyric must be classed as theoretical since it does not aim at action. Speech itself is not viewed by Sopatros as an activity.

The next question discussed (v, p. 5-9) is the origin of rhetoric. According to Homer and Plato, rhetoric existed among the gods and heroes. The first speech of prosecution was that by Theseus at Athens against Hippolytus. Rhetoric became dangerous to practice under the tyrants, though Phalaris had acquired his tyranny by a persuasive speech. Corax was the first teacher of rhetoric; Tisias was his student; Gorgias brought the art to Athens and was followed by Antiphon, Thucydides, and Isocrates. The art flourished most in the time of Demosthenes, but declined under Macdenonian rule, only to revive in the time of Hadrian and Antoninus Pius. Cicero lived earlier and well understood the art (an unusual note among Greek rhetoricians). Famous rhetoricians in modern times (*nun*, p. 8) have been Lollianus, Hermagoras, Minucianus, and Hermogenes. The latter came from Tarsus and spoke before the emperor Hadrian (a mistake for Marcus Aurelius) when he was eighteen years old, but by the time he was twenty-five he lost his sanity.

Sopatros then notes (p. 9) that some have wondered why Hermogenes, while writing a *technē rhētorikē*, did not define rhetoric nor explain in what sense it is an art. There are three questions which should be asked: What art is it? Who is the artist? How do we effect the work of the art? The first question can be subdivided into three: Is it an art? If so, what sort of art? Is it a noble art or a false art? The questions falling under the rubric of the artist are whether the orator philosophizes and whether he gives laws. Hermogenes and Minucianus neglected giving a definition of the orator or of rhetoric. Porphyry, in his commentary on Minucianus, says that the orator will speak on every political question, but that Minucianus' treatise is rightly limited to judicial and deliberative rhetoric: "it is superfluous to speak about the whole art when making an examination of only a part of it" (p. 9). A school of contentious critics rejects this view, for the orator will speak everywhere. Panegyric requires a knowledge of all sorts of occasions; deliberative and judicial rhetoric in turn require a knowledge of panegyric. Every epilogue is essentially an invective or encomium. Thus it is impossible to treat two kinds of rhetoric apart from rhetoric as a whole. "Every species is the same in genus" (p. 11). Yet, Sopatros continues, in support of Porphyry it can be argued that for an orator to use materials of panegyric does not make him a panegyrist, any more than one using grammar is a grammarian. Although species inheres in genus, everything that is predicated of a species is not predicated of the genus. Thus Sopatros agrees with Porphyry that the study of rhetoric can be limited to works of judicial and deliberative oratory, with the question of the art and the artist neglected. He does, however, make some interesting observations about the artist, which like his earlier reference to Cicero shows some indirect knowledge of discussions of *bonus orator* such as we find in Cicero and Quintilian. This topic is found only in Sopatros among the Greek rhetoricians, though it is of course possible that it had been touched on by Porphyry. An artist, Sopatros says (p. 14), is a man knowing how to speak well. This applies to all orators, but it does not logically follow that an orator should be a good man. The definition would apply to a philosopher or others, and we need to define more narrowly a political orator, who will be a man knowledgeable in political affairs who can argue on either side of a question in accordance with probability.

Definitions of rhetoric are then considered. That which Sopatros prefers is one he attributes to Lollianus (p. 17): "an artistic faculty of persuasive speech on a political subject having as its goal to speak well." This definition is frequently cited by others and usually attributed to Dionysius of Halicarnassus' work *On Imitation*.[48] Sopatros may have found it in Lollianus without any source indicated.

The function of Sopatros' prolegomenon is to place the study of rhetoric, as seen in Hermogenes' *On Staseis*, into a system of knowledge as understood by the Neoplatonists. The references to Porphyry are evidence that the latter had tried to do much the same and an indication that he was the key figure in beginning this effort of synthesis, definition, and division. The Neoplatonists did not, however, develop a new theory of the contents of the discipline. As in the case of dialectic, they took over earlier thought. They set this into a new framework and then wrote com-

---

[48] See Dionysii Halicarnasei *Quae Extant*, VI: *Opuscula II*, ed. Hermann Usener and Ludwig Radermacher, Stuttgart: Teubner, 1965, pp. 197-200.

mentaries on authoritative texts. The usual method, as practiced by Sopatros in this commentary, is to give a lemma, or quotation of a few words from Hermogenes, and then to explain the passage, to identify allusions, to give examples from the classics, to note controversies or divergent authorities, and sometimes to criticize the contents. In writing their commentaries, Sopatros and others are mindful of the general philosophical education to which the study of rhetoric contributes at an introductory level. Not only could a student learn the process of definition and division and the contents of rhetorical theory, but the commentaries served to enhance verbal skills, building vocabulary, and they include some philosophical material. Sopatros, for example, has occasion to refer to the Platonic theory of forms (p. 19). He appears to be writing for advanced students who already know something about dialectic or for teachers, but he does not show much interest in applying the system to declamation or to speech on contemporary issues: rhetoric is for him an academic discipline of intellectual value in itself.

Syrianus

A second important commentator on Hermogenes was Syrianus. Born in Alexandria, he studied with Plutarch in Athens and succeeded him as head of the Neoplatonic School there in 431/2. He wrote commentaries on Homer, Plato, and Aristotle, but only that on the *Metaphysics* survives, probably because there was no commentary on that work by his more famous student Proclus. Our manuscripts describe the commentaries on Hermogenes as the work of Syrianus the Sophist; there is no reasonable doubt that they are the work of the philosopher, but they may be an early work.[49]

[49] See *R-E* IVA, 1728-75, and Gloeckner, pp. 63-64.

Syrianus' introduction to his commentary on stasis is limited to what little was then known about Hermogenes and derives from Philostratus.[50] Some of the questions which Sopatros had discussed in his prolegomenon are, however, worked into early parts of the commentary: whether rhetoric is *technē, epistēmē,* or *empeiria*; the existence of rhetoric among the gods and the heroes; how panegyric is sometimes employed in political discourse. Hermogenes' own preface is treated in the form of lemmata and comments, but the discussion of the fourteen kinds of stasis is a paraphrase without keys to the Hermogenic texts. This form of commentary is parallel to that practiced by later Alexandrian Neoplatonists, and Syrianus may have learned it in Egypt. There are references to Dionysius of Halicarnassus, Minucianus, Evagoras, Aquila, Metrophanes, Cornutus, Apsines, and once to Porphyry (II, p. 14 Rabe). Although Syrianus sometimes agrees with Minucianus about matters of stasis, he found his definitions invalid; those of Hermogenes he regarded as better, even if sometimes incomplete.[51] Since Hermogenes has provided no definition of stasis, Syrianus furnishes one (II, p. 48 Rabe): "a simple rhetorical proposition affording demonstration of one contention about the issues in a political question, in accordance with which term occurs the division of the headings which contribute to proof." He explains the definition briefly.

Syrianus also composed a commentary to Hermogenes' *On Ideas*.[52] Its introduction is worth quoting in its entirety since it reveals the attitude toward Hermogenes in the Fifth Century as expressed by an intellectual leader of the time.

---

[50] For text see Syriani *In Hermogenem Commentaria*, II, ed. Hugo Rabe, Leipzig: Teubner, 1893. Walz IV, pp. 1-846 contains the composite commentary.

[51] See Gloeckner, pp. 60-63.

[52] For text see Syriani *In Hermogenem Commentaria*, I, ed. Hugo Rabe, Leipzig: Teubner, 1892.

SYRIANUS

Almost all the treatises which have come to us from the technical writer Hermogenes are remarkable and filled with political wisdom of a practical sort. I have in mind his work *On Staseis*, on which many others both sophists and Platonic philosophers, have thought it not unworthy to write commentaries, and his work *On the Method of Deinotēs* and his *Notes for Public Speaking*, which he himself mentions,[53] but more than any of the other works, his treatise *On Ideas* is worthy of admiration, for it is the best on the subject and the most worked out in accordance with the art and in no way failing in the perfect critical control of discourse. Since, however, much of the contents is not easy for everyone to understand and since up to now I have not met with a commentary on it, I thought it necessary, my dearest child Alexander, to put together some brief notes to the best of my ability for the more accurate reading of the book. But if someone can compose something still better than this which will contribute to the task, I shall feel complete gratitude to him for furnishing us with a guide in fact, not in words. As it is, with prayers to the gods of speech to favor us and our undertaking, let us begin the task. (I, pp. 1-2 Rabe)

The commentary takes the form of lemmata and notes. In the first of these Syrianus supplies a definition of "idea," which is wanting in Hermogenes' text as we have seen:

An idea is a quality of speech, harmonious with the person and subjects involved, in terms of thought, diction, and the whole interconnexion of the harmony. A species (*eidos*) differs from an idea in the same way that a genus differs from a species and the whole from the part. Species encompasses ideas, and ideas are subordinate to species. It is impossible for the judicial, delib-

[53] He means *On Invention*, but perhaps he had not seen it.

erative, and panegyrical species of speech to exist apart from a mixture of many ideas. (II, pp. 2-3 Rabe)

Thus rhetoric (genus) consists of species (judicial, etc.) and they in turn of ideas. Syrianus elucidates and often illustrates about two hundred passages in Hermogenes' text, though many of his notes are quite brief. There are several references to Dionysius of Halicarnassus, three to Basilicus the Sophist, two to Apsines and Iamblichus, and one to Porphyry.

Marcellinus

A third extant commentary to Hermogenes *On Staseis* is that bearing the name of Marcellinus. Some scholars have sought to identify Marcellinus as the author of the *Life of Thucydides*, but this is unlikely if, as now generally believed, the life is a Sixth-Century reediting of a much earlier work.[54] Marcellinus seems to have drawn on a lost earlier commentary on Hermogenes by Athanasius of Alexandria, but not to have known the work of Syrianus or George of Alexandria.[55] Byzantine scholars regarded Marcellinus' commentary as of comparable authority with that of Sopatros and Syrianus and preserved it in a work also containing portions of their commentaries.[56] This composite commentary (IV, pp. 1-864 Walz) has an anonymous prolegomenon, the end of which can be identified as the work of Marcellinus, and it seems likely that the prolegomenon as a whole is a revision by a later editor, probably the

[54] See OCD², s.v. "Marcellinus."
[55] See R-E XIV, 1487-88.
[56] The chief MS is *Parisinus Graecus* 2923 of the Eleventh Century, but portions of the text appear in other commentaries, and some of the attributions to the three authors may be wrong. See Hugo Rabe, "Aus Rhetoren-Handschriften: 11. der Dreimänner-Kommentar W IV," *RhM* 64 (1909), 578-90.

one who created the composite commentary, of Marcellinus' original introduction.[57]

This prolegomenon (PS, pp. 258-96 Rabe) integrates philosophical concepts beyond those found in Sopatros' preface into an approach to the study of rhetoric. It has a number of parallels with Sixth-Century Alexandrian commentators on Plato and Aristotle, such as David and Elias.[58] The author begins with the three intellectual faculties of *nous, dianoia,* and *doxa* (mind, thought, and opinion), to which are referred respectively *epistēmē, technē,* and *empeiria*. Each is defined. The existence of rhetoric is shown by historical example: rhetoric existed among the gods, heroes, and men, leading to Corax and Tisias in Sicily and Gorgias and the Attic Orators. The history of rhetoric among men is considered in terms of five peristatic, or circumstantial, headings: person, place, time, manner, and cause. Since rhetoric among men was caused by democracy it is necessary to explain the different kinds of constitution: monarchy, aristocracy, democracy, and their vitiated forms—tyranny, oligarchy, and ochlocracy (pp. 271-74 Rabe).

The author then turns to the definition of rhetoric. He first defines definition, including genus, species, and differentia, and then applies the process to definition of rhetoric, examining and rejecting many definitions. The definition of Plato's *Gorgias* is reviewed at length, its inconsistency with the treatment in the *Phaedrus* noted, and the conclusion reached that Plato's criticism of rhetoric fits sycophancy, but does not apply to "our rhetoric" (PS, p. 283 Rabe). The Neoplatonists teach a philosophical rhetoric. The definition which the author ultimately accepts is the same which we found in Sopatros, attributed there to Lollianus, elsewhere to Dionysius of Halicarnassus, but here to no authority.

[57] See PS, pp. lxxvi-lxxxv.
[58] See Rabe, "Der Dreimänner-Kommentar" (supra, n. 56), 579-80.

Next the *erga* of rhetoric are briefly defined as to deliver a proemium for good will, a narrative for credibility, an *agōn* for demonstration, and a summary for reminding. The *telos*, or end of rhetoric, is not to persuade, but to use persuasive methods. The general introduction concludes with a discussion of the *eidē* of rhetoric which are associated with the three Platonic faculties of the soul, deliberative with the appetitive, judicial with the passionate, and panegyrical with the rational. Aristotle had given highest rank to deliberative oratory, but late antiquity and Byzantium elevate epideictic to the noblest form. Each of the *eidē* has its *telos*, its time, its place, its persons.

The general introduction is followed by an introduction to *On Staseis* which considers its objective, utility, authority, form of teaching, title, and application (*PS*, pp. 287-96 Rabe). The objective is regarded as entirely intellectual: an understanding of the division of questions; even the utility of the work is described in terms of planning a speech rather than giving one. The author knows no more about Hermogenes than is found in Philostratus, and he seems to know of only three works: *Progymnasmata*; *On Staseis*; *On Ideas*. He regards these as making up a whole treatment of the art, but the Hermogenic corpus of later times seems not yet to have existed.

The prolegomenon concludes (*PS*, pp. 293-96 Rabe) with consideration of the topic which we saw discussed by Porphyry and Sopatros. Why does Hermogenes (or Minucianus in Porphyry's case) not provide a definition of rhetoric? The importance of this question results from the study of rhetoric as a matter of definition and division and from the fact—awkward for Neoplatonists—that Plato in the *Gorgias* rejected the claim that rhetoric was an art. According to the author of the prolegomenon, the true reason Hermogenes did not define rhetoric is that he was its "ally" in its state of danger, attacked by Plato. He did not wish to reply directly to Plato, but approached the subject obliquely, showing that rhetoric is a system which in fact fulfills the definition of art. This passage subsequently recurs in a part of the commentary attributed to Marcellinus (IV, p. 53 Walz) and is the basis of the attribution of the prolegomenon, or at least some of it, to Marcellinus.

George of Alexandria

A fourth commentary is that by George, sophist of Alexandria, continued by his student Zeno. He has usually been called Georgios Monos, but Monos is a title meaning "unique."[59] His work consists of fifty-four lectures on Hermogenes' *On Staseis* without lemmata in the Egyptian style. The writing is diffuse and repetitious, but the author had a good knowledge of classical literature. As rhetorical authorities he cites Athanasius, Aquila, Eustathius, Metrophanes, Minucianus, Porphyry, and Sopatros, but not Syrianus or Marcellinus. He may have been a contemporary of the last two, whose works had not yet reached Egypt; this would give a date in the early Fifth Century.

Other commentators of late antiquity include Athanasius, mentioned as a source for Marcellinus and George, Eustathius who is cited by George, Photius the Rhetor, and Phoebammon.[60] Parts of their works may be included without identification in later anonymous commentaries.

[59] Portions of the text are printed in Walz VII, 1, pp. 655-64, 690-95. A better text, unprinted, exists in *Parisinus Graecus* 2919 with the title *Scholia, with God's Help, for Diaeresis from the Lectures of the Same Georgios, Sole Sophist of Alexandria*. See Ludwig Schilling, "Quaestiones Rhetoricae Selectae," *Jahrbücher für classische Philologie, Supplementband* 28 (1903), 663-92, and Hugo Rabe, "Aus Rhetoren-Handschriften: 7. Georgios," *RhM* 63 (1908), 517-26. On the name see John Duffy, "Philogica Byzantina IV," *GRBS* 21 (1980), 265-68.

[60] See Gloeckner, pp. 78-88 and 90-92; Schilling, (supra, n. 59), pp. 715-33; Hugo Rabe, "Aus Rhetoren-Handschriften: 4. Athanasios, ein Erklärer des Hermogenes," *RhM* 62 (1907), 586-90; Schmid-Stählin, pp. 935-36.

For example, *Parisinus Graecus* 3032 contains an anonymous commentary, perhaps compiled in the Ninth Century, which appears to contain excerpts from a commentary by an unknown author of the Fourth or Fifth.[61] The anonymous commentary of Walz VII six times cites a rhetorician named Paul "the famous."[62] "Famous" apparently only to his own students, since "most sophists were not even able to name this man who was so distinguished in the art" (VII, p. 34 Walz). Paul was apparently a vigorous defender of Hermogenes and may well have lived around A.D. 400, since his name appears between those of Sopatros and Athanasius in one list.[63] It seems clear that by the Fifth Century the paramount authorities on rhetoric were Aphthonius and Hermogenes and that the process of developing a standardized curriculum based on progymnasmata, stasis theory, invention, and style was well under way. An integral part of this concept of a curriculum was the composition of prolegomena both to individual works in the course and to the course as a whole.

Prolegomena

Teachers of rhetoric, especially those of a philosophical bent, often began their lectures with introductions which explained the nature of the subject and its relation to other things. Aristotle, for example, begins the *Rhetoric* with a discussion of the relationship of rhetoric to dialectic, the faults of previous treatments, and the utility of rhetoric, and then proceeds to define it. Quintilian begins the *Institutio* with elementary and grammatical education, but in the second half of Book Two examines definitions of rhetoric (2.15), its utility (2.16), whether it is an art (2.17),

[61] See P. H. Richter, "Byzantinischer Kommentar zu Hermogenes," *Byzantion* 3 (1926), 153-204.
[62] *Paulos ho panu*, see W. Stegemann in *R-E* XVIII, 2374-76.
[63] See Rabe, "Athanasios" (supra, n. 60), p. 587.

of what other arts it is composed (2.18), whether nature or theory contributes more (2.19), whether rhetoric is a virtue (2.20), and what is its material, and continues at the beginning of Book Three with a survey of writers on rhetoric and other introductory questions. We have seen that Porphyry discussed the definition of rhetoric in his commentary on Minucianus, doubtless in an introduction, and it is possible that his introduction in other ways provided a model for later prolegomena as his commentary provided a model for later commentators on Hermogenes. The prolegomena of Sopatros and Marcellinus, just considered, are indications of the philosophical approach to rhetoric in the late Fourth Century.

Commentaries on the Aphthonian-Hermogenic corpus in manuscripts of the Middle and Later Byzantine Periods are accompanied by prolegomena, some to the study of rhetoric as a whole, others to individual works in the corpus. Some are quite philosophical and addressed to teachers or advanced students, others quite elementary. Some, such as that we have just attributed to Marcellinus, date from late antiquity, others are Byzantine and carry the names of known scholars such as John Doxapatres or Maximus Planudes, but the material in them is very similar to that found in prolegomena which can be dated to the Fifth or Sixth Centuries. Hugo Rabe's *Prolegomenōn Syllogē* is a collection of thirty-three such prolegomena.[64] In the prolegomena to rhetoric as a whole, Rabe detected two traditions, both in existence by the Fifth Century. One tradition organizes the material around the four questions of Aristotle's *Posterior Analytics* (2.1.89b23): Does something, in this case rhetoric, exist? What is its definition? What are its qualities? What is its end or purpose? Marcellinus' prolegomenon belongs essentially to this tradition,

[64] Hugo Rabe, *Prolegomenon Sylloge*, Leipzig: Teubner, 1931.

with some expansion. A second tradition is organized around a series of ten questions which cover and expand the ground of the four questions. A good example of this tradition is number four in Rabe's collection which Walz (VI, pp. 4-30) had wrongly attributed to John Doxapatres, a teacher of the Eleventh Century. Rabe showed that it is more likely the work of a rhetorician of the late Fourth or early Fifth Century, living in Asia.[65] The ten questions which it outlines at the beginning (PS, p. 18 Rabe) and then discusses are: Did rhetoric come from the gods and exist among them? Did rhetoric exist among the heroes? How did rhetoric come among men? How did rhetoric flower in Athens? These four questions, as we have noted, appear in Marcellinus also as replacements for the question Does rhetoric exist? Fifth is the definition of rhetoric, its *telos*, and its *ergon*. (This too is found in Marcellinus.) Sixth are the species of rhetoric, as at the end of Marcellinus' general introduction, but in greater detail. The seventh question we have not met before: How many rhetorics are there and of what sort? There are five, we are told (p. 37 Rabe): each is an antistrophe, the first and highest to philosopy, the second to politics, of which Miltiades, Cimon, Themistocles, and Pericles in the Fifth Century are examples, the third to dialectic, of which Demosthenes, Lycurgus, and other good fourth-century orators are examples, the fourth to sycophancy, of which Aristogeiton and Hegemon are examples, and the fifth to pure flattery, in which the leaders are Demades and Aristodemus. The eighth question deals with kinds of delivery, a traditional subject of rhetorical theory for which the Hermogenic corpus provided no discussion. Three kinds of delivery are briefly sketched: *syntonos*, most valued in judicial oratory, which involves a strong, rapid, and rough explosion of breath and an impression of anger;

---

[65] Ibid., pp. xxxviii-xxxix.

aneimenos, which is its opposite, soft, gentle, and mellifluous and is apparently to be used in reading poetry; and *mesos*, which is suitable for reading aloud a law or giving a lecture or reading a letter.

The ninth question deals with the kinds of constitution, a matter which Marcellinus had discussed as part of his historical survey. Our author notes (p. 41 Rabe) that the Athenians in the time of the Ten Orators lived under democracy, the Lacedaimonians under aristocracy, "but we now happily live in a monarchy with faith and orthodoxy."

The tenth question is, In how many ways ought the rhetoricians to teach rhetorical knowledge? The answer is a valuable glimpse into how rhetoricians lectured on the classics and can be compared to the various kinds of material found in some collections of scholia, such as those to Demosthenes. There are seven methods outlined. First, by allegory, when the material is interpreted to mean something different from what it says. Second by preface, when the teacher identifies the stasis headings and enthymemes and gives a synopsis of the argument. Third is by art, when the teacher identifies specific examples of stasis and argument, apparently going through the text with a running commentary. Fourth is by history, identifying the historical background, characters, and causes. Fifth is by figure, naming each figure of speech. Sixth is by idea, identifying which of the Hermogenic ideas of style is being employed. Seventh is by clarification, when the teacher elucidates the thought by paraphrasing it. Although this system of seven methods is characteristic of later Greek antiquity, many of the techniques were practiced earlier and are noted by Quintilian (2.5.7).

The prolegomena to rhetoric are analogous to prolegomena to philosophy composed by the Neoplatonists. Some of these, such as Ammonius' introduction to Aristotle's *Categories*, are divided into ten headings, though there is little overlap in content with the ten questions about rhetoric. Others—for example, David's Introduction to philosophy—are based on the four Aristotelian questions.[66] They also have some analogies to the Latin *accessus* writings of the Middle Ages.

A few other prolegomena can be attributed to specific teachers of late antiquity. The first in Rabe's collection bears the name of Trophonios the Sophist, of whom nothing is known; however, the fifth, which resembles the prolegomenon of Marcellinus, is attributed to Troilus. He may well be the sophist of Constantinople listed in the *Suda*, and is probably the friend of Synesius by that name (*Ep.* 26, 73, and 118). The historian Socrates (7.1 and 27) mentions Troilus as a native of Sidon, a Christian, and an adviser to the procurator Anthemius early in the Fifth Century. The twelfth prolegomenon, introductory to *On Staseis*, is an excerpt from a longer introduction by Athanasius of Alexandria edited by a certain Zosimos. Athanasius may be identified with the source used by Marcellinus and George of Alexandria, in which case he lived in the late Fourth or early Fifth Century. Zosimos, less certainly, might be Zosimos of Gaza or Zosimos of Ascalon, to be discussed in the next chapter as members of the School of Gaza. Athanasius' prolegomenon seems to have been a work of some originality for the time; in contrast to others, it defends Aristotle's definition of rhetoric.

Most interesting of all is prolegomenon number twenty-eight. Although preserved anonymously in the text of Syrianus, where it clearly does not belong, it can be identified as the work of Phoebammon by references in a passage of John of Sicily which was taken over by John Doxapatres (VI, pp. 67 and 73 Walz; *PS*, pp. 405 and 412 Rabe). The name Phoebammon was common in Egypt, and the au-

[66] See L. G. Westerink, *Anonymous Prolegomena to Platonic Philosophy* Amsterdam: North-Holland, 1962.

thor may be the sophist of Antinoöpolis mentioned by John Moschus (*Pratum Spirituale* 143), in which case he lived in the Sixth Century. His commentary to *On Staseis* (*PS*, p. 386 Rabe) is lost, though there are some references to it in Byzantine rhetoricians, and he is probably the author of the extant *Scholia on Rhetorical Figures*.[67]

Phoebammon's prolegomenon is introductory to *On Ideas* and is of special interest because it reveals the existence of opposition to Hermogenes' concepts and to the theory of imitation. It is possible that this developed in Alexandria in opposition to the teachings of Athenian Neoplatonists as seen in Syrianus' commentary and in the protheoria to Damascius' *Life of Isidore*.[68]

Phoebammon himself believes firmly in the utility of the Hermogenic ideas, both as a basis for criticism of the classics and as a way of achieving stylistic excellence in composing speeches. He quotes extensively from those opposed to the theory, but refers to them only as "they." Hermogenes he regularly refers to as *ho technikos*, the authority on the art. To judge from Phoebammon's quotations, the critics rejected the logical concept of both characters and ideas of style and the practical possibility of imitation of them. They took their start from Porphyry's analogy "as soul to body, so thought to speech" and argued that "it is not possible to know the quality of the characters if they are entirely like a living body." Authorities differ on the number of characters, and in fact the number is unknowable, since any mixture is possible. If two styles are alike, this has resulted from chance. Most of these arguments are old; Quintilian, for example, had thought (12.10.66-67) that there were innumerable characters of style, and the authorities cited by the critics are all prior to Hermogenes.

[67] See W. Stegemann in *R-E* xx 326-43.
[68] See A. Brinkmann, "Phoebammon *Peri mimeseos*," *RhM* 61 (1906), 117-34.

They include Demetrius' *On Style*, a work otherwise very little known in this period. It is not entirely clear whether the criticisms represent an extreme form of Platonism, grounded in the Platonic demand that discourse be like a living body, or whether that premise is borrowed from the Neoplatonists for controversial purposes only, since the critics seem to reject the whole Platonic theory of ideas.

Phoebammon replies to the critics on largely practical grounds: it is difficult to know the unique features of everything, easier to grasp a general idea of which each instance is a part; there is such a thing as a generally plain style, even if it is sometimes more amplified, sometimes more reduced; although one cannot know completely the style of Demosthenes or Plato, it is possible to get a general grasp of it. Later orators would have been reduced to silence if they had thought that they had to be exactly like Demosthenes. Quintilian had argued something similar about imitation of Cicero (12.11.28). Phoebammon thinks that the name given to a character, as to a person, is only a convenient symbol; Hermogenes, he says, sought to find a name for each form of style and metaphorically transferred that name to the idea. Thus Phoebammon does not appear to believe in the independent existence of the ideas, like Platonic forms, and indeed no Neoplatonist seems to have so argued. Phoebammon's discussion is dominated by the triad nature-theory-practice, and he presents his opponents as lazy: they want to rely on nature and not undertake the hard work necessary to attain excellence of style. Once having disposed of the opponents, Phoebammon continues his introduction to Hermogenes' *On Staseis* with the topics traditional in such introductions: the objective, utility, title, authenticity, arrangement, and parts of the work.

Figures of Speech

Hermogenes' *On Invention, On Ideas*, and *On Method* all include discussion of the use of figures, but there was a continuing need for handbooks which named, defined, and exemplified figures in ways which could be routinely learned by students of rhetoric. Some such works concentrated on the figures found in a single author, such as the treatise of Tiberius *On the Figures of Demosthenes*, composed in the late Third or early Fourth Century.[69] Examples from Demosthenes dominated many such handbooks, but general handbooks usually used a variety of examples and eventually came to add some from Christian sources. Byzantine rhetorical *corpora* often include a work on figures, but no one work gained the authority of Aphthonius and Hermogenes on their subjects, and Byzantine lists of figures are often anonymous compilations. Individual Greek authors from earlier times who made important contributions to the theory of figures include Caecilius of Calacte working in the Augustan period, and Alexander, son of Numenius, in the Second Century. Caecilius' work is lost, Alexander's survives in an epitome (III, pp. 1-40 Spengel).

Phoebammon's handbook (III, pp. 41-56 Spengel) is called *Scholia* and appears to be excerpts from a larger work; it may also have been reworked by an editor who added some Christian examples.[70] There is no specific reference to Hermogenes, but the treatise is frequently preserved in manuscripts together with works of Hermogenes, and figures discussed by Phoebammon were sometimes transferred into the work of Alexander on the same subject by Byzantine teachers seeking to compile a comprehensive

[69] See Tiberii *De Figuris Demosthenicis*, ed. Guilelmus Ballaira, Rome: Bibliotheca Athena, 1968.
[70] See Brinkmann, "Phoebammon" (supra, n. 68), p. 119, and Stegemann *R-E* (supra, n. 67), 333-34.

treatise. As in his prolegomenon, Phoebammon is systematic and emphasizes nature over art. At the outset he states four questions: What is the utility of figures? Why are they so-called? Do they exist by nature or by art and deliberate act? Are they of one sort or more than one, and what are the differences? In reply, figures are said to be useful in preserving "the qualities of the ancients" and in avoiding satiety, since a hearer is pleased by them. Thus figures make a speech more persuasive. The definitions of figures given by Zoilus, Caecilius, Athenaeus, and Apollonius Molon are rejected in favor of the "perfect" definition: "a figure is an alteration in thought or diction, for the better, occurring without a trope," that is, without departing from the proper meaning of the words. This definition is in fact that of Alexander (III, p. 11 Spengel), but he is not named. Phoebammon's account, especially of figures of thought, shows much influence of Alexander. Its unusual feature is that the two traditional species of figures of speech and figures of thought are each subdivided into four headings: figures resulting from *endeia* or omission, from pleonasm or supplement, from metathesis or inversion, and from enallage or alteration. The four categories clearly accord well with the interest in definition and division which characterize Neoplatonic rhetoric. These categories were known to Quintilian (9.3.27) and therefore not invented by Phoebammon, but they are not utilized in any other extant treatise. They may have been originated by grammarians who discussed figures of speech and have been extended by Phoebammon to the figures of thought.[71] They fit figures of speech much better than they do figures of thought, but even here the scheme is not followed out in all its logical possibilities. One might, for example, have expected that asyndeton, which is Phoebammon's first figure

[71] Stegemann, ibid., 335-36.

of speech by omission, would be balanced by polysyndeton, or figure by pleonasm, but the latter was not on the canonical list and had been omitted by Alexander and other writers. The term occurs only in scholia and there rarely, though the device itself is common enough in late Greek writing. Some historically important figures discussed by Alexander are oddly omitted by Phoebammon, for example, antithesis and homoioteleuton. Of the Gorgianic figures only paronomasia is included, and treatment of it is unsatisfactory.

Application of the system to figures of thought works reasonably well in the case of endeia and pleonasm, but is strained by metathesis and enallage, and a number of inconsistencies arise between the treatment and statements Phoebammon has made in the preface. In some cases the text may be defective. The last two pages of the treatise are apparently spurious, since they do not accord with what has gone before, and perhaps were added to include several figures not discussed by Phoebammon.

Among other treatises on figures from late antiquity the most interesting is perhaps an anonymous work *On Figures of Speech* (III, pp. 110-60 Spengel). Its compiler was a Christian who has specifically sought to write a discussion of figures based on the Hermogenic treatises *On Invention* and *On Method*, which he regards as genuine works. This suggests a late date, perhaps in the Sixth Century. There are similarities between the treatise and an anonymous commentary to *On Invention* suggesting that they may be by the same author or at least draw on the same source. Examples are drawn chiefly from Homer and Demosthenes, but Gregory of Nazianzus' Funeral Oration for Basil is cited once (III, p. 134 Spengel).[72] Acceptance of Greg-

---

[72] See *R-E* I, 2331, and Schmidt-Stählin, p. 941.

ory's works among the classics can also be seen in the treatise of Pseudo-Zonaios, which may belong to this period.[73]

Neoplatonic Commentaries on the *Phaedrus* and the *Gorgias*

The writing of commentaries on dialogues of Plato by Neoplatonists encouraged the development of a theory of literary interpretation.[74] It can be seen in Iamblichus, but was most fully developed by Syrianus' student Proclus in Athens in the middle of the Fifth Century. This theory takes its start from the statement in the *Phaedrus* (264c2-5) that a speech should be a living body in which all parts, like limbs, constitute a unity. From this authoritative principle the Neoplatonists inferred that a dialogue of Plato, by definition a work of the highest artistic merit, must have a single unified purpose; all its literary features, including setting, characters, and rhetorical qualities, should be interpreted in accordance with that purpose. A literary artist is analogous to the demiurge and creates a microcosm of reality through the use of symbols; the function of a commentator is to discover the artist's intention. These principles can be seen in all Neoplatonic commentaries to Plato, including that by Hermeias of Alexandria to *Phaedrus*.

Hermeias was the student of Syrianus in Athens and married his niece, but subsesquently returned to his native Alexandria to teach philosophy. What is known about him personally comes chiefly from Damascius' *Life of Isidore*, where his industry and uprightness are praised, but he is said to have been lacking in true love of knowledge and quickness of intellect; what he knew he learned from books

[73] See *R-E* I, 2331-32.
[74] See James A. Coulter, *The Literary Microcosm. Theories of Interpretation of the Later Neoplatonists* (Columbia Studies in the Classical Tradition II), Leiden: Brill, 1976.

COMMENTARIES ON PHAEDRUS AND GORGIAS

or from the lectures of Syrianus.[75] This seems to apply to his commentary on the *Phaedrus*, which is apparently an editing of Syrianus' lectures together with some material from a lost commentary by Iamblichus.[76]

Hermeias begins by saying that Socrates sought to bring different people to philosophy in different ways. In this dialogue Phaedrus, who is excited by rhetoric, is brought to the true rhetoric, which is philosophy. Hermeias wishes to set forth the "material" of the dialogue as an aid to understanding of its *skopos*, or intention. He then gives a brief summary of the dialogue (pp. 1-8 Couvreur). The only unusual point made is that Lysias' intent in the speech which Phaedrus reads was not the composition of a rhetorical exercise, but the sexual seduction of Phaedrus. Hermeias then turns to the definition of the *skopos* of the work, setting forth views of other unnamed interpreters. Some say the dialogue is about love, some about rhetoric. In his judgment, love and rhetoric are two sources of movement of the soul, love being external, rhetoric internal. Other commentators say the dialogue is about the soul or about the Good, but all these interpretations miss the real intent. The parts must cohere, "as in a living creature." Iamblichus says that the dialogue is about the good in every aspect (p. 9); this interpretation seems to Hermeias basically correct, but before expounding it he reviews objections to the *Phaedrus* which others have made: that it was childish of Plato to write both for and against love; that it was be-

[75] See Johann Rudolf Asmus, *Das Leben des Philosophen Isidorus von Damascius aus Damaskos*, Leipzig: Felix Meiner, 1911, pp. 44-45.

[76] See Amandus Bielmeier, *Die neuplatonische Phaidrosinterpretation. Ihr Werdegang und ihre Eigenart* (Rhetorisches Studien XVI) Paderborn: Schöningh, 1930, pp. 29-30. For the text see Hermeias von Alexandrien, *In Platonis Phaedrum Scholia*, ed. Paul Couvreur (Bibliothèque de l'école des hautes études CXXXIII) Paris: Bouillon, 1901, reprinted Hildesheim and New York: Olms, 1971. See also R-E VIII, 732-35.

neath him to make fun of Lysias; that he should not have employed such poetic language. These objections are answered in terms of Plato's goals and practices as seen in other dialogues. The *Phaedrus* is ethical and corrective, refutative, protreptic to philosophy, physical and theological in its treatment of love, logical in its treatment of rhetoric.

Hermeias then (p. 11) repeats the theory of the *skopos*, his complaint that interpretations are based only on a part, and the requirement that the whole should cohere like a living organism. His interpretation is that Plato begins with apparent beauty in the figure of Phaedrus, beloved by Lysias out of ignorance of true love. Phaedrus, for his part, is a lover of beautiful works, which is higher than a love of a beautiful body. Socrates in the palinode advances to love of the beauty of the soul, which is virtue and knowledge, then to love of the beauty of the gods, then to intellectual beauty, the source of beauty, the god Love, and Beauty itself. The second half of the dialogue returns to consideration of the beauty of the soul and beauty in speech, thus fitting the end to the beginning. The thought as a whole may be divided into three parts which correspond to aspects of a living organism: one lacks self-control; one is prudent; one is divine. Those who say that the dialogue is about love are not entirely wrong, but they focus only on activity, whereas the dialogue deals with essence, potentiality, and activity. Aristotelian concepts are thus brought into the interpretation.

Hermeias then lists the characters in the dialogue and begins his commentary in the form of lemmata and notes, the Athenian method. These are arranged in three books of which the second, constituting one half of the bulk of notes, is devoted to the palinode, which constitutes only one-quarter of Plato's text.

How an understanding of the *skopos* is applied to interpretation of the text can be seen immediately in Hermeias'

COMMENTARIES ON PHAEDRUS AND GORGIAS

treatment of Plato's opening words, *O phile Phaidre*. *Philon*, he says, refers to beauty and its vocative case calls us to itself. The next words, "Where are you going and where are you coming from?" are to be taken symbolically: Phaedrus is coming from his infatuation with specious beauty. Lysias is in the city and represents the visible world; Phaedrus goes outside the walls and seeks a higher perception; Socrates is an image of right opinion (pp. 13-14).

Hermeias makes occcasional comments on the style of the dialogue and some use of Hermogenic terms, as one would expect in a work emanating from the school of Syrianus.[77] The important rhetorical ideas of the *Phaedrus*—valid content, logical definition and division, unity—are brought out, but Hermeias makes no attempt to apply the concept of philosophical rhetoric to speech in his own day. Aristotle is occasionally cited, but only one reference seems to be to the *Rhetoric*. "According to Aristotle," he says (pp. 233-34), "rhetoric is an antistrophe to dialectic, that is, it is wound around the same things and equally woven in. For the two have the same material and they use probable epicheiremes [sic] and they are called faculties and they take up opposite sides of a case. According to Plato the orator uses the definitional and divisional method. For how can we move from blaming love to praising it without knowing the nature of what is said?"

Hermeias' commentary is the only one on the *Phaedrus* to survive from antiquity and is the major source for the marginal scholia to the dialogue found in manuscripts, as well as for the fragmentary commentary by Michael Psellus in the Eleventh Century.[78] For the *Gorgias* we also have only one ancient commentary, that by Olympiodorus.

Olympiodorus was head of the Alexandrian philosophi-

---

[77] E.g., p. 17 Couvreur (supra, n. 76). See Bielmeier, ibid., pp. 91-93.
[78] See Bielmeier, ibid., pp. 52-56, and A. Jahn, "Michel Psellos über Platons Phaidros," *Hermes* 34 (1899), 315-19.

cal school in the middle of the Sixth Century. Other works attributed to him are commentaries on Plato's *First Alcibiades* and *Phaedo* and on the *Categories* and *Meteora* of Aristotle, as well as a life of Plato and a prolegomenon to philosophy.[79] Like Hermeias, he was not an original thinker and his works are largely compendia of earlier commentaries or the lectures of his teacher Ammonius, who was the son of Hermeias. His commentary on the *Gorgias* consists of fifty *praxeis*, or lectures, in the Egyptian manner, probably representing the notes written up by one of his students.[80]

Olympiodorus begins with an introduction in which he explains that Plato wrote dialogues, despite his strictures on imitation, because we do not live in the ideal state. He then surveys the dramatic situation of the dialogue, its *skopos*, its division into parts, its characters and what they represent, and why Plato set the dialogue in its historical situation, which he regards as soon after Gorgias' first arrival in Athens in 427 B.C.

Olympiodorus says (p. 3 Westerink) that the *skopos* of the *Gorgias* cannot be rhetoric, as some have claimed, for that is discussed in only one part of the dialogue, but is an understanding of the ethical principles which bring us to political happiness. The causes of everything are six: material, formal, productive, model, instrumental, and final. "Many rhetors, not looking at the truth, say that the material cause of politics is the living body, the formal is luxury, the productive cause rhetoric, the model tyranny, the instrument persuasion, and the end pleasure. We say, however, that the material is the soul, not just its rational

[79] See *R-E* XVIII, 207-27, and Westerink, *Prolegomena* (supra, n. 66), xiii-xx. For the text, Olympiodori *In Platonis Gorgiam Commentarii*, ed. L. G. Westerink, Leipzig: Teubner, 1970.

[80] See Rudolf Beutler, "Die Gorgiascholien und Olympiodor," *Hermes* 73 (1938), 380-90.

element but all three parts (rational, passionate, and appetitive), the form is justice and temperance, the productive cause is the philosophical life, the model is the cosmos . . . , the instrument is character and education, the end is the good" (pp. 4-5). Socrates, Olympiodorus believes, discusses the productive cause with Gorgias, the formal cause with Polus, and the final cause with Callicles. The dialogue is thus a unity, though divided into three parts. Socrates himself represents knowledge, Chaerephon right opinion, Gorgias distorted opinion, Polus injustice, and Callicles swinish hedonism.

In his commentary Olympiodorus carefully works out the argument implicit in his approach, often going beyond Plato's thought and including extensive digressions. He praises Gorgias' original answer to Socrates' question, that the art of which he claims knowledge is rhetoric, and explains (pp. 27-28) that there are two kinds of rhetoric, the true which is an art and the false which is *empeiria*. Gorgias' mistake in defining rhetoric (p. 31) is a confusion between its activity and its instrument: when Gorgias says that rhetoric is "about" words he does not realize that they are its instrument. "It is worth asking why Gorgias came to the idea that words underlie rhetoric. We say that it is because rhetoric thinks about words and seeks an arrangement of proemia, *katastasis*, *agōnes*, and the like. He should not simply have said "words," but a certain kind of words. One should realize that rhetoric persuades not only through words, but through silence. . . . And delivery also underlies rhetoric, enforcing persuasion" (pp. 31-32).

Olympiodorus' own views of rhetoric are set forth in the introduction to the twelfth lecture when he is about to take up Socrates' famous definition of rhetoric as a form of flattery, analogous to cookery. He says that rhetoric is both an art and not an art. By the definition of the Stoics it is an art, "for it has a system and is learned and practical and it looks to a useful end" (p. 70). By Socrates' definition it is not an art, since it lacks knowledge. But Socrates is talking about popular rhetoric. True rhetoric is divine and can only be practiced by first becoming a philosopher (p. 73).

Olympiodorus shows a knowledge of Aristotle's *Rhetoric* (e.g., pp. 16 and 88) as well as familiarity with Hermogenes (pp. 24, 52, and 71), but specifically cites neither. He mentions Aelius Aristides several times, probably drawing on Porphyry's treatise against Aristides.[81]

Neoplatonic commentaries on the *Phaedrus* and the *Gorgias* are the capstones of rhetorical theory in late antiquity, the clearest integration of it into a philosophical system. Study of them helps to explain the approach to the teaching of rhetoric at a more elementary level, the content of the prolegomena, and some of the approach to be found in commentaries on Hermogenes written in late antiquity. To complete the picture of how rhetoric was understood from the Fourth to the Six Centuries we need to turn now to the activities of the sophists.

[81] See Friedrich Walter Lenz, "The Quotations from Aelius Aristeides in Olympiodorus' Commentary on Plato's *Gorgias*," *American Journal of Philology* 67 (1946), 103-28.

CHAPTER THREE

The Schools of the Sophists

"Sophist" is commonly used in the time of the Roman empire to mean a teacher of rhetoric. Many sophists took introductory students from the school of the grammarian, taught them progymnasmata and supervised their systematic reading of Demosthenes and the classics, and when they were judged ready for it, lectured to them on rhetorical theory and criticized their practice of declamations. Libanius in Antioch is an example of all of these activities. Sophists regularly declaimed themselves before their schools, and some acquired great reputations as orators, attracting advanced students from all over the world. This was especially true in Athens. The students there were often in their late teens and twenties, had studied rhetoric elsewhere before moving on to Athens, and were primarily interested in refining their abilities at declamation. Only a few Athenian sophists of the Fourth Century show much interest in theory or the composition of handbooks, and their chief activity other than declamation was the delivery of panegyrical orations in the various forms described in the handbooks of Menander. At a time when the theatre was in decay, listening to a sophist was a major form of recreation in many cities and provided many spectators with inspiration and delight. Sophists like Libanius often acquired leadership roles in their communities and sometimes even political influence. Unlike earlier sophists, they show little hostility to philosophy. Nor did the Neoplatonists share Plato's distrust of rhetoric. Hellenism was closing ranks.

Official support of the teaching of rhetoric in Greek had begun in the Second Century when Antonius Pius appointed Lollianus to a municipal chair of rhetoric in Athens (Philostratus *Lives of the Sophists* 1, p. 526 Kayser).[1] In a letter addressed to the cities of Asia, but applicable to the entire empire, he also accorded tax relief to sophists, grammarians, and physicians, the number being limited to five each in provincial capitals, four in other cities where law courts met, and three elsewhere (*Digest* 27.1.6). The political, military, and financial chaos of the Third Century doubtless partially disrupted these arrangements, but the inclusion of the regulation in the *Digest* shows that it remained in effect until the Sixth Century, when it was abolished by Justinian. As we shall see, Constantinople had the requisite five official sophists in the Fifth Century. Since Corinth was the capital of Greece and seat of the courts, Athens was entitled only to three, and Libanius twice speaks of "the three" in Athens (Or. 1.24-25 and 2.14).

In the Fourth Century the national system of education was standardized by law.[2] The price edict of Diocletian, published in 301, set salaries of sophists at 250 denarii per pupil per month, as compared with 200 for grammarians. Additional developments can be seen in Book Thirteen, Title Three, of the *Theodosian Code*.[3] Official sophists were exempted from public obligations and court summons and their salaries were to be paid by the local municipalities. At some times and in some cities this became difficult, and in Gaul, at least, the imperial government provided a minimum subsidy. According to Saint Augustine (*Confessions* 1.16), salaried teachers in Carthage also received fees from

---

[1] See Ivars Avotins, "The Holders of the Chairs of Rhetoric at Athens," *HSCPh* 79 (1975), 313-24.

[2] See L. Hahn, "Ueber das Verhältnis von Staat und Schule in der römischen Kaiserzeit," *Philologus* 76 (1920), 176-91.

[3] For translation, see Clyde Pharr, *The Theodosian Code and the Novels and the Sirmondian Constitutions*, Princeton Univ. Pr., 1952, pp. 387-90.

their students, and this may have been true generally. Although emperors and governors sometimes meddled, the formal appointment of an official sophist lay with the municipal council which paid him, and contests were held to fill vacancies (see, e.g., Libanius 1.35, 37, and 86-87). The emperor Julian provided that appointments were to be made on the basis of character and eloquence. Imperial support of the schools in late antiquity should be viewed as a general effort to maintain the cultural life of the cities and specifically as an attempt to provide a pool of educated persons for appointment to positions in the state bureaucracy.

The Sophists of Athens

From the fourth century to the Sixth Century Athens was the greatest educational center of the classical world. She owed this position to the fame of the philosophers and rhetoricians who taught there and the ability of the students they attracted from all over the world. It is, however, a modern fallacy to speak of a "University of Athens."[4] There was no organized faculty, no university building, no system of examinations, no degrees. The Neoplatonic School consisted of its scholarch, with whom were associated a small number of senior philosophical scholars, and a group of advanced students. It owned property and had a considerable endowment from gifts.[5] The rhetorical schools consisted of the separate schools of sophists and their students, usually housed and declaiming in the sophist's house. One such house, complete with auditorium, has been excavated

[4] As done, for example, by John W. H. Walden, *The Universities of Ancient Greece*, New York: Scribners, 1909.

[5] See John Patrick Lynch, *Aristotle's School. A Study of a Greek Educational Institution*, Berkeley and Los Angeles: Univ. of California Pr., 1972, pp. 168-98, and John Glucker, *Antiochus and the Late Academy* (Hypomnemata LVI), Göttingen: Vanderhoeck and Ruprecht, 1978, pp. 322-29.

on the north slope of the Acropolis. Although there were only three official sophists, numerous private schools existed as in other cities: a passage in Eunapius (p. 491 *ad fin.*) may imply that the total number of sophists teaching in Athens at one point in the Fourth Century was twelve to fifteen. Rivalry among sophists and between the students of each sophist was sharp. Students coming to Athens to study with one sophist were sometimes kidnapped by the followers of another and forced to join his school; an oath of loyalty to the teacher was required of all (Libanius 1.16 and 20). Student riots, like that which ended in the trial in Corinth described in Chapter One, were not infrequent. The whole atmosphere of the city encouraged jealousy, ambition, and notoriety. The prospect of the excitement was for some an inducement to study there (Libanius 1.19).

We know something about the life of sophists and students in Fourth-Century Athens from the accounts of studies there by Libanius and Gregory of Nazianzus, but our major source is Eunapius' *Lives of the Philosophers*, which is a continuation of Philostratus' account of earlier periods of sophistry.[6] Eunapius was born in Sardis around 346 and went to Athens to study rhetoric at the age of sixteen (p. 493). He stayed five years and then returned home to teach rhetoric until his death about 414. This was apparently a normal pattern, also followed by Libanius.

Eunapius is an entertaining writer, but a maddening historical source because of his casual treatment of detail. His preface announces that he will describe *erga*, not *parerga*, but what chiefly interested him was the personal character of the teachers: he admires a loftiness of soul, combined with gentleness of manner and love of truth and beauty.

[6] Trans. Wilmer Cave Wright, *Philostratus and Eunapius* (LCL), Cambridge: Harvard Univ. Pr., 1952. See also Fritz Schemmel, "Die Hochschule von Athen im IV und V Jahrhundert *post Christum natum*," *Neue Jahrbücher für Pädagogik* 22 (1908), 494-513.

The sophists appealed to him particularly because of their efforts to preserve the old eloquence of Greece at a time when everything else, he felt, was slipping into decay. The title of his work, in contrast to that of Philostratus, is significant: he sees sophistry as a philosophical movement embracing Hellenic wisdom and eloquence in a Neoplatonic synthesis, and he has almost no interest in rhetorical theory or in the teaching of rhetorical techniques.[7]

In the early Fourth Century the most eminent official sophist in Athens was apparently Julian of Caesarea in Cappadocia (Eunapius, pp. 482-85). We have already met him at the trial described in Chapter One.[8] The death of Julian, sometime around 330, produced considerable excitement among the sophists who vied for his chair. Eunapius (pp. 487-90) gives a confused report, which may perhaps be reduced to the following succession of events. From among the many applicants, the city council elected six finalists to participate in a contest before the governor, who was given the right to make the final choice. Two who were so elected were Epiphanius, known as the author of a work on stasis theory and a commentary on Demosthenes,[9] and Diophantus. It is possible that they were already the holders of the other two chairs and that the contest was intended not only to choose a successor for Julian, but also to establish a priority among the official holders of chairs, or it is possible that they were included to help determine a standard of excellence, but it is also possible that more than one vacancy existed at this time. Both Epiphanius and Diophantus certainly emerged from the con-

---

[7] The attitude is characteristic of the period, see Lellia Cracco Ruggini, "Sofisti greci nell' impero Romano," *Athenaeum* 49 (1971), 402-25, esp. 410-16.

[8] He may be the Julian to whom Nilus attributes a fragment about epicheiremes, see Gloeckner, pp. 92-93.

[9] Ibid., pp. 93-94.

test with official chairs. Two of the remaining four candidates failed to get a unanimous vote from the council, and Eunapius says that they had only the name and no authority. These are probably Sopolis and Parnasius, who were sophists in the sense that they were competent teachers of rhetoric but lacked the charisma expected in holders of a chair. The two serious candidates for the third chair were Hephaestion and Prohaeresius, both associated with Julian and friends of each other. Hephaestion declined to compete against Prohaeresius, but the other candidates bribed the governor and drove Prohaeresius out of town. With the arrival of a new governor and with the endorsement of Constantius II, Prohaeresius was able to return. The governor then assembled the sophists for the final decision, but to the horror of most he announced that he would propose a new theme to be handled ex tempore and that Prohaeresius was invited to participate. As the governor was about to propose a theme, Prohaeresius saw two of his enemies in the back of the audience and, confident of his own extemporaneous ability, dramatically called on the governor to ask them to propose the theme. From Eunapius' account it is clear that the theme proposed was a judicial problem like those found in Hermogenes' *On Staseis* and involved stasis of definition, but we are not told what it was. The actual theme was difficult because it seemed to allow little opportunity for adornment and thus taxed the competitors' ingenuity. As usual, Prohaeresius put on a virtuoso performance; it seems clear that he was given the appointment, but Eunapius characteristically fails to say so. In 336 the three sophists in chairs are explicitly said to have been Epiphanius the Syrian, Diophantus the Arab, and Prohaeresius the Armenian (Eunapius, p. 495).

When Eunapius first met Prohaeresius in 362 (p. 485), the latter was eighty-seven years of age, which would mean he had been born in 275. His hair was thick, curly, and silvered, "resembling the foaming sea. . . . He had such vigor in speech and his aged body was so animated by the youthfulness of his soul, that the author of these words thought him ageless and immortal and attended him as a god." Prohaeresius had studied with Ulpian in Antioch before joining Julian's school in Athens, and he held a chair as Julian's successor from the early 330s to 367.

Sometime between 345 and 350 Prohaeresius was summoned to Gaul by the emperor Constans, who entertained him and asked him to return home by way of Rome, "desiring honor for the quality of men over whom he had attained rule" (Eunapius, p. 492). Since Prohaeresius was a Christian, it is possible that Constans saw in him a promising spokesman to the pagan aristocracy of the city, acceptable because of his skill as a sophist. Prohaeresius had some success in Rome; his statue was set up with an inscription "Rome the Queen of Cities to the King of Discourse" (Eunapius, p. 492), and he was asked to nominate a teacher of rhetoric for a chair there. He sent his student Eusebius of Alexandria, who seemed well suited since he knew how to fawn and flatter the great (Eunapius, p. 493). This is of course as much a criticism of the Romans as of Eusebius. Prohaeresius also had his own motive in seeing Constans, for he successfully sought from him an improvement in the food supply of Athens, much as Second-Century sophists had sought imperial benefits for their cities, and Constans conferred on Prohaeresius the honorary title of stratopedarch.

Eunapius says (p. 492) that this title required confirmation by Anatolius, praetorian prefect of Illyricum, probably because of the death of Constans early in 350. Anatolius did not become prefect until 357/8; an interval of nearly ten years is thus unobserved in Eunapius' account.[10] When

[10] See A.H.M. Jones, J. Martindale, and J. Morris, *The Prosopography of the Later Roman Empire [PLRE]*, I, Cambridge Univ. Pr., 1971,

Anatolius did come, he posed a problem for declamation on which he wanted to hear the sophists speak (Eunapius, p. 490). There was much discussion among them about the appropriate stasis to be used, but Prohaeresius got private information of the issue the prefect favored and carried off all the honors. Himerius was one of the sophists trying to discover the preferred stasis. We have extracts of a speech of greeting by Himerius to Anatolius (Oration 32 Colonna) which possibly dates from this occasion or a return visit.

The visit of Anatolius does not seem to have resulted in any change in the tenure of the sophists. There had, however, been a competition in 353, judged by the governor, Strategius, who rebuked the Athenians for their unwillingness to call professors from abroad to their chairs and invited Libanius to apply (Or. 1.81-84). Libanius was at this time teaching in Constantinople and unhappy there, but he chose to go to his native Antioch instead. Since Diophantus outlived Prohaeresius, the competition probably resulted from the death of Epiphanius, but we do not know the identity of the successful candidate. The chief possibilities include Milesius, who was admired by Anatolius but perhaps too lethargic for the office, an unnamed Egyptian sophist who was later beaten up by his students and left for Macedon, Sopolis, Sopolis' son, or Parnasius, but not Himerius, who was still seeking a chair in the reign of Julian.

Eunapius was an enthusiastic pagan and plays down Prohaeresius' Christianity, although he does report the story (p. 493), found in Jerome's chronological note on 363 and

---

pp. 59-60, s.v. "Anatolius III." E. Groag suggested that Anatolius held some other office in Greece earlier, see *Die Reichsbeamten von Achaia in spätrömischer Zeit* (Dissertationes Pannonicae I, 14) Budapest: Nemzeti Museum, 1946, p. 29. Certainly Anatolius had heard Epiphanius speak (Eunapius, p. 491) and the latter probably died in 353, "long before" the arrival of Eunapius in 362 (p. 494).

in Orosius (7.30.3), that Prohaeresius refused to take advantage of the exemption offered to him when Julian the Apostate prohibited teaching of the classics by Christians. There is an extant letter by Julian to Prohaeresius (*Epistle* 14) in which he compliments the latter's eloquence, compares it to that of Pericles, but declines to send him a detailed account of his return to Constantinople unless Prohaeresius is planning to give up oratory to write a history of Julian's reign. Gregory of Nazianzus never mentions Prohaeresius in his accounts of his student days with Basil in Athens; this suggests that Gregory did not regard him as an outstanding Christian influence.

Some idea of Prohaeresius' oratory can be had from Eunapius' descriptions. He clearly had unusual extemporaneous ability, something apparently admired by the public but not generally cultivated by the sophists, who were fond of quoting a remark of Aelius Aristides, "We are not among those who vomit, but those who polish" (Eunapius, p. 488). In his speech before the prefect on Constans' gift, Prohaeresius introduced the story of Celeus and Triptolemus and Demeter's visit among men in order to give them the gift of grain. Thus despite his Christianity, he made use of mythological allegory as did other sophists. On Prohaeresius' death Diophantus delivered a funeral oration in his honor, which concluded "O Marathon and Salamis, now have you been silenced. What a trumpet for your trophies have you lost" (Eunapius, p. 494). Which is to say that Prohaeresius' declamations on historical themes were best remembered.

Himerius

The only Athenian sophist whose oratory is preserved is Himerius. Eunapius did not know him personally, but gives (p. 494) a brief sketch of his career. Born in Bithynia, probably around 310, he studied in Athens and then taught rhetoric there privately. When Julian became emperor Himerius went to his court in hopes of advancement but returned to Athens disappointed. Eunapius does not say that he ever obtained an official chair, but perhaps implies that he did after Prohaeresius' death. Of the seven sophists, including Himerius, to whom Eunapius accords separate discussion, all the others are known to have held a chair, and there does not seem to have been anyone else to overshadow him in the last third of the Fourth Century. Photius, who extracts extensively from speeches of Himerius not otherwise preserved, describes him (*Bibliotheca*, Codex 165 *ad fin.*) as head of "the school." As noted in Chapter Two, he was probably the teacher of Sopatros, the author of a commentary on Hermogenes' *On Stasis*

Speeches by sophists were sometimes taken down in shorthand, as happened in the competition in which Prohaeresius secured his chair. Students may also have recorded or copied the speeches of their teachers. Publication, even within the academic community of Athens, would increase the teacher's fame, attract students, and help achieve permanent recognition. In the case of Himerius it may have contributed to his appointment. The extant speeches, insofar as they can be dated, seem to come from early in his career, and we know that some were read by Eunapius (p. 491). He says that they had the ring of political oratory. That is a valuable indication that his major effort went into judicial and historical problems, even though these are not well represented in the extant corpus. Only orations one to seven in the edition of Colonna fall into this category.[11] They include a speech in the character of Hyperides on behalf of Demosthenes, a speech for Demosthenes against Aeschines, an accusation against Epicurus for impiety, a prosecution of a rich man for mistreatment of a poor man,

[11] Himerii *Declamationes et Orationes cum Deperditarum Fragmentis*, ed. Aristides Colonna, Rome: Officina Polygraphica, 1951.

a speech for Themistocles against the king of Persia, a funeral oration in the character of a polemarch of the classical period, and an Areopagitica. The *Polemarchus* is complete; the others survive only in the *eclogai*, or selections, made by Photius in the Ninth Century, which give little feeling for the argumentation as a whole.

The remaining speeches, some preserved complete, some in *eclogai*, are panegyrics in a variety of forms. The serious work of declamation was carried on in the schools in the morning, but after the baths and dinner, sophists brought together their students for *homiliai* and *symposiai*, and these furnished the occasion for speeches on birthdays, weddings, or departures from the school. Leading sophists also spoke in the theatre on official occasions, such as festivals or the arrival of an important visitor to the city, and Himerius' works include examples of this public as well as private epideictic.

Among the epideictic forms employed by Himerius are the monody, the epithalamium, the propemptikon, the protreptikon, the lalia, the dialexis, and the prosphonetikon. The political style of the first seven speeches is replaced in these works by the style of the prose poem, often drawing heavily on the language and images of Greek lyric poetry, emotional, often employing the first person, weaving webs of myth as expression of attitudes and sentiments, but with rhythms foreshadowing the stress accent of medieval Greek.[12]

As an example of Himerius' art in its fully developed form we may briefly consider Oration Forty-eight, Himerius' address to Hermogenes, governor of Achaea, on a visit to Athens. It is the longest of his extant speeches, and

---

[12] See Eduard Norden, *Antike Kunstprosa*, Leipzig: Teubner, 1909, pp. 428-31, and D. Serruys, "Les procédés toniques d'Himérius et les origines du cursus byzantin," *Philologie et linguistique. Mélanges offerts à Louis Havet*, Paris, 1909, pp. 475-79.

the addressee is a known person who held office in Corinth sometime between 350 and 358.[13] Himerius was not yet an official sophist, and his speech was probably one of several in which the sophists of the city vied for the governor's attention.

Many of Himerius' panegyrics carry titles identifying their form. This one does not. As a speech of greeting to an official it is a *prosphonetikos*, but the first half (sections 1-16) has some features of the more informal and personal lalia. The structural elements of this extended proemium are progymnasmatic forms. Himerius begins abruptly with a *mythos*:

> They longed once for Philoctetes as well, after the plague, did the Greeks, and much to the gods did they pray. He, as his suffering abated, taking his bow into his hands, sought to know whether he could still shoot his target-lovers. Now that same Philoctetes did Odysseus summon to battle, arriving and giving token of his art,— that Odysseus who also activates almost the whole poem of Homer, making possible for it to be strummed with verse and music; for the latter busies himself in his poem a little with Achilles, the son of Thetis, describing his battle on the Scamander and his race (with Hector), but Odysseus is everywhere in the epic and with him for the most part the poet is found to take pains. For the victory of Philoctetes and for whatever this Philoctetes accomplished at Troy with his bow, Odysseus took the credit among the Greeks.
>
> You, my friend [the governor], order us, taking up not the bow of Heracles, but the songs of the Muses, to shoot for the Greeks. Behold, I obey you in this too. But

---

[13] See *R-E* VIII, 864-65 (which, however, says Asia instead of Achaea); Groag, *Reichsbeamten* (supra, n. 10), pp. 36-38; *PLRE* (supra, n. 10), I, pp. 424-25, s.v. "Hermogenes IX."

O that I had moved my lyre long ago, since I desired to address you in the midst of the Greeks, but now I wish to denounce with you, my children [his Athenian audience], the Attic Cupids, because stilling their songs for a long time they allowed him [the governor] to be tended by the Ephyrian [Corinthian] Cupids. . . . (48.1-2)

It is possible to analyze this passage, as it is much of later Greek artistic prose, by means of the "seven methods of teaching" as outlined in the tenth question of the Prolegomena, discussed in Chapter Two. The myth is first an allegory, in which Philoctetes stands for Himerius and Odysseus for the governor, Hermogenes. Interpreting it "by preface" would involve stripping away the myth and allegory and summarizing the basic argument: the governor has come to Athens from Corinth and called for oratorical displays; his visit has been long delayed; the fault lies with the Athenians. The composition can be analyzed "by art" in accordance with the inventional and stylistic techniques described in the Hermogenic *On Invention*, probably a work of the Fourth Century. The composition as a whole is *pneumatikos*, which is appropriate to panegyric. The *pneuma* beginning "Now that same Philoctetes . . . ," for example, contains an *enstasis*: "that Odysseus who also activates almost the whole poem . . . ," for this answers a possible objection that the responsibility for action lies with Achilles. This is supported by an epicheireme: "for Homer busies himself with Achilles . . . ," followed by an ergasia: "but Odysseus is everywhere in the epic," then an enthymeme: "and with him for the most part . . . ," and finally an epenthymeme: "for the victory of Philoctetes . . . , Odysseus took the credit among the Greeks." Commentary "by figure" would point out the period, cola, and commata within the *pneuma* and identify such devices as the chiasmus in the first sentence of the speech and the use of the unusual epithet "target-lovers" to mean arrows. Analysis "by idea" would probably point out the use of long vowels and o sounds in the Greek of the first sentence, as well as the poetic vocabulary and metaphor, and conclude that Himerius seeks impressiveness. Finally, the whole passage could be paraphrased "by clarification."

The mythos of Philoctetes which starts the speech (section 1) is followed by a *psogos*, or invective against Attic Cupids for delaying the coming of the Mousegetes, who is Apollo, but here becomes another image for the governor (2). That is followed (3) by an ecphrasis of winter, the season through which they have been waiting, a chria about Anacreon (4), a synkrisis of Anacreon and Himerius (5), and a second psogos (6-7), this time against the governor for not coming earlier. The image of the governor as leader of the muses is maintained. In one of many rhetorical questions, Himerius asks, "Did not God [the emperor] send you to Greece in order that speeches may flower their ancient flower?" The figure emphasizes the connexion between sophistry and pagan culture. The speech continues with a *prokatastasis* in which Himerius declares that he knows why the governor's arrival has been delayed, and an elaborate mythos ensues about the Nile (8), with an ecphrasis of Egypt in time of flood (9). The long wait for the Nile flood makes it even more wonderful when it does come, and that cannot be until the proper festival. Possibly we should associate Hermogenes' visit with the Thargelia, the festival of Apollo in early summer. There follows (10) another myth, drawn from Alcaeus, about Apollo's journey in the winter to the land of Hyperboreans, with his return in the summer and then an ecphrasis of singing birds (11).

The complaint that the governor has not previously come has now been turned into a compliment about how good it is to have him, and we are ready to move on to the governor's virtues. Or almost ready, for first (12) we are treated to a Neoplatonic excursus on the soul, reminiscent of the *Phaedrus*. It is appropriate because of Hermogenes' known philosophical interests. Then at last Himerius is ready to describe the governor's education, career, and virtues as traditional in panegyric (17-33). Even so, he breaks up the narrative with a chria about Pythagoras (18-19) and a myth about Dionysius (26), inspired by the governor's travels.

The speech as a whole is a remarkable tour de force in a highly developed art form. Beauty is sought in every possible way in content, description, and sound. Himerius should probably be imagined delivering it in an elevated chanting tone, with carefully planned gestures. His audience would have been made up of connoisseurs who would recognize the allusions, the figures, the enthymemes, and appreciate the rhythms. The speech is to the Fourth Century what the poems of Pindar were to the early classical period. Modern critics generally have more taste for Pindar than for Himerius, but the primary reason for that may be the freshness with which Pindar seems to strike his lyre and the oppressive weight of a thousand years of literary history which mutes to our ears the bell-like tones of Himerius.

As known to Photius in the Ninth Century, the speeches of Himerius were accompanied by *protheōriai*, introductory remarks made by the sophist to explain to his students the treatment which he will follow. Two of these are preserved and are valuable indications of how Himerius viewed his art. Oration Nine in Colonna's collection is an epithalamium, a prose marriage hymn, addressed to Himerius' student Severus. He seems to have been something of a favorite with the sophist, who also addressed to him the twenty-first and twenty-fourth speeches. The *protheōria* to Oration Nine runs as follows:

It might perhaps seem to someone beside the point to lay down rules about marriage speeches, for where Hymen and choruses and the freedom of poetic license are present, what occasion is there for rules of art? But since the man of learning must do nothing artless even in such speeches, it is worthwhile saying a little about them also. Now let the best rule for epithalamia be to look to the poets for the style, to the needs of the occasion for the contents, to the subject for the rhythm. If the speech aims at all of these things, the composition will exhibit considerable clarity. Of its four parts, the first contains the beginning of the speech, presenting by means of polished enthymemes the thought from which the speaker takes his demonstration; in the second part we render the institution of marriage, naturally commonplace though it is, pleasurable by the novelty of the epicheiremes and the figures of thought, sweetly intermingling moreover some obscure allusions which will not escape an audience keen for these things. The third part contains the encomium of those who marry which, when brought forward in an inquiry about the praiseworthy, quickly fits the occasion. The speech ends with a description of the bride in which the speech attains as well a poetic grace, taking its rhythm from the subject.

Himerius aims at an aesthetic experience, and he thinks of this in something very close to the terminology of Hermogenes' "ideas." Clarity and sweetness are sought above all; thought, figures, and rhythms are among the techniques used to attain stylistic distinction. In the *protheōria* to the tenth speech the Hermogenic word "idea" is actually used, referring to the plain style.[14] Stress there is put on ethos, which is another Hermogenic idea.

[14] For a translation see Walden, *Universities* (supra, n. 4), pp. 238-39.

The sixty-eighth speech has no *protheōria*, but is itself a short protreptic to students to seek *poikilia* in composition. *Poikilia* is described as the variegated play of thought, style, allusion, and rhythm and compared to the various figures on the shield of Achilles or to the transformations of Proteus. Proteus is a good image for a sophist, but not the only one. In Plato's *Republic* (596d) Glaucon ironically calls the demiurge a "wondrous sophist," and Himerius here imitates him by calling the Neoplatonic creator and disposer of all things "the great sophist in the sky." Sophistic creativity is a microcosm of the universe.

The Schools of Antioch[15]

Among the cities of Asia in the Second Century, Ephesus, Smyrna, and Pergamum had been leading centers of sophistry, but in the Fourth Century they were eclipsed by Nicomedia and more especially by Antioch, which became one of the great cities of the world, often honored by the presence of emperors. Antioch was primarily an administrative, military, and trading center. Teachers and students did not dominate society in Antioch as they tended to do in Athens, and though some students were attracted from abroad, a majority were probably natives of the area. In the Third Century, Philostratus had lived in Antioch at the court of Julia Domna (*Lives of the Sophists*, p. 480), and Malchion successfully combined there the duties of a teacher of rhetoric and a presbyter of the Church (Eusebius *Church Hist.* 7.29), but the city reached its greatest rhetorical eminence as the home of Libanius. Other sophists who taught there, like Ulpian, Zenobius, Prohaeresius, and Acacius, are known chiefly through Libanius' references or those of Eunapius.

---

[15] For a general survey, see A. Harrent, *Les écoles d'Antioche. Essai sur le savoir et l'enseignement en Orient au IVe siècle (après J.-C.)*, Paris, 1898.

Libanius

Libanius was born at Antioch in 314 into a locally important family.[16] He always retained the social and political values of the local senatorial society, though he himself as a teacher enjoyed exemption from curial duties which were at this time a serious burden for hereditary landowners in municipalities. When he was ten he lost his father; when he was twenty he received a severe shock from a bolt of lightning, which left him permanently prone to nervous afflictions and headaches. For long he seems to have been a rather indifferent student, but then took up the study of the classics with zeal and in 336 fulfilled his ambition of going to Athens for further study of rhetoric. There he was coerced into becoming the pupil of Diophantus. Four years later he began his teaching career in a private capacity in Constantinople, where he was very successful, but by the beginning of 343 he had been forced out by rivals and

---

[16] Sources on Libanius' life include his own works, esp. Oration 1 and the letters, and Eunapius, pp. 495-96. For text see Libani *Opera*, ed. R. Förster, Leipzig: Teubner, 12 vols., 1903-27, and *Selected Works*, trans. A. F. Norman (LCL), 2 vols., London: Heinemann, 1969; 1977 (Or. 2, 12-24, 30, 45, 47-50). See Gottfried Sievers, *Das Leben des Libanius*, Berlin, 1868; reprinted Amsterdam: Rodopi, 1969; O. Seeck, *Die Briefe des Libanius*, Leipzig, 1906, reprinted Hildesheim: Olms, 1966; F. Schemmel, "Der Sophist Libanius als Schüler und Lehrer," *Neue Jahrbücher für Pädagogik* 20 (1907), 52-69; Schmid-Stählin, pp. 987-1000; R-E xii, 2485-2551; F. A. Wright, *A History of Later Greek Literature from the Death of Alexander in 332 to the Death of Justinian in 565*, New York: Macmillan, 1932, pp. 358-62; Roger A. Pack, "Studies in Libanius and Antiochene Society under Theodosius," Michigan Dissertation, 1935; Peter Wolf, *Vom Schulwesen der Spätantike: Studien zu Libanius*, Baden-Baden: Kunst und Wissenschaft, 1952; Paul Petit, *Libanius et la vie municipale à Antioche au IVe siècle après J.-C.*, Paris: Geuthner, 1956; idem, *Les étudiants de Libanius*, Paris: Nouvelles Editions Latines, 1957; A.M.J. Festugière, *Antioche païenne et chrétienne: Libanius, Chrysostom, et les moines de Syrie*, Paris: de Boccard, 1959; Glanville Downey, *A History of Antioch in Syria from Seleucus to the Arab Conquest*, Princeton Univ. Pr., 1961, pp. 373-446; J.H.W.G. Liebeschuetz, *Antioch. City and Imperial Administration in the Later Roman Empire*, Oxford: Clarendon Pr., 1972, pp. 1-39 on Libanius.

accepted first the official chair of sophistry at Nicaea and a year later the more important chair at Nicomedia. Here he met a future saint, Basil, and here a future emperor, Julian, first heard of him. Libanius' earliest surviving oration, the panegyric of Constantius and Constans, belongs to 349, his last year in Nicomedia. He was then, without any enthusiasm on his part, summoned back to Constantinople as official sophist, but soon began to try to arrange a return to Antioch and, after considerable difficulty, finally settled there in 354, becoming an official sophist in the city within a year. His *Hypotheses* to the speeches of Demosthenes were composed in Constantinople, but except for them and the panegyric composed in Nicomedia his speeches were composed after his return to Antioch. His life there might be divided into three periods. The first reached its climax with the reign of Julian and the official restoration of paganism, with which Libanius deeply sympathized. Julian's early death in 363 was a terrible blow. In the later sixties and seventies, the second period, Libanius was in partial eclipse, but there survive a large number of orations from the late 380s and early 390s, the third period of his career, when he vigorously pressed for social reforms and became a spokesman for paganism. In 391 he suffered great grief at the death of his only son. Libanius' latest work is to be dated in 392 or 393. The date of his death is unknown, perhaps around 394 when he would have been eighty years old.

We have more detailed information about the career, works, and personality of Libanius than about any other Greek of any period. The corpus comprises fifty-one declamations, ninety-six progymnasmata, sixty-four orations, the *Hypotheses* to the speeches of Demosthenes, and about sixteen hundred letters, mostly genuine. Much can be said in his favor: He writes excellent classical Greek, strongly influenced by Demosthenes, Isocrates, Plato, Aristides, and other classic writers. He represents the fading tradition of pagan classical culture of his age in its purest form. His long life, spanning the Fourth Century, was a time of many significant events, especially conflicts between pagans and Christians and attacks of barbarians on the empire from north and east. Unlike some sophists, he shows a continual awareness of contemporary events. He knew most of the leading men of his time, and he had opinions of his own which he argued forcefully. His works are thus mines of political, social, economic, prosopographical, and intellectual information, sometimes difficult of extraction in that, like other sophists, he is fond of indirect references and allusions and he views specific names, dates, and facts as vulgar. He is tolerant, humane, reasonably personable, despite the hypochondria which he cultivated in imitation of Aristides.[17] But for all his achievements he can be tiresome, repetitive, and unimaginative. What is rhetorically significant about Libanius is how little the form and content of political oratory seem to him to have changed since the time of Isocrates and Demosthenes, seven hundred years before, despite great changes in the political setting, and the extent to which he tried to deal with significant subjects and to accomplish a degree of persuasion. Study of him contributed to preservation throughout the Byzantine period of the "high style" classicism and a sense of the importance of oratory. To many readers he seemed to show that great oratory was possible under the Roman empire.

Discussions of Libanius naturally begin with his "Autobiography," which is Oration One in our texts.[18] Its proper

[17] See Roger Pack, "Two Sophists and Two Emperors," *CPh* 42 (1947), 17-20; A. F. Norman, "Philostratus and Libanius," *CPh* 48 (1953), 20-23; Roger Pack, "Julian, Libanius, and Others: A Reply," *CPh* 48 (1953), 173-74.

[18] See Georg Misch, *Geschichte der Autobiographie*, I. 2, Bern: Francke, 1950, pp. 566-75, and A. F. Norman, *Libanius' Autobiography. The Greek Text, Edited with Introduction, Translation and Notes*, London: Oxford Univ. Pr., 1965.

title is *On His Own Fortune* and it may be regarded as an epideictic oration to be read or recited to his students. Isocrates' *Antidosis* is the closest thing to a classical model, but that purports to be delivered in a law court and deals with Isocrates' professional career, whereas Libanius' speech has no specific dramatic setting and has much to say about his personal life. The work is introspective and could even be said to be addressed to himself: an attempt to evaluate the good and the bad which Fortune, whom he describes as a powerful goddess, has allotted to him throughout his life.[19] Libanius sets out to show that those who regard him as the happiest of men and those who regard him as wretched are equally wrong: Fortune has given him both blessings and misfortunes. Among his blessings he places first being a citizen of Antioch, which gives him an opportunity to praise that city, and then the family into which he was born. The technique of the speech is thus that of an ordinary encomium which follows chronologically through the life of the subject. The main part, ending with a peroration in sections 145-55, can be dated to A.D. 374. He was teaching in Antioch, his health was somewhat better than it had been (143), a change in the law had allowed him to will his property to an illegitimate son, who was his only child (145), and he seems to have regarded his career as rounded out. His chief regret (151-55) is how many of his pupils have died and how rhetorical studies in general have declined. Libanius always avoids direct reference to Christianity, but it was of course one of the influences he most regretted, and he also laments (e.g., 214, 234) the increased importance of Latin, a language which he refused to learn. The oration does not, however, have very much to say about the various causes he espoused or about

---

[19] See J. Misson, *Recherches sur le paganisme de Libanius*, Univ. de Louvain, 1914.

his intellectual concerns: it is basically a private history and seems not to have been published during his lifetime.[20]

Later Libanius composed a series of additions to this speech, continuing the course of fortunate and unfortunate events down almost to the end of his life. There seem to be seven separate sections, almost equal in length to the original speech, which they thus deprive of its artistic unity. The tone in these additions is even more personal. As a source of information about himself and as a psychological insight into the mind of later antiquity, *On His Fortune* is well worth reading, despite its lack of artistic unity.

Libanius' encomium of Constantius and Constans (Or. 59), delivered in Nicomedia late in 348 or early in 349, seems to have been much read in later years and many manuscripts survive. In the *protheōria* affixed to it Libanius notes that it has the unusual feature of being an encomium of two men at the same time. The second surviving speech is the *Monody on Nicomedia* after its destruction in the earthquake of August 358, clearly inspired by Aristides' *Monody on Smyrna* after a similar disaster.[21] After Libanius' return to Antioch he began to think about a suitable offering to the city and in 360 completed his finest sophistic product, the *Antiochicus* (Or. 11), of which he gave a demonstration at the local Olympic games that summer.

The *Antiochicus*[22] opens with a proemium (1-11) in which Libanius says that he has postponed speaking the praises of Antioch until his eloquence has matured and that he will show that the ancient and modern preeminence of the city are due to the same factors. He then takes these up one by

[20] Or. 2, 14-15 seems to indicate that Or. 1 had not been published in 381.

[21] See J. Mesk, "Libanius Or. LXI und Aristeides," *PhW* 57 (1937), 1326-28.

[22] See Glanville Downey, "Libanius' Oration in Praise of Antioch (Oration XI), translated with Introduction and Commentary," *Proceedings of the American Philosophical Society* 103 (1959), 652-86.

one, including the physical situation, the inhabitants and their histories, the harmony of the classes of the city and their virtues, the city's size, its military importance, the eloquence of its rhetoricians, the patriotism of its citizens. Toward the end (196-250) there is an unusually detailed and vivid ecphrasis of the city in Libanius' time, including its streets, buildings, and commerce. Like Himerius, Libanius incorporates the forms of progymnasmata into his oratory, but he is much less fond of myths and pure ornament and more given to narrative and the arguing of theses. The speech ends with a summation (265-71) and declaration that his debt to his city is repaid to the best of his ability.

To the social historian and the archaeologist the *Antiochicus* is an invaluable document. What did Libanius intend to accomplish by it? He demonstrates his ability to create a rich and smooth example of an important sophistic genre; he demonstrates his affection and admiration for his native city. Whatever he does beyond this is done by implication only, but certainly it is possible to see some philosophical and practical significance, as there is in similar works by Aristides or other great sophists. It has been suggested that an immediate objective was to attempt to counteract some of the steadily increasing importance of Constantinople, a city which Libanius never liked, and that he deliberately models his work on encomia of Rome.[23] In a wider sense what Libanius seems to describe is an ideal polis in the grand classical tradition. Epideictic orators ever since Pericles' *Funeral Oration* had felt entitled to go beyond actual conditions to describe what should be. Perhaps Antioch was as handsome a city as Libanius says, but it certainly was not characterized by the unanimity of spirit which he stresses. The speech ignores the Christians, who

[23] See A. D. Nock, "The Praises of Rome," *Journal of Egyptian Archaeology* 40 (1954), 76-82.

were very strong in Antioch, and concentrates on the culture and religion of pagan Greece. The mythical origin and early history of Antioch at one end and the flourishing contemporary life of the city at the other are stressed, but little is said about the difficulties of the first three centuries of the Roman empire. Libanius has no interest in Latin culture and prefers to think of Antioch as being much what she had been in Hellenistic times, just as his own oratory is that of earlier Greece.

Up to this point Libanius' career had not been very different from that of other successful sophists, but it subsequently took on a new and wider dimension. Several factors contributed to the development. The most important was probably Libanius' own mind and personality, but accidents of history contributed to the change. He had for one thing returned home to a position of special influence in a city which, unlike Athens, was of great importance at this time and which yet lacked the political rivalry and constant intrigue of Constantinople. Libanius could not be an intellectual leader in Constantinople; in Antioch he stood out and his opinion was sought on important matters. A second historical accident was the reign of Julian, with its restoration of official paganism. There suddenly seemed an opportunity for a renaissance of the Hellenic culture which was the basis of Libanius' life, belief, and teaching, and there was increased freedom of speech. His attempts to accomplish something in this direction and his inclination to speak out, once awakened, survived the death of Julian and lasted in varying degrees of intensity through the rest of Libanius' life. A final and later factor seems to have been his belated discovery, about 380, of how little he was making himself understood, the theme of his second oration,[24] and a resulting attempt to explain and accomplish

[24] The third speech, which assumes criticism from students, and the fourth, which replies to Eutropius, are somewhat similar.

his public goals. The whole direction of Libanius' intellectual development in the time from the *Antiochicus* until his death over thirty years later has been described as a discovery of how "disastrously far from attainment" was his ideal for his city and a movement from "the spirit of eulogy, on dry sophistic models, to that of an original and mainly adverse social criticism."[25]

Several of Libanius' orations relate to the emperor Julian.[26] Although he was delighted with Julian's accession, ideologically and personally, since he resented Constantius' treatment of himself, he was, nevertheless, initially very reserved with Julian: he would not give the impression of tainting his own public position with the qualities of a flatterer (Or. 1.118-23). Preparations for the Persian war brought Julian to Antioch for an extended stay, where he apparently came to understand Libanius' situation and made the appropriate request for a speech from Libanius.[27] The encomiastic *Prosphoneticus* (Or. 13) was the answer, and eventually the emperor and the sophist became friends. Julian, no mean orator himself, put a high value on eloquence as a Hellenic virtue, and this perhaps pleased Libanius as much as the revival of pagan cults. In any event, that theme is the first which Libanius touches on in the speech. Later, on New Year's Day 363, Libanius delivered a speech on the consulship to Julian, and this too notes the role of eloquence in Julian's transformation of the world (Or. 12.92).

Julian had need of Libanius' help since he experienced great difficulty with the residents of Antioch relating to the food supply, land reform, the recruitment of troops, and the reopening of pagan cults. Libanius played a statesman-

---

[25] See Pack, "Studies in Libanius" (supra, n. 16), pp. 12 and 3, respectively.
[26] See Norman, *Selected Works* (supra, n. 16), I, pp. vii-liii.
[27] See Pack, "Two Sophists" (supra, n. 17), pp. 18-19.

like role: in March 363 he published an appeal to the Antiochenes (Or. 16), rebuking their conduct toward Julian, and at the same time, he sent a plea to the emperor asking him to forgive the citizens' conduct toward him (Or. 15). Julian, on campaign into Persian territory, was dead of an arrow wound before he received Libanius' message. Before leaving Antioch, Julian recognized Libanius' value to him. He told him, "You seem to me to deserve to be enrolled among the orators for your eloquence, but among the philosophers for your deeds" (1.131). In fact, it was only as a practical philosopher that Libanius could claim the title; he did not share Julian's enthusiasm for metaphysical speculation and Neoplatonism. Libanius always retained his admiration for Julian, whose death was a stunning blow. He says that he considered suicide (Or. 1.135). He eventually composed in Julian's memory both an emotional *Monody* (Or. 17) and a formal funeral oration (Or. 18), in which Julian is presented as the Hellenic ideal, "a paragon of such virtue, both moral and political, whereby the way to personal salvation is revealed and the state and society purged of grossness and error and brought to perfection."[28]

In the years after Julian's death, Libanius drew back somewhat from public affairs. Having been identified with Julian, he had now lost influence and was regarded by the court with suspicion; he was very discouraged and much troubled by the gout. None of his numerous letters can be dated between 365 and 388 and the only oration in this period is the autobiographic first oration discussed above. The reign of Valens was as difficult a time for Libanius as for the empire as a whole, but Theodosius in 378 brought a new spirit. In the fifteen years which follow, Libanius used his position as a base for speaking out on many sig-

---

[28] See Norman, *Selected Works* (supra, n. 16), I, p. xxxvi.

nificant public matters, especially concerning the administrative and social evils evident to him in Antioch.[29]

One of the first speeches in this series is the oration addressed *To Those Who Called Him Tiresome* (Or. 2), datable to 381. Among the aspects of life in which he claims there has been a decline are religion, agriculture, administration, the army, and education. Other important speeches are *On the Plethrum* (Or. 10), dealing with the decadence he regarded as being introduced into the celebration of the Olympic games,[30] *On Forced Labor* (50), *On the Patronages* (47),[31] and *On the Prisoners* (45).[32] He also has much to say about the conduct of the governors of Syria, good and bad, but the most interesting speech is probably *For the Temples* (30).[33] This, which is datable to 386, takes the form of an address to the emperor Theodosius, but since Libanius seems not to have left Antioch and the emperor not to have visited there, it must be regarded as analogous to those elaborate orations which Isocrates and later sophists addressed to distant rulers. The speech is a spirited attack on the pillaging and destruction of pagan temples, especially those in country districts, by Christian monks. This, Libanius claims, is directly counter to the law and against the interests of the state. Animal sacrifice had been

[29] Pack, "Studies in Libanius" (supra, n. 16), p. 39, thinks that Libanius' son Cimon was his chief contact with the world of practical affairs and that Cimon's resentments were an important factor in Libanius' views.

[30] For translation see Downey, *A History of Antioch* (supra, n. 16), pp. 688-94.

[31] See Louis Harmand, *Libanius, Discours sur les patronages* (Publications de la Faculté des Lettres de l'Université de Clermont-Ferrand II, 1), Paris: Presses Universitaires, 1955.

[32] See Pack, "Studies in Libanius" (supra, n. 16), pp. 70-120, with English translation and commentary.

[33] See R. van Loy, "Le *Pro Templis* de Libanius," *Byzantion* 8 (1933), 7-39 and 389-404; Paul Petit, "Sur la date du *Pro Templis* de Libanius," *Byzantion* 21 (1951), 285-310; Liebeschuetz, *Antioch* (supra, n. 16), p. 39.

prohibited earlier, but sacrifice of incense and perfume was still legal and the temples remained open. Libanius does not attack Christianity as such, only its extremists, and of course he addresses Theodosius with great deference, especially at the beginning. Toward the end, however, comes a very striking passage (51-54) in which the orator seems almost to dare the emperor to take the ultimate step of prohibiting pagan worship. Five years later it was done.

Libanius is somewhat analogous to Demosthenes, Cicero, Juvenal, or other ancient social critics in that he is trying to arrest and reverse changes rather than to introduce new social and political principles as the basis of reform. He does so with vigor, and though tactful in treating the emperors, he is quite outspoken about conditions and officials. *On the Temples* is unusual in its presentation of powerful, sustained thought. More often Libanius goes along point by point (Or. 2 and 62 are especially good examples of this), but unlike Demosthenes or Cicero fails to array the parts into a greater whole. The result is that most of his speeches have little internal dynamics: they lack the counterpoint of artistic digression; they reach no stirring climaxes. One reason for this is doubtless that none of them is a product, as were the great speeches of Demosthenes, of open, spirited debate.

Most of Libanius' speeches can be dated from internal references or from information in his letters. We are less well informed about the circumstances of delivery and publication. The *Prosphoneticus* and the New Year's Day speech were apparently delivered before Julian. The *Autobiography* as a whole may never have been spoken to anyone. In between these extremes lie speeches which could have been read in his school or published as open letters to officials. It is interesting that several of the speeches whose success he describes with the greatest pride in his autobiography do not seem to have been published. The degree of rhetorical finish varies greatly; presumably the more rhetorically polished were intended for publication. Another doubtful and related matter is the extent to which Libanius' reform speeches accomplished a practical effect. In most instances he pleaded lost causes: paganism, municipal reform, classical education, but he contributed to the transmission of a modified Greek culture to the Byzantine period in which his works were much read.[34]

The speeches discussed above were occasional, even if highly visible, efforts by Libanius as a citizen orator. In his own school his major activity was of course teaching and exemplifying judicial and deliberative problems of declamation, but he also taught progymnasmata. From a purely artistic point of view the progymnasmata and declamations of Libanius are rather satisfying. They were apparently much admired for centuries after his death, and many of them are quite good reading. The declamations resemble those of the Second Sophistic and differ from Latin declamations, as represented, for example, by the collection attributed to Quintilian, in being less sententious in style and in being often connected with mythological or historical incidents.

Some of the declamations have introductory *protheōriai* which reveal something about the theme as Libanius viewed it. For example, the third is a speech for Menelaus asking the Trojans to give up Helen and the fourth is a similar speech for Odysseus. In the *protheōria* he says that the characterization and the style are to be based on what Homer says about the oratory of the two heroes and that similar arguments are to be used in the two speeches, but

---

[34] See esp. Paul Petit, "Recherches sur la publication et la diffusion des discourses de Libanius," *Historia* 5 (1956), 479-509. For a more optimistic view of Libanius' effectiveness, see Harmand, *Patronages* (supra, n. 31), pp. 105-6. Liebeschuetz, *Antioch* (supra, n. 16), pp. 23-39, is an excellent survey of Libanius' functions.

differently treated because of the difference in characterization. The sixth declamation, for Orestes on the charge of having killed his mother, has a particularly long and interesting *protheōria* about the characterization and style required: Orestes should not try to soothe the jury by a mildness of manner, because that will undermine the sense of outrage which is his best justification for his action. Seven of the declamations relate to Athenian-Macedonian relations in the fourth century; of these the most admired was the twenty-second, in which Demosthenes is presented as appealing to the Athenians to destroy the altar of pity. He is imagined to have taken refuge there, but to have been forcibly removed by orders of the assembly and given up to Philip of Macedon. The specific situation has no historical basis, but the wider circumstances of the time and the character of Demosthenes are based on reality,[35] and though the theme is startling, it is not in fact impossible or absurd as Roman declamations sometimes seem. The question of the destruction of pagan altars of course had contemporary meaning. This is even clearer in the case of the first declamation, Libanius' version of a speech for Socrates at his trial, which can be read as a defense of Julian.[36]

Libanius also composed declamations in which types of characters are the speakers. Probably the best of these, and the most entertaining of all his declamations, is the twenty-sixth, which is an example of a "figured" problem. A misanthrope (*dyskolos*) appears before the senate of his city, perhaps to be imagined as Cos or Marseilles,[37] and asks to be required to drink the hemlock. His problem is that he

---

[35] See Joannes Bielski, "De Aetatis Demosthenicae Studiis Libaniis," *Breslauer Philologische Abhandlungen* 48 (1914), 66.
[36] See H. Markowsky, "De Libanio Socratis Defensore," *Breslauer Philologische Abhandlungen* 40 (1910), esp. pp. 169-70.
[37] See Valerius Maximus 2.6.7-8.

has allowed himself to be trapped in a marriage to a garrulous woman and he can no longer bear his life. This impossible situation is made probable by a very effective presentation of the character of the speaker. He describes the steps by which his natural fears were allayed as he was led into the marriage by a friend and he vividly presents the streams of words emanating from his loquacious bride. The first half is largely a narrative of his situation, the second an answer to the various objections which might be raised.

Libanius' declamations were composed as part of his work as a teaching sophist. They were models for his students and public demonstrations of the training which he offered. Most of them were doubtless given on several occasions and often revised and improved. A picture of his school can be reconstructed from references in his autobiography and his letters.[38] It is tempting to compare him as a teacher with Quintilian, of whom, however, he knew nothing. Each took a broad view of his function *in loco parentis*; each was concerned with the total education of young men, not simply with technical rhetoric as might be said of Hermogenes, for example; in both schools reading of the classics was given much more emphasis than was true with some rhetoricians. Libanius says (*Ep.* 1036) that his course was based on Homer, Hesiod and other poets, Demosthenes, Lysias and other orators, Herodotus, Thucydides, and other historians.[39]

The Schools of Constantinople

When, late in the Third Century, Diocletian established a permanent seat of the emperors at Nicomedia, he made special provision for intermediate and higher education

[38] See Schemmel, Wolf, and Petit (*Les étudiants*), supra, n. 16.
[39] See A. F. Norman, "The Library of Libanius," *RhM* 107 (1964), 158-75.

there.[40] Grammar, rhetoric, and philosophy were taught as elsewhere, but an attempt was made to provide instruction in both Greek and Latin. Latin was neither common in the East nor popular with Greek intellectuals, but it was the language of Roman law and administration and a necessity for public officials.[41] One of those appointed to teach Latin rhetoric was Lactantius, who later became famous as a Father of the Church (Jerome *De Viris Illustribus* 80).

At Constantinople, almost from the time of its founding (324-30), grammarians, sophists, and philosophers were appointed to official chairs. Libanius held such a position from 349 to 353. He mentions (Or. 1.39) another sophist, Bemarchius, a pagan who seems to have taken a speaking tour of the East in support of Constantius' religious policy. Another sophist of the time was Hecebolius, with whom Julian studied (Socrates Scholasticus 3.1) and to whom he addressed a letter (*Ep.* 63).[42] Aemilius Magnus Arborius, a distinguished Gallic rhetorician and uncle of the poet Ausonius, was brought to Constantinople to teach Latin rhetoric. In 370 the emperors issued regulations for students coming to either Rome or Constantinople in search of an education (*Theodosian Code* 14.9.1). The objective was perhaps to prevent the unruly conditions which prevailed in Athens. Students had to secure a travel permit from their home towns and have birth certificates and letters of recommendation. When they arrived they registered with the master of tax assessment and his office kept an eye on

[40] See Fritz Schemmel, "Die Hochschule von Konstantinopel im IV Jh. post Christum natum," *Neue Jahrbücher für Pädagogik* 22 (1908), 147-68.

[41] See Henri-Irénée Marrou, A *History of Education in Antiquity*, trans. George Lamb, New York: Sheed and Ward, 1956, pp. 255-64 and 425; Henrik Zilliacus, *Zum Kampf der Weltsprachen im oströmischen Reich*, Helsingfors, 1935; reprinted Amsterdam: Hakkert, 1965.

[42] Other names are known, see Schemmel, "Der Sophist Libanius" (supra, n. 16), pp. 151-52.

them. Ordinarily, they could expect to stay until they were twenty-one years old, but if they failed to show signs of serious study they could be sent home.

If we may believe the emperor Constantius, the person who contributed most to the academic reputation of Constantinople in the Fourth Century was Themistius, whose oratory has been briefly described in Chapter One.[43] Themistius apparently never taught rhetoric; his subject was philosophy, with emphasis on Plato and Aristotle. In his numerous orations, however, we see what rhetoric could and could not accomplish in the later empire. It could be more than the honeyed phrases of Himerius in an academic setting. It could be more than the efforts of Libanius to secure reforms and teach students in a provincial capital. It could in fact be the exposition of Hellenic ideals in the capitals of the world and in the highest forum of the empire. Themistius had a public visibility lacking to any Greek orator at least since Herodes Atticus and perhaps since the fourth century. The costs were that he could not be very critical or pressing, which is a major feature of great oratory as seen in Demosthenes. He could give general moral advice, as we saw him do to Constantius, but had to shy away from the details of its application. His role is thus rather like that of a Christian bishop. In the long run his major achievement was to express classical Greek ideas in forms acceptable to Christian rulers and advisers and thus to transmit aspects of Greek culture to the Byzantine period, when he continued to be admired.

A generation after the death of Themistius, higher education in Constantinople was given a new structure by an edict of the emperor Theodosius II, issued February 27, 425 (*Theodosian Code* 14.9.3). This edict prohibited professors who did not hold official appointments from teach-

[43] For Constantius' sentiment, see his letter to the senate, 21a (pp. 23-24 Dindorf). For bibliography on Themistius, Chapter 1, n. 27.

ing on public property, though they were allowed to teach in private homes. Conversely, those who had been appointed to teach "in the auditorium of the capital" were not to give private instruction. The effect was to control education officially. There were thirty-one official appointments: ten Latin grammarians, three Latin rhetoricians, ten Greek grammarians, five Greek sophists, two professors of law, and one of the secrets of philosophy. The number of five Greek sophists is of course consistent with the rule of Marcus Aurelius discussed at the beginning of this chapter. The edict states that each professor was to have his own classroom. Another edict (*Theodosian Code* 15.1.53) provided that large classrooms were to be made available adjacent to the north portico and mentions food shops, presumably patronized by the students. The capitol was apparently a large centrally located building, but no parts of it are known today.

These provisions are often described as the foundation of the "University of Constantinople."[44] They do constitute something beyond the informal organization of schools at Athens and elsewhere, although no word for university appears and there is no provision for examinations or degrees. Like the earlier regulations for students in Constantinople, the foundation of the "university" is probably primarily an attempt on the part of the government to control the general situation in the capital city. Choice of the faculty was made by the senate. After twenty years' teaching experience, including service elsewhere, a professor could expect the title of Count of the First Order. Information about the "university" in the following centuries is very slight; it

[44] See Walden, *Universities* (supra, n. 4), pp. 141-51; Louis Bréhier, "Notes sur l'histoire de l'enseignement supérieur à Constantinople," *Byzantion* 3 (1926), 73-74, and 4 (1927), 13-25; Marrou, *History* (supra, n. 41), pp. 307-8; M. L. Clarke, *Higher Education in the Ancient World*, Albuquerque: Univ. of New Mexico Pr., 1971, p. 130.

FIFTH-CENTURY ATHENS

probably collapsed in the Eighth Century, but something like it was later revived.[45]

Athenian Schools in the Fifth Century

The best known Athenian sophist of the Fifth Century was Lachares.[46] Marinus (*Life of Proclus* 11) describes him discussing philosophy with Syrianus and Proclus about 430, but the *Suda* reports that he flourished in the time of the emperors Marcian and Leo (450-474). Damascius, in his *Life of Isidore*,[47] mentions Lachares as a sophist among the Athenian philosophers; Damascius had seen a picture of him, which he describes as that of a philosopher, and had read some of his speeches, which he says were carefully worked but lacking nobility. According to the *Suda*, Lachares published *Rhetorical Selections in Alphabetical Order* and *Dialexeis*. This latter term has various possible meanings, ranging from the philosophical type practiced earlier by Maximus of Tyre to the rhetorical showpieces of Procopius and Choricius delivered at festivals. None of Lachares' speeches survives, but we do have a portion of his work *On the Colon, the Comma, and the Period*.[48] Here he criticizes lack of understanding of classical prose rhythm by writers of his own times, and quotes extensively from Dionysius of Halicarnassus, more briefly from Cassius Longinus and Hermogenes. What is strange about the work

[45] See Louis Bréhier, "L'enseignement classique et l'enseignement réligieux à Byzance," *Revue d'histoire et de philosophie réligieuse* 21 (1941), 34-69; F. Fuchs, "Die höheren Schulen von Konstantinopel im Mittelalter," *Byzantinisches Archiv* 8 (1926); P. Speck, review of Lemerle, *BZ* 67 (1974), 385-93; below, Chapter 5, nn. 19, 31; Chapter 6, nn. 10, 14, 46.

[46] See Schmid-Stählin, pp. 1101-2; *R-E* XII, 332-34.

[47] See Rudolf Asmus, *Das Leben des Philosophen Isidorus von Damascius aus Damaskos*, Leipzig: Meiner, 1911; *Damascii Vitae Isidori Reliquiae*, ed. Clemens Zintzen, Hildesheim: Olms, 1967.

[48] See H. Graeven, "Ein Fragment des Lachares," *Hermes* 30 (1895), 289-313.

is that, although describing classical quantitative rhythm, it is written in the accentual rhythm which had begun to be common in the Fourth Century. Presumably Lachares thought that classical rhythms should be attempted in declamations, but that a technical handbook should be written in contemporary style.

Some picture of student life in Athens in the second quarter of the Fifth Century can be found in Marinus' *Life of Proclus*[49] and Damascius' *Life of Isidore*.[50] The latter survives, like some of the works of Himerius, in quotations made from it by Photius in the Ninth Century and in some passages in the *Suda*. The article on Superianus in the *Suda* is derived from Damascius and tells how Superianus took up the study of rhetoric for the first time when he was over thirty. He was regarded as a curiosity in Athens because of his extreme efforts to master the discipline, which extended even to beating himself. Ultimately Superianus succeeded to the extent of becoming one of the official sophists of the city, his fame almost equaling that of Lachares.

Damascius' *Life of Isidore* was a finished rhetorical work and is unusual in being accompanied by a *protheōria* in which Damascius describes the style in terms of Hermogenic ideas, though he concludes by pointing out that the biography was written for its content and not as an *epideixis*.[51] This interest in Hermogenic ideas among Athenian philosophers should doubtless be credited in the first instance to Syrianus.

---

[49] See Marini *Vita Procli*, ed. J. F. Boissonade, Leipzig, 1814; reprinted Amsterdam: Hakkert, 1966.

[50] See supra, n. 47.

[51] See A. Brinkmann, "Die Protheorie zur Biographe eines Neoplatonikos," *RhM* 65 (1910), 617-26.

The School of Gaza

Gaza, on the southern coast of Palestine, was a pleasant and prosperous city in the Fourth Century which clung to the old traditions. Julian's apostasy was greeted there with enthusiasm (Gregory of Nazianzus Or. 4.86) and Libanius thought well of its rhetorical schools (Or. 55.33-34). A change came in the reign of Theodosius II when Porphyry, bishop of Gaza, undertook a campaign against local cults with the support of the empress Eudocia which replaced the principal temple of the city with a church named in her honor. Porphyry's activities are well known from the biography of him by Mark the Deacon.[52] Eudocia was the daughter of an Athenian rhetorician named Leontius (Socrates Scholasticus 7.21.8) and had herself a knowledge of rhetoric. On a visit to Antioch she delivered an encomium of that city and was honored by the erection there of her statue. Like all speeches by women in antiquity it is lost, but we know that it ended with a quotation of *Iliad* 6.211 (Evagrius 1.20.3-5).

Christianity may for a time have inhibited classical studies in Gaza, but in the late Fifth and early Sixth Centuries it was the home of a series of classicizing sophists and writers who together constitute what is known as the School of Gaza.[53] The most important of these are Procopius and Choricius, but brief mention may be made of several others. Aeneas of Gaza was the author of a surviving dialogue entitled *Theophrastus*; Zacharias Scholasticus, later bishop

---

[52] See Marc le diacre, *Vie de Porphyre, évêque de Gaza*, text, translation, and commentary by Henri Gregoire and M.-A. Kugener, Paris: Les Belles Lettres, 1930.

[53] See Kilian Seitz, *Die Schule von Gaza, eine litterargeschichtliche Untersuchung*, Heidelberg: Winter, 1892; Glanville Downey, "The Christian Schools of Palestine: A Chapter in Literary History," *Harvard Library Bulletin* 12 (1958), 297-319.

of Mitylene, of a dialogue *Ammonius*. The latter imitates the setting, but not the contents, of Plato's *Phaedrus*. There seem to have been two rhetoricians in Gaza named Zosimus, one in the time of Zeno (473-491), the other in the time of Anastasius (419-518).[54] Neither is the historian of that name, though it is not impossible that he had some connexion with Gaza. The *Suda* attributes to the second Zosimus a rhetorical lexicon and commentaries on Lysias and Demosthenes. A life of Demosthenes attributed to Zosimus is preserved in manuscripts of Demosthenes and is clearly an introduction to a commentary on the orator which may be the chief basis for Byzantine Demosthenic scholia. The abstract of Anastasius' Prolegomenon, number twelve in Rabe's collection, is also the work of a Zosimus, described as a pupil of Theon, and he may be one of these rhetoricians. A final member of the school of Gaza is John, who lived during the reign of Justinian and is the author of an ecphrasis in hexameter verse describing an allegorical picture of Christ and the world of nature.[55]

Procopius of Gaza, who must not be confused with the historian Procopius of Caesarea, was born around 465, educated in Alexandria, and called to an official chair of rhetoric at Gaza, where he lived until his death around 527.[56] The bulk of his extant work consists of commentaries on the Old Testament (PG LXXXVII), but he taught and practiced classical rhetoric with no seeming embarrass-

[54] See R-E XA, 790-95; Seitz, *Schule von Gaza* (supra, n. 53), pp. 27-30; Downey, "Schools of Palestine" (supra, n. 53), pp. 309 and 313; Zosime, *Histoire nouvelle* I, ed. François Paschoud, Paris: Les Belles Lettres, 1971, pp. xviii-xix.

[55] See Paul Friedländer, *Johannes von Gaza und Paulus Silentiarius, Kunstbeschreibungen Justinianischer Zeit*, Leipzig and Berlin: Teubner 1912.

[56] See R-E XXIII, 259-72; Seitz, *Schule von Gaza* (supra, n. 53); Schmid-Stählin, pp. 1029-31; Downey, "Schools of Palestine" (supra, n. 53), pp. 310-11.

ment, as is seen in seven declamations.[57] The second and third declamation, and probably the first as well, though the manuscript evidence is lost, were labeled *Dialexeis*, disquisitions. Although some logical development is sought, they are primarily ecphrastic, describing the arrival of spring; it appears from Choricius that the sophists of Gaza annually participated in a rose festival.[58] Procopius' second declamation describes a walk out of the city, in which he is reminded of Plato's *Phaedrus*, and ends with an encomium of the rose; the third declamation deals with the loves of Aphrodite and frequently mentions roses. Its opening lines reveal something of Procopius' attitude toward his art:

> Painting and poetry, the one with colors, the other with words—for words are the colors of poetry—both imitate the figures of gods and men, their passions and their loves. Poetry reports the drops of semen from Uranus falling upon the sea, describes Aphrodite, and calls her "born from the foam," unless I forget the words of the poet [Hesiod, *Theogony* 189] where he says she was begotten "in the surging sea." Painting on the other hand gives a visual image to poetry's account, for it represents the figures of the sea and you might say that the waves are moved by the painting. In the middle of the scene the painter introduces Aphrodite and her irresistible beauty, just as Aphrodite should be shown. She is drawn in the car of the Tritons. These are men down to their flanks, their form completed below like fish. Round about is a chorus of Nereids, and you can see dolphins now

[57] For the text see Procopii Gazaei *Epistolae et Declamationes*, ed. Antonius Garzya and Raymundus-J. Loenertz, Eltal: Buch-Kunstverlag, 1963.
[58] See Choricius 16 = *Dialexeis* 9 and 39 = 24, discussed by Paul Friedländer, *Spätantiker Gemäldezyklus in Gaza*, Vatican City: Studi et Testi LXXXIX 1939, pp. 4-115.

diving with pleasure into the water, now leaping up from the waves. This is how the arts represent divine Aphrodite.

The analogy of painting and poetry (or rhetoric) is a commonplace. What is remarkable about this passage is that it seems to be describing a specific work of art and its very pagan tone. Is it possible that Procopius was originally a pagan rhetorician who later converted to Christianity and wrote commentaries on the Bible? The external evidence is against this thesis. Procopius' extant letters seem to show a Christian who was active as a sophist,[59] and Choricius' Funeral Oration for him treats him as a sophist throughout his life who was also a Christian (21-22) and a scholar (16).

Procopius' remaining four declamations are ethopoeiae: the words of a shepherd at the arrival of spring after a harsh winter (4), the words of a merchant when spring comes (5), what Aphrodite said when she caught her foot on a thorn while seeking Adonis (6), and what Phoenix said when Agamemnon sent him to plead with Achilles about the matter of Briseis (7). In none of these works does it seem reasonable to take the pagan elements as Christian allegories. Procopius simply worked in a literary tradition adopted for aesthetic effect. It was doubtless easier to do so in the relaxed cultural setting of Gaza than in Antioch or Alexandria, but the technique represents a separation of Church and society which is in contrast to the view of most of the Christian orators to be described in Chapter Four.

In addition to the declamations of Procopius, there are two *ekphraseis* describing works of art, one a picture of Phaedra and Hippolytus,[60] the other a remarkable clock at

---

[59] See R-E XXIII, 259-60 and 265-66.
[60] See Friedländer, *Gemäldezyklus* (supra, n. 58), pp. 4-18 and 23-86.

Gaza.[61] These are preserved in a manuscript (*Vaticanus Graecus* 1898) which also contains Procopius' declamations and part of the *Eikones,* or *Descriptions of Pictures,* by Philostratus the Elder, written in the early Third Century, as well as the similar work of Callistratus, who lived in the Fourth or Fifth Century.[62] We are thus dealing with the continuation of a minor sophistic genre. The objective of such works is the expression in words of the action depicted, which is regarded as in turn reflecting the sentiment of the writer as he views the picture. Ecphrasis thus becomes analogous to ethopoeia, but with the twist of transferring the experience from one art form to another rather than creating a speech out of a purely literary situation. A quotation from Procopius' account of the painting of Phaedra may help to make this clear.

Theseus is asleep and the members of his household take advantage of the opportunity. But sweet sleep holds not Phaedra. Instead of sleep, Love has taken possession of her heart. What is happening to you, woman? You suffer in vain from a love which cannot succeed. How will you persuade him who knows self-restraint? Why do you shame yourself by longing to approach a forbidden bed? Turn about a little and cast your glance on your spouse; scorn not what is available while you seek what you do not possess. Respect your husband even when he is asleep and take yourself out of the picture on which you fasten your eyes. For Hippolytus shows restraint, it seems, even in painting.

[61] See Hermann Diels, "Ueber die von Prokop beschriebene Kunstuhr von Gaza, mit einem Anhang enthaltend Text und Uebersetzung der Ekphrasis Horologiou des Prokopios von Gaza," Akademie der Wissenschaften zu Berlin, Philosophische-historische Klasse, *Abhandlungen* 1917, no. 7.

[62] See Philostratus, *Imagines*; Callistratus, *Descriptions,* trans. Arthur Fairbanks (LCL), London: Heinemann, 1931.

But what is this I experience? I am deceived by the art of the painter and think all this is alive, and my sight forgets that this is a painting [an imitation of Philostratus *Eikones* 2.8]. Let me speak about Phaedra, not to her. Her form proves her love. You can see her moist eye, her mind unsettled by passion, her body lacking support, her soul wandering, though her body is still alive. (16-17)[63]

In the opening years of the Sixth Century a statue of the emperor Anastasius was presented to the city of Gaza, and Procopius, as official sophist, delivered a panegyric of the emperor, addressing the statue as though it were the ruler himself.[64] The speech shows the influence of Isocrates' *Evagoras* and Aristides' *Panathenaicus* and closely accords with the rules of Menander. After an amplified proemium of thanks, the orator proceeds to an encomium of Epidamnus, the native city of Anastasius, and of its mother city, Corinth. The emperor is said to trace his ancestry through Heracles to Zeus (2). There is then praise of the early life of Anastasius and a narrative of his succession to the throne, which represents an act of God (5). The great deeds of the emperor are described, in war, foreign and domestic, and in peace (6-21). The latter include appointment of good judges, tax reform, and the abolition of the bloody games, as well as specific benefits to the cities of Hierapolis, Caesarea, and Alexandria. Then come the virtues of the emperor, ending in a synkrisis of him with Cyrus, Agesilaus, and Alexander (22-27). The brief epilogue returns to the gift of the statue and the gratitude of Gaza to the emperor. It would have been possible for Procopius to have eulo-

[63] Based on Friedländer, *Gemäldezyklus* (supra, n. 58), p. 10.
[64] See Karl Kempen, *Procopii Gazae in Imperatorem Anastasium Panegyricus*, Bonn: Karl Georg, 1918.

gized Anastasius in Christian terms; Eusebius of Caesarea had established such a tradition nearly two hundred years earlier. Procopius prefers the older, more pagan form; he even swears "By Zeus," a usage Christian bishops like John Chrysostom had tried to stamp out.

The rhetorical works of Procopius were apparently not well known in succeeding centuries, and they survive chiefly in a single manuscript. The works of his pupil and successor as official sophist, Choricius, were better known. Only the Madrid manuscript contains all of Choricius' speeches, but individual ones are preserved elsewhere, indicating their popularity. Photius (Codex 160) praises Choricius' clear and pure style, his character and morality, and his Christian faith, but criticizes his introduction of pagan mythology into his works. The dates of his life are unknown, but his speeches fall into the years 520-540.

Choricius' works consist of six epideictic orations (three encomia, an epithalamium, and two funeral orations), twelve declamations (*meletai*), and twenty-eight *Dialexeis*.[65] Of the epideictic speeches, the most interesting for our purposes is the *Funeral Oration for Procopius* because of the picture it gives of the life of a sixth-century sophist. Choricius observes the standard structure of a funeral oration. After a brief proemium, he discusses the career of Procopius (4-14) and his virtues (15-26), then offers a consolation to the audience (27-53) into which he inserts (31-33) a lament, and concludes with an exhortation (54) and brief epilogue (55). Excellence in a sophist is said (7) to consist in two things: the ability to astound an audience in the theatre and the ability to initiate the young into the rites of learning. As a teacher, Procopius never tolerated from his students non-Attic diction, irrelevant thought, poor rhythm,

[65] For the text see *Choricii Gazae Opera*, ed. Richard Foerster and Eberhard Richsteig, Leipzig: Teubner, 1929.

or composition which offended the ear (8); as an orator he roused the young to the love of speech, he amazed special guests, and he charmed the bystanders (9). One would have said that Demosthenes had returned to life (10). Personified Rhetoric is imagined seeking an Orpheus to bring back Procopius from the dead (11). Procopius' personal virtues are said to include his love of learning, his indefatigable toil, his temperance, piety, and charity. In the lament Procopius is imagined in his usual way of life, feeding the flock of his young students, gathering the leaders of the city to hear him, playing with his sister's children, and giving speeches at weddings. The consolation reaches a climax in the argument that Demosthenes too had to die, and at exactly the same age (sixty-two) as Procopius, but Demosthenes left Athens in crisis, whereas Procopius has sailed into a safe harbor. The classical models evident throughout Choricius' works include Demosthenes, Homer, Herodotus, Thucydides, Plato, Aristides, and Libanius;[66] he seems untouched by the great Christian panegyric of Gregory of Nazianzus and other fourth-century Fathers.

The declamations of Choricius resemble the prosopopoeiae of Libanius (esp. 26 = Libanius *Decl.* 7). Several are contrasting pairs: Polydamus and Priam; a young hero and an older father. All but one are prefixed by *theōriae* like the *protheōriae* of Libanius, concentrating on the presentation of character and appropriate argument, but not discussing style.

The *Dialexeis* of Choricius are proemia, intended to attract the attention of an audience to which the sophist is about to deliver a panegyric or declamation. They usually have some relation to the occasion and set the tone, but do not reveal the theme, of the speech which is to follow.

[66] See Seitz, *Schule von Gaza* (supra, n. 53), pp. 21-23; R-E III, 2424-31; Downey, "Schools of Palestine" (supra, n. 53), 311-13.

Some are connected with festivals and thus resemble the *Dialexeis* of Procopius, but others are more like diatribes. Choricius' panegyric of Marcian, bishop of Gaza (Or. 1) is introduced by a dialexis which, "more bold than usual, hunts out the good will of the audience for the occasion." "Since an opportunity for play is presented—for this is a festival and a single pleasure and joy are in the hearts of all—come then, I too shall make a display for my pupils. Lead the way, O Logoi—for show belongs to holidays—if ever you put on airs for me at another contest, all the more come now, very well-crowned, wearing splendid robes, and setting out variegated feats." The point seems to be that the festival audience expects a showy speech. This is not in fact entirely suited to the occasion, which is praise of a Christian bishop, and Choricius affects to speak what is suited to the occasion, but the audience may yet find in his words what they want. In fact, they find a colorful ecphrasis of the Church of St. Sergius.[67]

The Decline of the Schools

The educational system of late antiquity, including the sophistic schools, was destroyed during the reign of Justinian. The influences at work seem to be Christian opposition to paganism, the emperor's desire to secure greater centralization and control, and severe financial constraints. According to Procopius of Caesarea (*Secret History* 26.5-6), Justinian terminated the maintenance allowances which were given to physicians and teachers and confiscated the municipal funds used for local purposes. This included funds for local chairs of rhetoric. Furthermore, he prohibited paganism and forbad pagans to practice as advocates or to hold professorial chairs. It appears that the governor of Achaea inquired about the application of these injunc-

[67] Partial English translation in Glanville Downey, *Gaza in the Early Sixth Century*, Norman: Univ. of Oklahoma Pr., 1963, pp. 127-29.

tions and in a rescript of 529 was ordered to allow no one to teach philosophy or law in Athens (Malalas, p. 449 Bonn ed.).[68] It has generally been thought that this order was directed against the pagan Neoplatonists and that it resulted in the confiscation of the endowment of their school. Seven of the philosophers emigrated to Persia, but found conditions there uncongenial. The Persian king Chosroes negotiated permission for them to return home and live in peace without being forced to accept Christianity (Agathias 2.30-31). They were allowed to continue their studies in private and Simplicius even attained some fame during the mid–Sixth Century, but higher education was in fact destroyed outside of Constantinople, Alexandria, and, in theory, Rome.[69] The Slavic invasion of Greece in 579 probably was the actual end of Athens as an educational center.

Justinian's law code (11.19) drops all the provisions for education set forth in the *Theodosian Code* except for three: the provisions establishing the "University" of Constantinople, provision for payments to grammarians and sophists by the praetorian prefect of Africa, presumably in Alexandria (1.27.1-42), and provision for honoring grammarians, sophists, and teachers of law in Constantinople after twenty years of service (12.15). In 554 Justinian made an effort to reestablish higher education in Rome, of which he had recovered control. It was clearly his intention to centralize higher education. Law schools were limited to Constantinople, Rome, and Beirut (on the latter see Agathias 2.15.3-4), rhetoric to Constantinople, Rome, and Alexandria. The hopes for Rome did not materialize, and the last public teacher of rhetoric there until the Renaissance was Melior

[68] See A.H.M. Jones, *The Later Roman Empire, 284-602*, Oxford: Blackwell, 1964, I, p. 286.

[69] See Alan Cameron, "The Last Days of the Academy at Athens," *Proceedings of the Cambridge Philological Society* no. 195, n.s. 15 (1969), 7-29, and Glucker, *Antiochus* (supra, n. 5), pp. 322-29.

DECLINE OF SCHOOLS

Felix in 534.[70] Though there are few references to it, private instruction in rhetoric continued in some places and knowledge of Greek rhetoric can be seen in writers of the next two centuries. But the term "sophist" disappears from contemporary usage after the time of Justinian.

[70] See Henri-Irénée Marrou, "Autour de la bibliothèque du Pape Agapit," Ecole française de Rome: *Mélanges d'archéologie et d'histoire* 48 (1931), 157-65.

CHAPTER FOUR
Christianity and Rhetoric

Christianity has a distinctive rhetoric which originated in Jewish attitudes toward God and speech found in the Old Testament and which reflects the radical theology taught by Jesus and his apostles. Christian rhetoric presupposes the intervention of God in history and through the Holy Spirit in the minds of men. For the classical ethos of the speaker it substitutes divine authority given canonization in the Scriptures and the revelation accorded to the Church; for probable argument as a basis of proof it substitutes proclamation of the kerygma, or divine message, but preserves the forms of inductive and deductive argument; for supporting evidence it turns to miracles and the acts of martyrs; and for pathos the Christian orator threatens damnation or promises eternal life. Christian rhetoric has distinctive topics and a distinctive style based largely on the language of the psalmists and the prophets.[1]

Of all of the passages in the New Testament relating to rhetoric, the most influential are probably the first and second chapters of First Corinthians. Here Paul rejects the whole of classical philosophy and rhetoric: "I did not come proclaiming to you the testimony of God in lofty words of wisdom. For I decided to know nothing among you except Jesus Christ and him crucified" (2:1-2). "Yet among the mature we do impart wisdom, although it is not a wisdom of this age or the rulers of this age, who are doomed to

---

[1] See *CR & CST*, pp. 120-32. For an introduction to the relations of Christianity and classical culture in late antiquity see Ihor Ševčenko, "A Shadow Outline of Virtue: The Classical Heritage of Greek Christian Literature (Second to Seventh Century)," *Age of Spirituality: A Symposium*, ed. Kurt Weitzmann, New York: Metropolitan Museum of Art, 1980, pp. 53-73.

pass away. But we impart a secret and hidden wisdom of God, which was decreed before the ages for our glorification" (2:6-7). To those wise in the ways of the world, Christian rhetoric will seem foolishness, but "the foolishness of God is wiser than men" (1:25). This paradox is a prevailing theme among Christians and is carried out in Christian rhetoric by antithesis and irony. It is also characteristic of Christian rhetoric that whatever the text or the occasion, all details are made subordinate to one message, "Jesus Christ and him crucified." The Christian preacher regularly uses his text as a springboard to the central teaching of Christianity.

Since Christian truth cannot be demonstrated by rational argument, conversion and persuasion result from the grace of God, which allows acceptance or rejection of the message, and not from anything the orator can do. God tells Moses (Ex. 4:12) "I will be your mouth and teach you what you shall speak," and Jesus says to his disciples (Mark 13:11), "when they bring you to trial and deliver you up, do not be anxious beforehand what you are to say, but say whatever is given you in that hour, for it is not you who speak, but the Holy Spirit." This might seem to render the Christian orator superfluous, and some Christians thought that attempts at artistic expression were idle, or worse, a sign of pride in worldly achievements, but the Church always believed that the preaching of the gospel was necessary and came to understand it as part of the process by which God works among men. Moreover, many Christian leaders also came to feel that there was a place for eloquence in deepening and explaining the faith in such a way that it could be practiced in the Christian life. This was especially true after the passage of the apostolic age and the gradual realization that the kingdom of God was not to be immediately realized and that the Church was expected by God to function within human society.

Preaching in the early Church took a variety of forms.[2] The most striking are perhaps the missionary sermons seen in Acts, of which Paul's speech on the Athenian acropolis (Acts 17:22-31) is the most famous example. There are also references to "prophecy," or a kind of preaching based on the models of the Old Testament prophets, and examples of this can be found in later periods as well. But the most characteristic and persistent form of preaching in the Church has always been the homily. Homily in Greek means "conversation"; it implies informality of structure and in Christian contexts a reliance on authority and inspiration. The homily originated in elucidations and applications of scriptural readings in the Jewish Sabbath services and was practiced in this form by Jesus and Paul. Application includes exhortation to live a religious life and this aspect of the homily opened the way for it to be influenced by the diatribe, the vigorous, informal, philosophical, moral, and sometimes satirical preaching of Cynic and Stoic philosophers throughout the Greek-speaking world. This influence was felt by Jewish preachers in the Hellenistic period and continues strong in Christian preaching until at least the Fourth Century. A true homily, however, takes its start from a scriptural text, and its commonest form is the sermon in a Christian service explaining the reading of the day, but in later antiquity and the Middle Ages the term "homily" was often extended to include all kinds of Christian sermons except panegyric.

Because of the close tie of the homily to the text, exegesis of the Scriptures is an integral aspect of Christian rhetoric. In a sense, exegesis is the discovery of truth, and thus corresponds to dialectic, but it is based on the authority of the message and the desire of the interpreter to make it consistent with the one great message, the ke-

[2] See CR & CST, pp. 135-8.

rygma: homiletics corresponds to rhetoric, the expression of the truth to the congregation. This relationship is best seen in Saint Augustine's *De Doctrina Christiana*, which is the authoritative statement of Christian rhetoric for the West, but which was unknown to the Greek Church.

The close tie to the scriptural text contributes to many features of the homily. It often has no structure except that inherent in the text it illuminates. It tends to echo biblical language out of which it develops a stock of commonplaces, and it borrows the imagery and rhythmical devices of Hebrew poetry. Some of these, such as antithesis, assonance, anaphora, and isocolon, are identical with figures of speech in classical rhetoric, and a variety of other classical figures was gradually adapted by educated speakers addressing congregations accustomed to sophistic discourse. An early example of this are the works of Melito, bishop of Sardis in the Second Century.[3] Meretricious adornment might be inconsistent with Christianity, but the poetry of the Psalms and the passion of the prophets could be regarded as providing a mystical perception of the ineffable wisdom-not-of-this-world.

Classical rhetoric is one of the parts of classical learning and its partial adoption by Christians is closely connected with Christian adoption of parts of classical philosophy which had originated in Platonism, Aristotelianism, and Stoicism. Classical metaphysics and ethics contributed important ideas to Christianity, but dialectic became a fundamental skill in Christian disputation. Even Saint Paul was not able to avoid dialectic in dealing with matters of Church discipline. The question of the relationship of Christians to the Jewish law continually vexed him and brought him into conflict with followers of Peter. His response to this, as seen, for example, in Galatians, is to interpret and ex-

[3] Ibid., pp. 136-37.

tend by rational argument the teachings of Jesus as applied to new questions being asked. This continued to be the basic procedure of the Church, but there was a wide variation among Christians in the extent to which they were willing to appeal to human reason as well as to authority and faith. The Apologists of the Second Century, in their attempt to explain and defend Christianity, were necessarily addressing the pagan world and argued in terms which that society could understand; moreover they utilized Attic language and style in order to be taken seriously by an educated audience, though in their communications to each other they held to the humble *koinē*. The Christian exegete, seeking to interpret obscure portions of the Bible, used his trained mind in the best way he could, through the arts of definition, division, and syllogistic reasoning. A central figure in this effort is Origen (c. 184-254), who taught in Alexandria and in Caesarea in Palestine. He did important work on the text of the Bible and wrote numerous commentaries and homilies. In the latter he regularly goes beyond an exposition of the text to seek to persuade his audience not only to understand and believe the Scriptures, but to live in accordance with their teaching.[4]

Origen regarded the Bible as inspired in every respect and arranged by God in a series of levels of meaning (*On First Principles* 4.1.11). The lowest is the "corporeal" level of the literal meaning; higher is the moral meaning, which he identifies with the soul; highest is the spiritual or theological meaning. Only the latter is present throughout all parts of the Bible and its elucidation is the chief objective of the exegete and preacher. The spiritual meaning is entirely consistent with basic Christian truths and, unless it is explicit in the text, must be found by allegorical interpretation. The use of allegorical interpretation becomes the

[4] Ibid., pp. 138-40.

great characteristic of the Alexandrian School of exegesis and was transmitted by it to the West, where it remained a major influence. In the East, allegory is consistently employed in homilies and in religious poetry, but less often in exegesis. Eastern exegesis in the Fourth and Fifth Centuries was dominated by the methods taught in the School of Antioch, which was more content to accept the literal meaning of the text or to seek historical explanations for the content.[5]

In the Third Century there was increasing sign not only of the adoption of dialectic, but of the influence of rhetoric among Christians. The earliest extant example of the utilization of the structure and topics of classical epideictic oratory to create Christian panegyric is apparently the farewell speech of Gregory Thaumaturgus to Origen in 238. Its introduction in particular is that of a student of the sophists practicing panegyric, and throughout Gregory never mentions the name of Christ.[6] Around 270 Paul of Samosata, bishop of Antioch and closely tied with the Antiochene School of exegesis, was excommunicated by a synod of bishops. The major charges were theological, that a literal interpretation of Scripture led him to the view that Jesus was a man who became divine and not God who became man, but he was also accused of excessively flamboyant oratorical delivery (Eusebius *Ecclesiastical History* 7.29-30). One of Paul's accusers was Malchion, whom Eusebius tells us was made a presbyter because of his great faith, but was the head of a sophistic school in Antioch at the time.

The Fourth Century brought a radical change in the relationships of Christianity to rhetoric as the Church moved from being a persecuted sect to the position of official re-

---

[5] See Christian Schaeubin, *Untersuchungen zu Methode und Herkunft der antiochenischen Exegese* (Theophaneia XXIII), Cologne: Haustein, 1974.

[6] See CR & CST, pp. 140-41.

ligion of the Roman empire. The beginning of this process is the Edict of Milan, issued by Constantine in 313, which granted religious toleration to all beliefs. In the following decades the political slogans and language of public life were gradually colored so as to be accepted by both Christians and pagans; the disputes of the Church became important national issues and openly utilized devices of classical rhetoric and dialectic; emperors had occasion to address bishops and bishops to speak at court. A writer whose works are central to our understanding of this process in the early Fourth Century is Eusebius Pamphili of Caesarea.

Eusebius

Eusebius was born around 260 and trained in the school of biblical scholars in Caesarea in Palestine which had begun with Origen and in Eusebius' time was under the leadership of Pamphilus. Pamphilus fell victim to the persecutions of 310, but Eusebius escaped, became bishop of Caesarea, and played an important role at the Council of Nicaea in 325, the first great Council of the Church. He closely associated himself with policies of Constantine, although the extent to which Constantine regarded him as a trusted adviser is somewhat uncertain, and died around 340.[7]

Eusebius' importance in the history of rhetoric is principally connected with his creation of Christian historiography, his panegyrics of Constantine, both oral and written, and his role in debate at Nicaea. He made important contributions as well to the development of the political theory of a Christian empire and of orthodox Christology, as well as to chronology and Christian doctrine.[8]

---

[7] On Eusebius see *R-E* VI, 1370-1439; Schmid-Stählin, pp. 1359-72; F.L.F. Jackson, *Eusebius Pamphili. A Study of the Man and His Writings*, Cambridge Univ. Pr., 1933; D. S. Wallace-Hadrill, *Eusebius of Caesarea*, London: Mowbray, 1960.

[8] See the works cited in chapter 1, n. 26, and in n. 20 infra.

EUSEBIUS

Eusebius' *Ecclesiastical History* in ten books covers the progress of Christianity from the time of Christ to that of Constantine.[9] As expressed in the first chapter, its purpose was to preserve a knowledge of chronology, of events, and of men, but there was clearly present in the author's mind the desire to demonstrate the divine origin and authority of the Church.[10] Although Eusebius writes primarily for Christians, he is intensely aware of how recent and how precarious the Christian victory has been. The writing of history is a classical concept and Eusebius was familiar with pagan historians, but his selection and presentation of material reflects the values we have associated with Christian rhetoric rather than the conventions of secular historians. Instead of composing speeches for historical characters, he quotes extensively from original writings and documents, thus seeking to establish the authority of his work rather than give it dramatic brilliance. Although his sentences sometimes become long and his thought labored, he ordinarily presents a simple narrative with little stylistic adornment. His diction and style are an elevated *koinē* rather than sophisticated Attic. When he does wish to amplify or enrich his account or to express his emotions at some event, he follows the model of the Christian preacher and weaves quotations from Scripture into his narrative. A good example is the celebration of the Christian victory at the beginning of Book Ten.

Eusebius' work as a historian of the Church was continued by others in the Fifth and Sixth Centuries. Since there will be occasion to refer to their writings as sources it is convenient to review them here briefly. Eusebius' succes-

[9] See Eusebius, *The Ecclesiastical History*, trans. Kirsopp Lake and J.E.L. Oulton, 2 vols. (LCL), Cambridge: Harvard Univ. Pr., 1957; 1959.

[10] See George L. Kustas, "Literature and History in Byzantium," *The Past in Medieval and Modern Greek Culture*, ed. Speros Vryonis, Malibu, Calif.: Undina, 1978, pp. 55-69.

sors generally follow his lead in preferring the authority of documents to the composition of speeches, though some show a greater accommodation to secular learning and an appreciation for philosophy and rhetoric which grew among intellectual leaders in the Church.[11] They characteristically write in the elevated *koinē* rather than in the Attic of secular literature. The vast history by Philip of Side, which covered the whole period from the creation to A.D. 426, is lost, though some impression of its encyclopedic contents and ostentatious style can be gained from excerpts quoted by others.[12] Philostorgius' history of the Church from 300 to 430 is known chiefly from the excerpts made by Photius.[13] Philostorgius was an Arian, though he included a generous treatment of Gregory of Nazianzus and Basil the Great. His hero was Eunomius, bishop of Cyzicus and an important Arian leader of the later Fourth Century. Eunomius had been a student of Aetius, and Philostorgius explains (3.15) how Aetius' skill in disputation aroused ill will, though he had a gift from God which saved him from defeat in debate. The Arians were commonly represented by the orthodox as sophists and, according to Philostorgius (10.1), earned epithets reminiscent of Aristophanes' picture of Socrates in "Cloud-Cuckooland." He is at pains throughout to counteract this view and demonstrate Arian logic, sincerity, and faith in contrast to orthodox irrationality and manipulation of power politics.

The most respected of those who continued Eusebius' history is Socrates, called Scholasticus because he was a

[11] See Glen F. Chestnut, *The First Christian Histories: Eusebius, Socrates, Sozomen, Theodoret, and Evagrius* (Théologie historique XLVI), Paris: Beauchesne, 1977.

[12] See Quasten III, pp. 528-30.

[13] For text see J. Bidez, *Philostorgius Kirchengeschichte*, revised by F. Winkelmann, Berlin: Akademie-Verlag, 1972; English translation by Edward Walford, *The Ecclesiastical History of Sozomen and the Ecclesiastical History of Philostorgius*, London: Bohn, 1855, pp. 425-528.

EUSEBIUS

lawyer.[14] His work covers the period from 306 to 439 and shows considerable independence of judgment. Socrates admired Origen (2.21, 35, 45), who was by his time being accused of heresy, and he praises Socrates and Plato (3.23). He makes a distinction between philosophy, which is good, and dialectic or *philoneikia* the love of disputation, which is destructive and a major cause, he thought, of the theological controversies of the Fourth Century (2.34; 3.22-23). Yet he justifies the study of classical philosophy on the ground that "the Scriptures do not instruct us in the art of reasoning, by means of which we may be enabled successfully to resist those who oppose the truth. Besides, adversaries are most easily foiled when we can use their own weapons against them" (3.16).

The ecclesiastical history of Sozomen covers a similar period and draws on the work of Socrates, without acknowledgment, but it has other sources as well which give some independent value.[15] Sozomen is somewhat impatient with Church politics and theological detail, and he lacks Socrates' judgment, but he is the ablest stylist among the Church historians, showing an excellent literary education. In partial contrast, Theodoret, who also wrote a history of the Church covering the same period, was a theologian of note as well as an excellent stylist and an eloquent preacher, as seen in his discourses on providence.[16] The final Church historian is Evagrius who lived

[14] Text ed. R. Hussey, revised by W. Bright, Oxford Univ. Pr., 1893; English translation by A. C. Zeno, *SLN & PNF*, Second Series, II. See Chestnut, *Christian Histories* (supra, n. 11), pp. 167-89.

[15] For text see Sozomenus, *Kirchengeschichte*, ed. Joseph Bidez, revised by Günther Christian Hansen, Berlin: Akademie-Verlag, 1960; English translation by C. D. Hartfranft in *SLN & PNF*, Second Series, II. See Chestnut, *Christian Histories* (supra, n. 11), pp. 191-200.

[16] For text see Theodoret, *Kirchengeschichte*, ed. L. Parmentier, Berlin: Akademie-Verlag, 1956; English translation by B. Jackson, *The Ecclesiastical History of Theodoret* in *SLN & PNF*, Second Series, III. See Chestnut, *Christian Histories* (supra, n. 11), pp. 200-206.

in the Sixth Century and carries the account of events down to his own times.[17] Church history is a distinct genre both in style and in subject: ecclesiastical historians do not regularly discuss military events, which is the main subject of the secular historians of these centuries, and secular historians do not discuss the Church. Ecclesiastical historians find their models in the Bible, for example, in Acts; secular historians imitate Herodotus, Thucydides, or Diodorus. Church historians as a group resist ornamentation and digression; the secular historians, with the exception of Procopius, often seem to regard history as a convenient subject for sophistic display.

Eusebius was also a panegyrist and illustrates the stage in which Church leaders had occasion to address a wide public and were comfortable with some stylistic features of sophistry, but had not yet extensively adapted its language, its commonplaces, its references to classical literature, and its structure. Presumably Eusebius' preaching would have shown some of these same features, but none of his sermons survives. The earliest of his panegyrics is a speech he gave at Tyre in 316 or 317, which he quotes in full in the *Ecclesiastical History* (10.4).[18] The occasion was the reconstruction of the church there, which had been destroyed in the persecutions, and the speech honors Paulinus, the bishop of Tyre, who had directed the effort, but it is far from being a panegyric of him in classical terms. What Eusebius celebrates is primarily the victory of the Church over her enemies, and the visible and material church at Tyre is made a symbol for the greater and invisible spiritual Church (esp. sections 21-22 and 26). The topics of the speech are Christian and, as in homilies, quo-

[17] For text see J. Bidez and L. Parmentier, *The Ecclesiastical History of Evagrius*, 1893; reprinted Amsterdam: Hakkert, 1964.
[18] Text and translation in Oulton, LCL Eusebius (supra, n. 9), II, pp. 398-445.

tations and allusions to Scripture are woven into the language and imagery, but certain features are reminiscent of the sophists. There is a great deal of verbal amplification (e.g., 15-16) and some use of figures, such as an extended series of rhetorical questions (17-20) and a rather artificial paraleipsis (43-44). Further, some passages adopt progymnasmatic forms; this is especially true of the extended ecphrasis of the church at Tyre, which is valuable for an understanding of Christian architecture (37-45 and 64-68). The opposition of the Devil and Christ (58-61) might be viewed as a synkrisis, though it is not really handled in a sophistic way. The power of evil and the machinations of the Devil are a source of vigor in Christian oratory and help to give it an intensity lacking in the flowery but somewhat bland efforts of pagans in late antiquity. Great oratory needs its villains, as Demosthenes and Cicero had known.

In the *Life of Constantine* (4.46) Eusebius mentions delivering an oration at Constantinople on the thirtieth-anniversary celebration of Constantine's accession to the throne. The exact date was July 25, 336. A version of it survives, but combined with another oration which Eusebius delivered in Jerusalem at the Holy Sepulcher in the previous year.[19] The jubilee speech (chapters 1-10) refers to Constantine as present, but does not address him; the Jerusalem speech (11-18) addresses him directly. The two have common thematic elements and are both highly complimentary to Constantine, but the second part is more of a sermon setting forth Christian doctrine, while the first is more truly encomiastic. In the jubilee speech, however, Eusebius does not, as a traditional panegyrist might, review Constantine's ancestry, education, and advance to the

[19] See H. A. Drake, *In Praise of Constantine: A Historical Study and New Translation of Eusebius' Tricennial Orations* (Univ. of California Publications: Classical Studies xv), Berkeley and Los Angeles: Univ. of California Pr., 1975.

throne, and in the prologue he distinguishes his role as a Christian orator from that of a secular encomiast, but he does develop the topics of Constantine's virtues and describes some of his actions. The style is somewhat less biblical than in the speech at Tyre; there are at least two references to Homer (Prol. 1-2 and 6.4) and a rather tiresome parade of Pythagorean number theory (6.5-6 and 10-17). In neither speech is the name of Christ mentioned, though both set forth Christian views, more explicitly in the second speech, which was given on a specifically Christian occasion. On the occasion of the jubilee speech, given at court, some of the audience was presumably pagan; if they were philosophically minded they would not have found much of the thought offensive. Progymnasmatic influence may be seen in the description of the universe (6) and in the comparison of the past and the present as seen in penultimate chapter (9). An important feature of the speech is the concept of the Christian emperor, seen especially in the opening chapter, but taken up again later as well.[20] Eusebius applies imperial epithets to God and divine epithets to the emperor, while the empire is presented as an imitation of the monarchical power in heaven with the emperor as an image of the one all-imperial God. Such a view, though developed by Christians, was not unacceptable to Platonists, as seen in its appeal to Themistius. In his enthusiastic exposition of this idea Eusebius, however, helped to create some problems later in the century when the emperors inclined to Arianism and orthodox leaders sought to dissociate Church and state.

Constantine was a great leader, but Eusebius' praise of him is by modern standards vastly overdone. Many Christians gave way immediately and completely, once they had

---

[20] See Kenneth M. Setton, *Christian Attitude towards the Emperor in the Fourth Century*, New York: Columbia Univ. Pr., 1941, esp. pp. 40-56 and 79-81.

even a tolerable public leader to praise, to adulation as a way to strengthen the public position of the Church and to emphasize the new national unity. But Eusebius set the tone, and his part in the Arian controversy suggests a political pragmatism unseen in earlier centuries when the Church was under attack and scorned the pride of kings.

Eusebius' *Life of Constantine* is a panegyrical biography, not a speech, extended to the length of four books, but it includes topics which might have been found in a funeral oration, including an account of the emperor's parents, his youth, his actions and virtues, and his death.[21] Progymnasmatic forms are utilized, for example, a synkrisis of Constantine with Cyrus and Alexander the Great (1.7-8) and an ecphrasis of the Holy Sepulcher (3.34-39). As in the *Ecclesiastical History*, documents are quoted to give the work authority, and ornamentation is sought or pathos amplified by scriptural language. One chapter is devoted to a description of Constantine as an imperial Christian orator (4.29). Eusebius here says that Constantine spent much time studying divine knowledge and composing speeches,

> for he conceived it to be incumbent on him to govern his subjects by appealing to their reason, and to secure in all respects a rational obedience to his authority. Hence he would sometimes himself evoke an assembly, on which occasions vast multitudes attended in the hope of hearing an emperor sustain the part of a philosopher. And if in the course of his speech any occasion offered of touching on sacred topics, he immediately stood erect, and with a grave aspect and subdued tone of voice seemed reverently to be initiating his auditors in the mysteries of the divine doctrine; and when they greeted him with

[21] For text see Eusebius, *Werke I: Ueber das Leben des Kaisers Konstantin*, ed. F. Winkelmann, Berlin: Akademie-Verlag, 1975; English translation by Ernest Cushing Richardson in *SLN & PNF* Second Series, I, p. 471-559, which is utilized below.

shouts of acclamation, he would direct them by his gestures to raise their eyes to heaven and reserve their admiration for the Supreme King alone and honor him with adoration and praise.

A typical speech by Constantine, according to Eusebius, began by refuting polytheism, then asserted the sovereignty of God, gave an account of his providence, demonstrated the necessity of salvation, and concluded with the doctrine of divine judgment, where the emperor appealed to the conscience of his hearers and denounced the wicked.

As an example of Constantine's oratory, Eusebius appended to the *Life of Constantine* the emperor's oration *To the Assembly of the Saints*.[22] He says (4.32) that the speech was composed in Latin, but put into Greek by interpreters appointed to this service. The speech does not exactly conform to the outline given by Eusebius above, but certainly has some of the features he describes. Consistent with the tradition of Christian rhetoric, Constantine urges (Chapter 1) his audience to attend, not to the language, but to the truth of what he says, and to correct any error in the content. He prays that the Holy Spirit will furnish the words to him as he speaks (Chapter 2). The speech shows how the methods of Greek dialectic, in which the rhetorical schools furnished preliminary training, had been accepted in Christian disputation and also how Platonic philosophy was viewed by Christian leaders in the second quarter of the Fourth Century. These features could, of course, be illustrated from other authors of the period or earlier, but their use by the emperor gave them official blessing in the new relationship of Church and state.

An example of syllogistic reasoning is a passage (Chapter 4) where Constantine seeks to disprove the immortality of

[22] Text in *PG* xx, 1233-1316; English translation by Richardson in *SLN & PNF*, Second Series, I, pp. 561-80, utilized below.

the pagan gods. He sets this forth in an orderly sequence of major premise, minor premise, and conclusion: "Whatever has had a beginning, has also an end. Now that which is a beginning in respect of time is called a generation, and whatever is by generation is subject to corruption and its beauty is impaired by the lapse of time. How, then, can they whose origin is from corruptible generation be immortal?" The major premise is not proved, but assumed on the basis of experience. The minor premise is a sequence of definitions. The conclusion is cast as a rhetorical question.

A more elaborate form of argument (Chapter 6) appears to conform to the type described in the Second Book of the Hermogenic *On Invention*.[23] Constantine states first the "heading" which he will refute: "The great majority, in their folly, ascribe the regulation of the universe to nature, while some imagine fate, or accident, to be the cause." Then comes *lysis* from *enstasis*, furnishing the denial of the proposition. The end of this sentence is treated with what in *On Invention* is called *hypodiairesis*: "With regard to those who attribute the control of all things to fate, they know not that in using this term they utter a mere word, but designate no active power, nor anything which has real and substantial existence." Next a succession of two supporting arguments, called "enthymemes" in *On Invention*: "For what can this fate be, considered in itself, if nature be the first cause of all things? Or what shall we suppose nature itself to be, if the law of fate be inviolable?" Then an *ergasia*, or working out of the argument. "Indeed, the very assertion that there is a law of fate implies that such law is the work of a legislator; if therefore fate itself be a law, it must be devised by God." And finally an "enthy-

[23] See above, pp. 88-91.

meme" which states the speaker's conclusion: "All things therefore are subject to God and nothing is beyond the sphere of his power." The argument is essentially *a priori*, inherent in the speaker's assumptions and definitions, and its "working out" is rhetorically effective, rather than logically cogent. That is, the form seems to give logical defense to the proposition, but in fact only restates it in clearer forms. It is perhaps not surprising that Eusebius reports (*Life of Constantine* 4.29) that Constantine's audience usually received his words with loud applause, but were little convinced by them. The employment of dialectic in the Arian controversy and other disputes of the Church had similar results.

Later in the speech Constantine criticizes the use of dialectic by classical philosophers such as Socrates and Pythagoras. "The persuasive influence of argument," he says (Chapter 9), "has a tendency to draw most of us away from the truth of things, which has happened to many philosophers, who have employed themselves in reasoning and the study of natural science and who, as often as the magnitude of the subject surpasses the powers of investigation, adopt various devices for obscuring the truth." Apparently, his view is that truth is known by revelation; dialectic may be used in supporting it or combatting error, but is dangerous as a method for the initial discovery of truth. This explains why he can make an exception of Plato in his rejection of classical philosophy. Plato is "the gentlest and most refined of all, who first essayed to draw men's thoughts from sensible to intellectual and eternal objects and taught them to aspire to sublimer speculations." The studies of Origen and others had made it clear that Platonism had significant similarities with Christian truth and could be useful in developing its doctrine. Constantine summarizes these features as belief in a God who is the creator and controller of the universe and of a second deity who proceeds from him and is the obedient agent of his command, in other words a belief in something like the Father and the Son. God is the Word, but the Word is also the Son of God. He criticizes Plato's creation of a plurality of gods descending from this source, but praises his belief that the rational soul is the breath of God and his division of all things into intellectual and sensible, as well as his teaching about the immortality of the soul. Such a view implies an opening up of Christianity to the wisdom of this world and possibilities for the synthesis of Platonic and Christian rhetoric which were attempted later in the century.

The Arian Controversy

The place of rhetoric and dialectic in the Church was an important theme in the Arian controversy, in which Constantine and Eusebius were major participants. In 318, only five years after the Edict of Milan had brought religious peace to the world, an Alexandrian priest named Arius set off a dispute, the effects of which were to last for centuries and affect both the political history of Europe and the content of Christian theology. Socrates Scholasticus (1.5) describes the incident in the following words:

> [Alexander, bishop of Alexandria,] in the fearless exercise of his functions for the instruction and government of the Church, attempted one day in the presence of the presbytery and the rest of the clergy to explain, with perhaps too philosophical minuteness, that great theological mystery, the unity of the Holy Trinity. A certain one of the presbyters under his jurisdication, whose name was Arius, possessed of no inconsiderable logical acumen, imagining that the bishop was subtly teaching the same view of this subject as Sabellius the Libyan, from love of controversy took the opposite view to that of the Libyan and as he thought vigorously responded to

what was said by the bishop. "If," he said, "the Father begat the Son, he that was begotten had a beginning of existence, and from this it is evident that there was a time when the Son was not. It therefore necessarily follows that he had his substance (*hypostasis*) from nothing."[24]

It is unlikely that the incident was as spontaneous as the account implies. Arius was an old man with a history of disputation and heresy; probably he had been preaching the doctrine in Alexandria and the meeting may have been summoned by Alexander in the interest of Church discipline. Arius had been a student of Lucian of Antioch, and the split between Antiochene and Alexandrian Schools of exegesis was a part of the background to the discussion. Socrates' words "from love of controversy" need not be taken literally: it is a rhetorical topos constantly used by the orthodox of Arians throughout the Fourth and Fifth Centuries. But it is possible to see in Arianism a comparative willingness to use the rational methods of classical philosophy and, conversely, among the orthodox a desire to achieve a definition of the Trinity which transcended human reason.[25] That the issue was a sincere theological difference need not be doubted, but neither side was really capable of understanding the other and the rhetoric became increasingly shrill, as did the resort to external means of persuasion. Speaking about a later stage of the dispute involving the term *homoousios*, Socrates says (1.23): "While they occupied themselves in a too minute investigation of its import, they roused the strife against each other; it seemed

[24] Zeno's translation, *SLN & PNF*, Second Series, II, p. 3.
[25] See T. E. Pollard, "The Origins of Arianism," *Journal of Theological Studies* n.s. 9 (1958), 103-11; Harry A. Wolfson, "Philosophical Implications of Arianism and Apollinarianism," *Dumbarton Oaks Papers* 12 (1958), 5-28; G. C. Stead, "The Platonism of Arius," *Journal of Theological Studies* n.s. 15 (1964), 16-31.

not unlike a contest in the dark; for neither party appeared to understand distinctly the grounds on which they calumniated one another. Those who objected to the word *homoousios* conceived that those who approved it favored the opinion of Sabellius and Montanus; they therefore called them blasphemers as subverting the existence of the Son of God. And again the advocates of this term, charging their opponents with polytheism, inveighed against them as introducers of heathen superstitions."[26]

The controversy which originated in Alexandria was rapidly spread by letters written by Arius. He soon found a vigorous champion in the bishop of Nicomedia in Bithynia, who had been his fellow student under Lucian of Antioch and, like the bishop of Caesarea, bore the name Eusebius. Alexander reacted by calling a local synod in Egypt, at which Arius was excommunicated, and by writing letters to bishops throughout the Church about the danger. The forms of communication used by the two sides became standard in ecclesiastical controversy: disputation before synods, letters, preaching, publication of polemical tracts, and eventually the writing of commentaries on the Bible and of historical works from each point of view. In addition, Arius himself, but apparently not the orthodox, sought to popularize his views by writing songs which achieved some circulation among the working classes, and Arius published a work called *Thalia* defending his views in a mixture of prose and poetry.[27] External means of persuasion were quickly resorted to in the form of orders to desist issued by bishops, bans on preaching, removal from office of offending bishops, and excommunication.

Constantine is described by Socrates (1.7) as deeply grieved at the dissension and as regarding it as a personal misfor-

[26] Zeno's translation, *SLN & PNF*, Second Series, II, p. 27.
[27] See Gustave Bardy, "La Thalie d'Arius," *Revue de philologie* 1 (3rd series) (1927), 211-33.

tune. He sent Ossius (or Hosius), bishop of Cordova, to Alexander and Arius ordering them to stop the dispute and be reconciled:

> Let each one of you, showing consideration for the other, listen to the impartial exhortation of your fellow servant. And what counsel does he offer? It was neither prudent at first to agitate such a question nor to reply to such a question when proposed, for the claim of no law demands the investigation of such subjects, but the idle useless talk of leisure occasions them. And even if they should exist for the sake of exercising our natural faculties, yet we ought to confine them to our own consideration and not incautiously bring them forth in public assemblies nor thoughtlessly confide them to the ears of everybody. Indeed, how few are capable either of adequately expounding or even accurately understanding the import of matters so vast and profound![28] (Socrates 1.7; see also Eusebius, *Life of Constantine* 2.64-72.)

The emperor's appeal was entirely unsuccessful, but as a result of the embassy Ossius embraced Alexander's side in the controversy and influenced the emperor in that direction. Since strife continued, not only between leaders of the Church, but between congregations and lay followers, Constantine ultimately resolved to call a general council of the Church, the Council of Nicaea of 325. This is the first such assembly of the Eastern and Western bishops with authority to speak for all of Christendom.

Beginning with the Third Ecumenical Council, at Ephesus in 431, we have *acta*, or minutes, which give some account of the proceedings. For Nicaea and other Fourth-Century councils we are dependent on the descriptions in the ecclesiastical historians and in the writings of

---

[28] Zeno's translation, *SLN & PNF*, Second Series, II, p. 6.

THE ARIAN CONTROVERSY

the participants or later authors.[29] For the Council of Nicaea, Athanasius, Eusebius of Caesarea, Eustathius of Antioch, and Socrates Scholasticus are probably the most valuable sources. Few events in Church history are more complicated than the Council of Nicaea or have been more studied. The drama was intense, and the political and theological implications great. Here it is enough to point to some features of the Council which are of rhetorical interest.[30]

First, the Council demonstrates the tension between the tradition of simple, radical Christianity, unaffected by worldly philosophy, and the emerging tradition of Christian use of dialectic and classical philosophy. This is clear, for example, from a passage in Socrates Scholasticus (1.8):

> Now a short time previous to the general assembling of the bishops, the disputants engaged in preparatory logical contests before the multitudes; and when many were attracted by the interests of their discourse, one of the laity, a confessor, who was a man of unsophisticated understanding, reproved these reasoners, telling them that Christ and his apostles did not teach us dialectic, art, or vain subtleties, but simple-mindedness, which is preserved by faith and good works. As he said this, all present admired the speaker and assented to the justice of his remarks; and the disputants themselves, after hearing his plain statement of the truth, exercised a greater degree of moderation. Thus then was the disturbance caused by these logical debates suppressed at this time.[31]

[29] The evidence is collected by Hans-Georg Opitz, "Urkunden zur Geschichte des Arianischen Streites," *Athanasius Werke* III. 1. 1, Berlin and Leipzig: de Gruyter, 1934.
[30] The following account is indebted to Ralph E. Person, *The Mode of Theological Decision Making at the Early Ecumenical Councils*, Basel: Reinhard, 1978.
[31] Zeno's translation, *SLN & PNF*, Second Series, II p. 8.

201

Opposition to dialectic was thus grounded on the authority of Christ and the apostles, as seen for example in 1 Corinthians 1-2. It reflects of course the claims to exclusive truth made by Christianity, which altered the ground rules accepted in the pagan philosophical schools. Despite dogmatic qualities inherent in Platonism, the limits of discussion there were wide and the skeptical tradition of the Hellenistic Academy was never entirely abandoned. This could not be true in a Christian assembly which could not, in the last analysis, exalt human reason above divine inspiration.

Among extant works of Fourth-Century Fathers, the best representative of opposition to dialectic is probably Epiphanius of Salamis (c. 315-403), especially in his treatise on heresies known as *Panarion* or *Breadbasket*.[32] Epiphanius vigorously opposed virtually any departure from the customs of the early Church, all heresies, all compromise with classical culture, all the work of Origen, and all use of statues and paintings of Christ or the saints, thus anticipating the iconoclasts of the early Byzantine period.

Second, the formal sessions of the Council apparently did not include a fair presentation of Arius' views, although there was some argument about those views. Eyewitness sources contain no reference to any participation by Arius himself or any systematic presentation of his case. Rufinus and Sozomen, writing much later, indicate his presence, but may have assumed it without evidence.[33] Sozomen's account (1.17) describes a preliminary assembly of bishops which apparently debated the issues while waiting for others to arrive. Among the voting members of the Council Arius had few supporters, and the question which faced the formal session of the Council was not what he had said or

[32] See Epiphani Episcopi Constantiae *Opera*, ed. G. Dindorf, vols. II-III, Leipzig: Weigel, 1861, and Quasten III, pp. 384-96.

[33] See Person, *Theological Decision Making* (supra, n. 30), p. 59.

the heretical quality of what he taught, but the composition of a creed in accordance with which he could be judged heretical and the unity which Constantine so desired could be imposed upon the Church. The stasis was one of definition, turned upside down: viewed as a trial—and the Council did judge and anathematize Arius—the bishops might be compared to a jury which first found the defendant guilty and then wrote the law which he had broken. The issues facing other councils of the Church can also be formulated in terms of stasis theory. At Nicaea the judicial functions, in the view of Constantine and most of the bishops, were, however, subordinate to its deliberative functions.

Third, the Council of Nicaea illustrates the importance of external rhetoric in the late empire. Constantine called the Council, provided transportation and housing for the bishops (*Life of Constantine* 3.6), and dominated proceedings. Threat of loss of bishoprics, excommunication, or exile hung over the participants. The sessions were held in a large audience room in the imperial palace. Apparently the procedure was modeled on that of the senate, in which the emperors traditionally asked for advice, listened to the *sententiae* of the members, and then acted on the advice. Ceremony, so congenial to late antiquity, must have contributed to inhibiting opposition and the expression of divergent opinions: it operated as an external rhetoric. On the first day the bishops all took their place in the splendid chamber and a hush fell. A procession of members of the imperial family entered, followed by the emperor himself, "like some heavenly messenger of God, clothed in raiment which glittered as it were with rays of light, reflecting the glowing radiance of a purple robe and adorned with the brilliant splendor of gold and precious stones" (*Life of Constantine* 3.10). All stood until the emperor took his seat on a golden throne. One of the bishops, probably Eusebius of

Caesarea, then delivered a short speech of thanks to God on behalf of Constantine. The emperor sat silent for a moment, gazing with serenity on the assembled company, and then "in a calm and gentle tone," delivered a short speech, of which Eusebius preserves the official version (*Life of Constantine* 3.12). In it, the emperor gives thanks to God at seeing the bishops assembled in harmony, he reminds them of his victories over the enemies of the Church, but expresses his belief that internal strife in the Church is far more dangerous than any war. A second time he mentions his joy in his victories and his distress at dissension: "Delay not, then, dear friends. Delay not, ministers of God and faithful servants of him who is our common lord and savior. Begin from this moment to discard the causes of that disunion which has existed among you and remove the perplexities of controversy by embracing the principle of peace. For by such conduct you will at the same time be acting in a manner most pleasing to the supreme God, and you will confer an exceeding favor on me, your fellow servant."[34] The emperor spoke in Latin, and his speech was translated into Greek, though in the subsequent discussion he spoke directly in Greek (*Life of Constantine* 3.13).

The details of what followed are not clear. It is probable that charges were made against the Arians and letters and documents supporting the charges read, as is the custom at later councils.[35] At some point Eusebius of Caesarea presented a creed, probably that of his own church, and assured the bishops of his orthodoxy. This may have been an attempt to mediate for the Arians or to get the Council to remove the provisional excommunication which a synod at Antioch had laid on Eusebius himself. Subsequently,

[34] Adapted from Richardson, *SLN & PNF*, Second Series, I, p. 523.
[35] See Person, *Theological Decision Making* (supra, n. 30), pp. 58-71.

THE ARIAN CONTROVERSY

the text of what became the Nicene Creed was presented, probably the work of a committee, and its terms discussed. The Creed contained the word *homoousios*, describing the Son as "of the same nature" as the Father. Constantine supported use of the word, despite its lack of biblical authority, and tried to give an interpretation of it that would allow acceptance of it both by the orthodox and by those who had some sympathy with Arius' views. The former pressed for more restrictive words and for anathemas against specifically Arian terms. Eusebius of Caesarea, after much thought, convinced himself that he could sign the creed; he had throughout had some sympathy with the Arian position and is sometimes called a "semi-Arian." All but two of the Arian bishops followed him, according to Eustathius (Theodoret *Ecclesiastical History* 1.18), not because they had been persuaded, but to save their bishoprics.[36] Arius himself was exiled and subsequently died in a public lavatory in Constantinople; the scene is luridly described by orthodox writers (e.g., Athanasius *Ep.* 54).

Fourth, much of the work of the Council went into finding words which would describe the Son. In the debate, the tension was not so much between orthodox and Arian as between those orthodox bishops who wanted to exclude as specifically as possible all Arian interpretation and the emperor, who was anxious for a creed to which as many as possible could subscribe. The most conspicuous rhetorical feature of theological debate from the Fourth Century on becomes the use, or failure to use specific epithets: *homoousios*, *homoiousos*, and *homosios*, and later other terms such as *Theotokos*, "Mother of God" as applied to the Virgin Mary. This obsession with the definition of words had not characterized earlier Greek public address; it primarily arises from conditions in the Church, but resembles

[36] Ibid., pp. 71-83.

other developments in later antiquity, including the increased concern with definition and technical terms in rhetorical theory, the greatly expanded use of honorific titles and epithets in public life, and the codification of the law under Theodosius.

Fifth, the basis of theological disputation at the Council of Nicaea and subsequently was a combination of scriptural authority and the tradition of the Church.[37] Historically and pragmatically, orthodoxy is whatever view won out, but theologically and semantically it is the true doctrine, inherent in the Christian faith as originally revealed. Both Arians and their opponents claimed to be orthodox and both cited a considerable number of passages of Scripture as the basis of their beliefs. In practice, the resulting logical deadlock was broken by what could be called majority contemporary opinion: the number of bishops and the moral authority and ecclesiastical power which they could muster. The Church equated their decisions with the Holy Spirit moving in the minds of men; Constantine said, "That which has commended itself to the judgment of three hundred bishops cannot be other than the doctrine of God," and Socrates Scholasticus in reporting this says (1.9), "Even if those who constituted that synod had been laymen, yet as being illuminated by God and the grace of the Holy Spirit, they were utterly unable to err from the truth." Human reason and argument from probability or expedience were allowed little or no role in theory, though expediency certainly played some part in practice. It is characteristic of the mind of late antiquity that it could reject human reasoning powers, despise the world of men, and yet easily accord divine inspiration to a council of bishops. Legally, the power of the Council came from the

[37] Ibid., pp. 129-59.

signatures of the bishops who subscribed to the creed and the power of the emperor who implemented it.

Asterius the Sophist

An early adherent of the Arian cause was Asterius of Cappadocia, who had been a teacher of rhetoric, but gave up teaching after his conversion to Christianity (Socrates, *Ecclesiastical History* 1.36).[38] He is astringently described by Athanasius (*On the Synods* 18) as a "many-headed sophist" who compared the locust and caterpillar to Christ, claimed that the wisdom of God was other than Christ, and boldly went around the East preaching to indignant audiences. Most Arian writing is lost, but portions of Asterius' homilies survive, some only discovered in the mid-Twentieth century.[39] Here is how he begins a homily for the Octave of Easter based on the Eighth Psalm. It is possibly this passage, or something like it, that Athanasius had in mind when he referred to Asterius' comparison of locusts and Christ:

> The divine vine, existing before all time, sprouted from the tomb and has brought forth the newly enlightened, like fruit on the altar. Let the things which have been shown declare to us the new vintage. The vine has been harvested and the altar, like a wine vat, is overflowing with grapes. Here are the wine-pressers, the harvesters, those who climb trees for the fruit, singing cicadas, and today they reveal to us, in the fullness of grace, the paradise of the Church. Who are the wine pressers? The prophets and the apostles, foretelling to us in song the vintage. "Unto the end, the presses." Who are the cicadas? Those who receive the new light, bedewed from

[38] See Quasten III, pp. 194-97.
[39] See Marcel Richard, *Asterii Sophistae Commentaria* (Symbolae Osloensis Supplementum 16) Oslo: Brøgger, 1956.

the fountain and taking their rest on the cross as on a tree and warmed by the sun of justice and lighted by the spirit and singing things of the spirit, saying, O Lord, our Lord, how wondrous is thy name in all the earth.[40]

The allegorical imagery is cultivated with the extravagance of a sophist, as it had been done by Melito in the Second Century, but differs only in degree from the traditional incorporation of biblical language in the homily.

Athanasius

The great champion of orthodoxy in the Fourth Century, and an opponent of Arius, Eusebius, and Asterius as well as of the Arian emperors Constantius and Valentinian, is Athanasius of Alexandria (c. 295-373).[41] One does not have to be a Christian to admire the fortitude and determination with which he persisted in his cause, but it takes a considerable sympathy with orthodox Christianity to admire his rhetoric and dialectic. He was a skilled dialectician, but he continually misrepresents his opponents and seeks to impugn their motives and morality, and his argumentation is often technically invalid. He is, however, the best example of a consistent attempt to apply dialectic to Christian disputation. As an orator he was not particularly remarkable, to judge from his few extant homilies which are ill arranged and saccharine in tone. It is possible that some of his indifference to the preacher's art reflects the undemanding character of his Alexandrian congregation.[42] We are told by Gregory of Nazianzus (Or. 6.35) that Athanasius had studied philosophy, and it is likely that he had studied rhetoric as well. He makes considerable use

[40] *Homily* 14, pp. 105-6 Richard.
[41] See Quasten III, pp. 20-79.
[42] See Robert W. Smith, *The Art of Rhetoric in Alexandria. Its Theory and Practice in the Ancient World*, The Hague: Nijhoff, 1974, pp. 100-104.

of Platonism in his defense of orthodox Christianity[43] and has been shown to use the topics of Aristotle and of the progymnasmatic thesis as described by Aphthonius in disputation.[44] His language is fundamentally that of the *koinē* and his style simple, but he makes some use of the commoner figures of speech.

Athanasius has relatively little to say about rhetoric as such, but that little is negative. For example (*Against the Gentiles* 17): "nobody who pronounces a panegyric upon anyone accuses his conduct at the same time, but rather, if men's actions are disgraceful, they praise them up with panegyrics, on account of the scandal they cause, so that by extravagant praise they may impose upon their hearers and hide the misconduct of others."[45] He claims that he speaks "as lies within our power, first refuting the ignorance of the unbelieving; so that what is false being refuted, the truth may shine forth of itself" (ibid. 1). God's truth has no particular need of eloquence. Something of his typical rhetorical and dialectical manner can be seen in the following passage from the first "oration," actually a pamphlet, *Against the Arians* (1.11):

You Arians say and believe, at the suggestion of Satan, that there was a time when the Son was not. This is the first of your outworks which we must assail. Tell us then, you blasphemers, what was it which had a being before the Son had any? If you say the Father had, this is a more unpardonable statement than the other. For to say of him that he was heretofore or at some time or other is appalling insolence. For he has always been what

[43] See E. P. Meijering, *Orthodoxy and Platonism in Athanasius. Synthesis or Antithesis?* Leiden: Brill, 1968, esp. pp. 114-31.
[44] See G. Christopher Stead, "Rhetorical Method in Athanasius," *Vigiliae Christianae* 30 (1976), 121-37.
[45] Translation of Archibald Robinson, *SLN & PNF*, Second Series, IV, p. 13.

he is now, the Father of the Son, and therefore so likewise is the Son the Son of the Father. But if you had rather say that the Son was heretofore, when he was not, there cannot be a more foolish and absurd contradiction.[46]

He constantly introduces such phrases as "at the suggestion of Satan" to create a wicked and perverse ethos, and he puts words in the mouths of his opponents which they would never have said. Neither alternative of the dilemma here expressed would be acceptable to an intelligent Arian. When the Arians argue from Scripture, Athanasius accuses them of blaspheming holy writ, when they argue from reason, he accuses them of being unscriptural.

Probably the best known of Athanasius' writings is his *Life of Saint Anthony*, composed about 357. It is the model for the lives of the saints, or hagiography, the most popular literary form of the Byzantine period, with influence also in the West, and it reinforced among radical Christians, especially within the monastic movement, a distrust of rhetoric as un-Christian. The ideal of the Christian orator as developed by Gregory of Nazianzus and John Chrysostom later in the century thus must be viewed as developed in a context in which there were powerful forces moving in the opposite direction. Athanasius' model for Anthony is John the Baptist, or at times even Christ (e.g., 58) but the biography is an encomium and shows the influence of classical encomia, such as Xenophon's life of Agesilaus.[47] It utilizes some of the structural principles of panegyric (e.g., 67) and shows some signs of familiarity with progymnasmatic forms, such as the chria and the prosopopoeia.

[46] See the anonymous translation of *The Orations of S. Athanasius Against the Arians* (Ancient and Modern Library of Theological Literature), London: Griffith Farran, n.d., p. 21.
[47] See S. Cavallin, *Literarhistorische und textkritische Studien zur Vita S. Caesarii Arelatensis*, Lund: Gleerup, 1934, pp. 5-17.

ATHANASIUS

Anthony was a hermit, living on a mountain in the Egyptian desert, withdrawn from the cities of men. Yet he is presented as knowing almost everything that is going on in the world, and the world comes to him, a wiseman, for advice and help. Such figures become common in later antiquity, not only in Egypt, but also in Asia.[48] Athanasius wanted to preserve the discipline of monasticism as established by Anthony (94). He clearly also wanted to use the authority of Anthony in combating Arianism (e.g., 82), and he wanted to counter paganism by a dramatic equation of the demons who continually beset Anthony with the Greek gods (37).

As a hermit, Anthony had little use for rhetoric, but a group of solitary monks eventually collected around him and, according to Athanasius, he finally addressed them in a speech of which an extended version is given (16-43).[49] This is perhaps a dramatic device on the part of Athanasius, but there is no doubt that the contents of the speech are consistent with the values of monasticism, and the speech is an excellent example of radical Christian rhetoric. Anthony begins by saying, "The Scriptures are enough for instruction, but it is a good thing to encourage one another in the faith and to stir it up with words." (16). The function of the speech is thus exhortation to the holy life; its material is Christian doctrine, supported by quotation from the Bible and by the personal experience of Anthony: his contests with devils and the miracles he has been able to perform in Christ's name. The devils add a great deal of excitement, even more than in the speech of Eusebius,

[48] See Peter Brown, "The Rise and Function of the Holy Man in Late Roman Society," *Journal of Roman Studies* 61 (1971), 80-101.
[49] Translation by Archibald Robertson in SLN & PNF, Second Series, IV, pp. 200-208, utilized below. The collection of sermons and epistles attributed to Anthony in PG XL, 961-1102, is spurious.

culminating in a prosopopoeia (41) where Satan, rather pathetically, begs Anthony not to curse him undeservedly.

Subsequently Athanasius touches on various other aspects of Christian rhetoric exemplified by Anthony. He is untaught and illiterate (72), and in fact probably knew only Coptic, not Greek. He had no need of letters, for his speech "was seasoned with the divine salt" (73). Without dialectical training, he is yet able to dispute with philosophers (74), for he has revealed knowledge and faith, which is better (77). "You," he says to the philosophers, "by your eloquence do not hinder the teaching of Christ, but we by the mention of Christ crucified put all demons to flight, whom you fear as if they were gods" (78). "You still do not believe and are seeking arguments. We, however, make our proof 'not in the persuasive words of Greek wisdom,' as our teacher has it [1 Cor. 2:4], but we persuade by the faith which manifestly precedes argumentative proof" (80).

Some other Egyptian monks acquired fame as preachers. In some cases their style was allegorical and contributed to the development of Christian mysticism. Good examples are the *Spiritual Homilies* attributed to Macarius the Egyptian, which were translated into English by John Wesley, founder of Methodism. The attribution was made as early as the Sixth Century, but contemporary sources on Macarius know nothing of any writings by him.[50] More often the style was gnomic, imitating the sayings of Jesus.[51] Like Anthony, the monks are often described as throwing short biblical quotations in the face of temptation, and they created gnomic *sententiae* of their own which were quoted and preserved.

Many of the monks were illiterate, and their native lan-

[50] See Quasten III, 161-68.
[51] See the translation of the *Apophthegmata Patrum* by Ernest A. Wallis Budge under the title *The Wit and Wisdom of the Christian Fathers of Egypt*, London: Oxford Univ. Pr., 1934.

guage was usually Coptic, but they attracted the admiration of educated Christian Greeks like Athanasius or later Palladius (c. 363-431). Palladius came from Galatia, but lived over ten years in Egypt before becoming bishop of Helenopolis in Bithynia. His *Lausiac History*, so called because of its dedication to Lausus, chamberlain of Theodosius II, is the best picture of Egyptian monasticism at the end of the Fourth Century.[52] It contains brief accounts of seventy-one individuals, mostly holy men and women, but a few backsliders, whom Palladius met or had heard about. He writes not to glorify them, he says (Prologue 7), but to help readers to holiness, and his rhetoric is like that of Anthony. He contrasts his work (Prologue 1) to three other forms: First, works written with inspiration of grace for the salvation of those who follow the teachings of the savior. These may be thought to include orthodox theological tracts such as those by Athanasius. Second, works intended to please men and women with corrupt purpose and to reassure their desire for fame; this clearly refers to secular panegyric. Third, works inspired by madness and written with the energy of the Devil to turn the minds of the foolish against the Christian life; this refers to pagan attacks on Christianity, like Julian the Apostate's *Against the Galilaeans*, and also to works by Arians and other heretics. Palladius employs the *koinē*, and his literary pretensions in the *Lausiac History* are modest, though there are occasional echoes of Greek biography. His *Dialogue on the Life of Saint John Chrysostom* is more literary in intent and shows some familiarity with Plato, but the style is unpretentious.[53]

[52] See Palladius, *The Lausiac History*, translated and annotated by Robert T. Meyer, London: Longmans Green, 1965, and Quasten III, pp. 176-80.
[53] See Palladii *Dialogus de Vita Sancti Johannis Chrysostomi*, ed. Paul R. Coleman-Norton, Cambridge Univ. Pr., 1968, and Herbert

In marked contrast to the model of Saint Anthony, in the second half of the Fourth Century major leaders of the Church adopted features of classical rhetoric on an unprecedented scale. Although they regularly criticize pagan mythology and the vanity of wordly display, they put a high value on education and eloquence and borrow not only stylistic, but also structural features from sophistry. The result is Christian panegyric in its fullest form.

Several factors help to explain this development. First, with the Christianization of the state, Church leaders had need for public address on a larger and more varied scale. At the same time, individuals began to exhibit in their lives combinations of Christian virtues and public virtues associated with the classical tradition. When Gregory of Nazianzus delivered a funeral oration for his brother Caesarius, he praised his exemplification of Christian faith, but also his work as a skilled physician and his eloquence. Second, several of the most influential Christian thinkers, including Gregory, Basil, and John Chrysostom, had studied rhetoric with leading sophists and been moved by their enthusiasm for speech. Third, Julian's prohibition of teaching of the classics by Christians provoked realization that Christians had a right to share in the common inheritance of Hellenism. This can be seen, for example, in Gregory of Nazianzus' invective against Julian and in Basil's work *To the Young On How They Should Benefit from Greek Literature.* Fourth, the Neoplatonists of the late Third and Fourth Centuries had neutralized the traditional hostility between rhetoric and philosophy. Rhetoric had become an introduction to dialectic, and the interest in dialectic and other aspects of Neoplatonism on the part of Christians tended to encourage their interest in rhetoric as well. Fifth, Arianism and other heresies led to a competi-

---

Moore, *The Dialogue of Palladius Concerning the Life of Chrysostom*, London: Macmillan, 1921.

tion between orthodox and heretics for public support in which the techniques of rhetoric and dialectic were useful.

Gregory of Nazianzus

The most important figure in the synthesis of classical rhetoric and Christianity is Gregory of Nazianzus, whose speeches became the preeminent model for Christian eloquence throughout the Byzantine period. Gregory was born to a wealthy family living near Nazianzus in Cappadocia in 329 or 330. His education began in Nazianzus and continued in Caesarea, the capital of the province, in Caesarea in Palestine under a rhetorician named Thespius (Jerome *De Viris Illustribus* 113 or 117), and in Alexandria, where he became familiar with Christianized Platonism. About 350 he went to Athens, where for nine years he continued his studies of rhetoric under Prohaeresius and Himerius. There he was joined by his friend Basil. Their experiences are described in Gregory's autobiographical poem,[54] in his funeral oration for Basil, and in other works. After Basil's departure, Gregory taught rhetoric briefly in Athens and probably also in Cappadocia on his return there (*Ep.* 3). It was, he says (*Autobiography* 113-14), his goal to turn "illegitimate letters" to the service of those which were "genuine," but he soon abandoned rhetoric as a career, was baptized, and was ordained into the clergy. This last step was forced upon him by his father and meant that he no longer had the option of entering permanently into the monastic life to which Basil had been urging him. His career shows a continuing tension between his duty as a priest, and later a bishop, and his longing for the contemplative life.[55] From 379 to 381 Gregory occupied the pulpit

[54] See Christoph Jungck, *Gregor von Nazianzus, De Vita Sua. Einleitung, Text, Uebersetzung, Kommentar*, Heidelberg: Carl Winter, 1974.
[55] On this conflict see Rosemary Radford Ruether, *Gregory of Nazianzus, Rhetor and Philosopher*, Oxford: Clarendon Pr., 1969, pp. 18-54.

of the Church of the Anastasis in Constantinople and used his eloquence to defend orthodoxy against Arianism. It is likely that he was called to Constantinople primarily because of his reputation as an orator. In 381 he became bishop of Constantinople—the term "patriarch" was not in use until the Sixth Century—but his position was vigorously challenged by the Arians at the ecumenical council of that year and, ill-suited for a leadership role in church politics, he resigned his position and returned to Cappadocia. There he served briefly, unhappily, and in ill health, as bishop of Nazianzus, and finally succeeded in retiring to his family's country estate, where he wrote poetry and letters until his death around 390. It is possible that he edited his speeches into the ancestor of the present corpus in this final period of his life.[56]

Gregory's surviving works include forty-five orations, two hundred and forty-four letters, and a considerable amount of poetry.[57] The speeches are arranged in modern texts in roughly chronological order, beginning with those of 362

[56] On Gregory's life see the works cited in nn. 54 and 55 supra; also Paul Gallay, *La vie de S. Grégoire de Nazianze*, Lyon: E. Vitte, 1943. Byzantine panegyrics of Gregory Presbyter and Nicetas the Paphlagonian include accounts of his life, see PG XXXV, 243-304, and James J. Rizzo, *The Encomium of Gregory Nazianzen by Nicetas the Paphlagonian* (Subsidia Hagiographica LVIII), Brussels: Société des Bollandistes, 1976.

[57] For the text of the speeches we are still largely dependent on PG XXXV-XXXVI, but Or. 1-3, 20-23, and 27-31 are available in Sources chrétiennes, vols. CCXLVII, CCL, and CCLXX, Paris: du Cerf, 1978; 1979; 1980. Editions of other speeches are cited below, nn. 72, 78, and 87. For the letters see the edition, translation, and notes by Paul Gallay, Saint Grégoire de Nazianze, *Lettres*, 2 vols., Paris: Les Belles Lettres, 1964; 1967. See Quasten III, pp. 236-54. On Gregory's prose style see Marcel Guignet, *Saint Grégoire de Nazianze et la rhétorique*, Paris: Picard, 1911; Ruether, *Rhetor and Philosopher* (supra, n. 55), pp. 55-128; Manfred Kertsch, "Bildersprache bei Gregor von Nazianz. Ein Beitrag zur spätantiken Rhetorik und Popularphilosophie," *Grazer Theologische Studien* 2 (1978), which discusses Gregory's use of the images of water and the sun.

GREGORY OF NAZIANZUS

relating to his forced ordination and ending with those delivered after his final return to Cappadocia.[58] In his encomium of Cyprian (Or. 24, PG xxxv, 1185), Gregory classifies the speeches of that Latin Father into three groups based on their objectives: the moral edification of all; the teaching of Christian dogma; the celebration of the lives of men. This classification may be applied to his own works if the categories are somewhat broadened into moral, dogmatic, and panegyric.[59] From a theoretical point of view, the three categories correspond to deliberative (the future actions of the audience), judicial (judgment of truth as known from the Scriptures and events in the past), and epideictic. The first two categories may take the form of homilies or thematic sermons. Of the homilies which Gregory spoke regularly in church, only one, Oration Thirty-seven on Matthew 19:1, is included in the corpus, but the fourth theological oration is homiletic in treatment, and Oration Fourteen, *On Love of the Poor*, is a sermon not connected with a specific day or event. The other preserved speeches are largely occasional, relating to events in his own life or the times in which he lived.

Gregory's three earliest orations relate to the sudden ordination of himself by his father in the Christmas season of 361.[60] Stunned by this action, for which he was spiritually unprepared, he fled to Basil's monastery, but re-

---

[58] Some speeches (e.g., 14 and 15) are out of order, but the grouping by the three periods before, during, and after Gregory's tenure in Constantinople is correct; see Ruether, *Rhetor and Philosopher* (supra, n. 55), pp. 178-79.

[59] For further refinement, see Adolf Doners, *Der hl. Kirchenlehrer Gregor von Nazianz als Homilet*, Münster: Westfälischen Vereinsdruckerei, 1909, p. 18.

[60] See Jean Bernardi, *Grégoire de Nazianze, Discours 1-3. Introduction, texte critique, traduction et notes* (Sources chrétiennes CCXLVII) Paris: du Cerf, 1978. English translation by Charles Gorden Browne and James Edward Swallow in *SLN & PNF*, Second Series, VII, pp. 203-29, utilized below.

turned by Easter of 362 and sought to explain his reaction to the uncomprehending Christian community of Nazianzus. Oration One is a brief panegyric of Easter, purely Christian in structure and context, and affects to put aside the speaker's hostilities in the glory of the resurrection. Oration Three is a short invective against those who summoned him back and then failed to greet him when he came. In between is the *Apologeticus*, which is a major speech combining both classical and Christian elements. Its length suggests that it is an enlarged version for publication of what he may have said at the time.

The *Apologeticus* has no explicit classical references, though some of its thought is indebted to classical writers and the style is that of a student of the sophists. Its quotations are entirely from Scripture, and the inspiration of Christian rhetoric is declared at the outset: "Let the most blessed David be the beginning of my speech and even more him who spoke through David and even to this day speaks through him.[61] Since the best order for one beginning everything, both speech and action, is to begin from God and in God to make his ending" (2.1). Gregory seeks to explain his flight, primarily on the ground that he regarded himself as unworthy of the priesthood. "I do not see," he says (2.16), "with what knowledge [*epistēmē*] or trust in what faculty [*dynamis*] one would have the courage to undertake this office. For in reality it seems to me to be the art [*technē*] of arts and the science of sciences to lead man, the most manifold [*polytropon*—Homer's word for Odysseus in *Odyssey* 1.1] of creatures." Gregory then elaborates an elevated picture of the priesthood and, as the model to which he cannot attain, delivers an encomium of the ministry of Saint Paul (2.52-56), followed by warnings of failure from the Old Testament prophets (2.57-68)

[61] This may be a Christian imitation of the opening of Aratus' *Phaenomena* or of Theocritus' *Encomium of Ptolemy*.

GREGORY OF NAZIANZUS

and the story of Jonah (2.106-9), treated as a chria applied to his own circumstances.

It seems clear that the picture of the idealized Christian preacher which Gregory draws is influenced to some extent by the idealized classical orator of Isocrates and the later sophists and by the philosophical orator of Plato's *Phaedrus*.[62] The passage quoted above utilizes some of the technical language of philosophical rhetoric, including *epistēmē*, *dynamis*, and *technē* and there are other passages which resemble ideas in the *Phaedrus*. For example, Gregory describes the divinity of the soul, which struggles "that it may draw to itself and raise to heaven the lower nature, by gradually freeing it from its grossness, in order that the soul may be to the body what God is to the soul, itself leading on the matter which ministers to it, and uniting it, as its fellow-servant, to God" (2.17).[63] The soul, as in Plato,[64] has wings and the object of the preacher's art is that they may develop and the soul fly up to God (2.22). Later in the speech Gregory incorporates a small Socratic dialogue reminiscent of the *Gorgias* or the second half of the *Phaedrus*: " 'Tell me, my good sir, do you call dancing anything and flute-playing?' 'Certainly,' they would say. 'What then of wisdom and being wise, which we venture to define as knowledge of things divine and human?' " (2.50).[65]

Closest to the thought of Plato is what Gregory says about the knowledge which the preacher must have, both of truth and of the souls of his audience. "We must really walk in the King's Highway [Num. 20:17] and take care not to turn aside from it either to the right hand or to the left, as the

[62] Gregory's understanding of the priest's role includes the concepts of statesman, pastor, physician, and teacher. See Bernardi's discussion (supra, n. 60), pp. 38-50.

[63] Translation by Browne and Swallow (supra, n. 60), p. 208.

[64] E.g., *Phaedrus* 246a and 251b. See George Kennedy, "Later Greek Philosophy and Rhetoric," *Philosophy and Rhetoric* 13 (1980), 192-96.

[65] See Browne and Swallow (supra, n. 60), p. 215.

Proverbs [4:27] say. For such is the case with our passions, and such in this matter is the task of the good shepherd, if he is to know properly the souls of his flock and to guide them according to the methods of a pastoral care which is right and just and worthy of our true Shepherd" (2.34).[66] This knowledge few have. Gregory then lists some of the subjects which the preacher should thoroughly understand (2.35-38): the world, matter, soul, mind; the types of truth, the covenants, the first and second coming of Christ, the incarnation, and the like. He is troubled, he says, by his own lack of complete understanding of mysteries and also by the difficulty of conveying that knowledge to the souls of his listeners, which is of course a major problem also in the realization of Platonic philosophical rhetoric:

> I have now briefly dwelt upon the subject to show how difficult it is to discuss such important questions, especially before a large audience, composed of every age and condition and needing like an instrument of many strings to be played upon in various ways; or to find any form of words able to edify them all and illuminate them with the light of knowledge. For it is not only that there are three sources from which danger springs, understanding [*dianoia*], speech [*logos*], and hearing [*akoē*], so that failure in one, if not all, is infallibly certain; for either the mind is not illuminated, or the language is feeble, or the hearing, not having been cleansed, fails to comprehend, and accordingly, in one or all respects, the truth must be maimed; but further, what makes the instruction of those who profess to teach any other subject so easy and acceptable—the piety of the audience—on this subject involves difficulty and danger. (2.39)[67]

[66] Ibid., p. 212.
[67] Ibid., p. 213.

The dangers and difficulties of addressing different kinds of souls are then examined at some length. Classification of the audience by age and condition resembles that in Aristotle's *Rhetoric* (2.1388b-1391b); the three sources of danger correspond to Aristotle's three factors in the speech act: speaker, speech, and audience (*Rhetoric* 1.1358a38).

Gregory's picture of the priesthood, with its rhetorical demands, influenced John Chrysostom's dialogue on that subject,[68] and its subsequent history deserves tracing through the Byzantine period. It was also known in the West: Rufinus translated the *Apologeticus* and several other orations by Gregory into Latin, and the concept is found in a somewhat diluted form in the *Pastoral Care* of Gregory the Great, who had read Rufinus' translation of the *Apologeticus*.[69]

Gregory's fourth and fifth speeches are an invective against Julian the Apostate, composed soon after Julian's death in 363 and published immediately.[70] He perhaps read them aloud to a group in Nazianzus, but they are primarily intended for circulation in written form and bear the title *Steliteutikoi*, as if they were to be inscribed on stone as a public indictment against Julian.

The first invective opens in exultation at Julian's death; the rest of the work attacks the character, principles, and actions of the Apostate, following a generally chronological sequence from his birth to his death on campaign against the Persians. Various compositional segments having their origins in progymnasmatic forms may be noted, including synkriseis of Julian and Gallus (4.30-33) and of Julian and Constantius (4.34-38), the latter with an ecphrasis of their

---

[68] See J. Volk, "Die Schutzrede des Gregors von Nazianz und die Schrift über das Priestertum von Johannes Chrysostomos," *Zeitschrift für praktische Theologie* 17 (1895), 56-63, and Quasten III, pp. 243-44.

[69] See Tyranni Rufini *Orationum Gregorii Nazianzeni Novem Interpretatio*, ed. Johann Wrobel, Vienna: Tempsky, 1910, preface.

[70] See *PG* XXXV, 532-720. English translation by C. W. King in *Julian the Emperor*, London: George Bell, 1888, pp. 1-121.

funerals from a comparative point of view. There are also narrations, including the punishment of Marcus (4.88) and, in the second invective (5.1-32), of God's punishment of Julian, an ecphrasis of the fire of Aetna (4.85), and a description of Julian's arrival in the Greek underworld set in the concluding exhortation of the second speech (5.33-42). The whole has considerble vigor, but some tastlessness in Gregory's unflattering description of Julian as he knew him in Athens as a student, while historical veracity is bent for vicious effect in the accounts of Julian's death, some of which Gregory must have known were not true.

Gregory says (4.17) that his speech is "woven out of sacred words and thoughts," but there is much more classical allusion than in the earlier speeches. One of the things which Gregory most holds against Julian is his effort to prevent Christians from teaching the classics. He argues at length (4.100-110) that pagans have no exclusive right to the language and literature of Greece. Here he confesses his own love for words:

> All other things I have left to those who like them, riches, nobility, glory, power, which are of the lower world and give delights fleeting like a dream. Words alone I cleave to, and I do not begrudge the toils by land and sea that have supplied me with them. May mine be the possession of words and his too, whoever loves me, which possession I embraced and still embrace first of all after the things that be first of all—I mean religion and hope beyond the visible world—so that if, according to Pindar 'what is one's own weighs heavily,' speech in their defense is incumbent upon me; and it is especially just for me, perhaps more than anyone else, to express my gratitude to words for words by word of mouth. (4.100)[71]

[71] See King (supra, n. 70), p. 67.

Another interesting and related passage is that (4.111-117) on Julian's plans for a pagan "church," or school with services and readings. Gregory asks what "virtues" will be taught and describes flagrant violations of those virtues as found in classical mythology, of which he shows a thorough knowledge.

Gregory's love for words and his great success as a speaker constituted a psychological conflict with his desire for the contemplative life. He was inept at ecclesiastical politics and resentful of public duties, and he appears to have felt somewhat guilty about his reputation for eloquence. Oration Nineteen, *On His Speeches to the Tax Adjuster Julian*, resulted from Gregory's appeals to this imperial official on behalf of the poor and the demand that he deliver an oration in response to certain official concessions. The date is late in 374 after he had been silent for many months since the death of his father. The speech consists of an introductory section setting forth his feelings about speech, followed by discussion of Christian virtues and an exhortation to the tax adjuster.

What, asks Gregory (19.1-4), is this wisdom and knowledge which he is supposed to have and which leads him to be beseiged at every festival? He cannot find it in himself; he seeks to be dead to the world, to live a life hidden in Christ. If he cannot do that, he would choose to continue through life as a student rather than be a teacher. But he is continually approached by those who want him to speak and who try to strike a flame of speech from him, like a spark from a flint. They offer rewards, appeal to his sense of pity, remind him of his God-given eloquence, his duty to his father's church. His silence has enhanced public desire to hear him. In response he will give them something better than silence, not in a soft, smooth, and sweet style, but in one that is manly and severe. (The terminology is not specifically that of the Hermogenic ideas, but resembles them.) As usual, he does not denigrate speech, but idealizes its need for knowledge and inspiration and authority to the point where he can claim to be inadequate to the challenge.

Gregory was known to the Byzantines as "the Theologian," a title which came to him above all from the five Theological Sermons (Orations 27-31) which he delivered in Constantinople in 380 in an effort to combat Eunomianism, the radical Arianism which then dominated the city.[72] These speeches represent the pinnacle of his efforts as a preacher, just as his panegyric of Basil represents his most brilliant utterance as a classical orator. The five sermons are sometimes called homilies, but only the fourth, which examines ten scriptural texts on which the Arians laid great weight, is truly homiletic. The others are philosophical disquisitions in which Gregory's theses are supported by syllogistic argument (see, e.g., 31.7) and by rhetorical methods. The first sermon (Or. 27) is introductory to the series, the second (28) deals with the Father, the third and fourth (29-30) with the Son, and the fifth (31) with the Holy Spirit.

The five sermons can be analyzed in terms of highly developed forms of composition which have their artistic origins in progymnasmata. The first sermon is largely a psogos, an invective against the Arians as sophists who are concerned with the wrong things in the wrong way at the wrong time. Amplification of the charges comes, as frequently in Gregory, in the form of lists which pour out from a seemingly inexhaustible abundance. The stasis is

---

[72] For text and commentary see Arthur James Mason, *The Five Theological Orations of Gregory of Nazianzus*, Cambridge Univ. Pr., 1899, and Joseph Barbel, *Gregor von Nazianz, Die Fünf theologische Reden*, Düsseldorf: Patmos, 1963. English translation by Edward R. Hardy and Cyril C. Richardson, *Christology of the Later Fathers* (Library of Christian Classics III), London: SCM Press, 1954, pp. 113-214.

stochasmos: what the Arians say is wrong in fact, but Gregory supplies not only an *anaskeuē*, or refutation of his opponents, but a *kataskeuē*, or confirmation of his own beliefs. The bases of his premises are commonly accepted rational views, as would be the case in dialectic, rather than appeal to authority. Except in the homiletic fourth sermon, there is occasional reference to the ideas of philosophers, especially Plato, as supporting evidence, and there are allusions to Greek mythology and literature, as in the second sermon (28.25), where we meet Palamedes, Daedalus, and the Cretan labyrinth and a reference to the *Iliad* (28.30). Some of the argument in this speech (e.g., 28.10) bears a similarity to the sophist Gorgias' treatment of the existence of the gods and the question of being and nonbeing.[73] Gregory says (28.11) that he is forced to dispense with simplicity of exposition and turn to an intricate style: God has deliberately obscured creation in order to prevent us from throwing away understanding of it as something too easily attained.

The high point of the oration on the Father, and perhaps of the series as a whole, is the extended description of the works of God's creation in all their beauty and diversity (28.22-30): man and his body, animals, fish, birds, plants, the earth, sea, air, the heavens, and angels, up to the veil which separates us from vision of God himself. This passage, which is in outline a list, is given constant impetus by exclamations and rhetorical questions, and may be regarded as an ecphrasis of creation which, in the sublimity and completeness of its vision, goes beyond the ordinary art of a sophist. The sermon on the Father as a whole has a splendid upward movement from the sophistry of the heretics to reasoned argument against their view of God to the unknowable greatness of God himself glimpsed

[73] See *The Older Sophists*, ed. Rosamond Kent Sprague, Columbia: Univ. of S. Carolina Pr., 1972, pp. 42-47.

in all creation. Although there is ample dialectical skill, the persuasive effect is a rhetorical achievement, the power of the preacher to paint in words the wonders of the Father's world.

The sermon on the Father begins with refutation and ends with exposition of Gregory's own views; the sermon on the Son reverses this order.[74] In the early part of the speech there is an interesting adaptation of the theory of political constitutions as taught in the rhetorical and philosophical schools. Gregory says (29.2) that there are three views of God through which the world has historically developed: *anarchia*, *polyarchia*, and *monarchia*. Within the latter there has, however, been a development from the monotheism of the Old Testament to the duality of Father and Son of the Gospels to the Trinity. The rhetorical high point of this speech, corresponding to the ecphrasis of the works of creation in the sermon on the Father, is the description of the nature of Christ (29.19-20). The combination of divine and human in one person lends itself to antithesis and paradox, again based on a list. The fourth sermon, a homily on the Son, has a corresponding but less elevated passage on the names of God (30.17-20), and the fifth, at the corresponding place in the composition, a description of the Holy Spirit (31.29-30). In this last speech Gregory repeatedly represents the dispute with the Arians as one involving the spirit and the letter of the law, a heading of stasis theory (e.g., 31.18 and 24). An historical progression is again noted, from idols to the law to the gospel (31.25). Why, Gregory asks, was there not a sudden revelation? "That no violence might be done to us, but that we might be moved by *persuasion*. . . . That which is

---

[74] On the structure and argument of the third theological sermon see Johannes Focken, "De Gregorii Nazianzei Orationum et Carminum Dogmaticorum Argumentandi Ratione," Dissertation Berlin, 1911, pp. 51-54.

voluntary is most durable and safe." At the end of the sermon Gregory seeks an image or synkrisis. To what can God be compared? He tries and rejects various possibilities: "Finally, then, it seems best to me to let the images and the shadows go, as being deceitful and very far short of the truth; and clinging myself to the more reverent conception, and resting upon few words, using the guidance of the Holy Ghost, keeping to the end as my genuine comrade and companion the enlightenment which I have received from him, and passing through this world *to persuade all others also to the best of my power to* worship Father, Son, and Holy Ghost, the one Godhead and power. To him belongs all glory and honor and might forever and ever. Amen."[75]

Closely associated with the five theological sermons is Oration Forty-two, Gregory's speech resigning the bishopric of Constantinople. The audience was made up of Gregory's congregation and of the Christian bishops convened for the Council of 381, over which Gregory had been presiding. Always uncomfortable with ecclesiastical politics, he knew he was facing failure in leading negotiations among the princes of the Church, for the theological issues of the day, on which he was both clear and eloquent, were complicated by issues of personality, prestige, and power. Though only in his early fifties, and the son of a father who had lived to be nearly a hundred, he felt old and sick, and he determined to withdraw. This speech is difficult to classify, for it contains judicial, deliberative, and panegyrical elements: it is a defense of his actions (42.1-2), a celebration of the victory of orthodoxy, an attempt to instruct the Council in Christian doctrine (42.15), and an effort to persuade the bishops to accept his own resignation with good

---

[75] See Hardy and Richardson, *Christology* (supra, n. 72), p. 214.

will (42.25). He shows bitterness, nevertheless, about the life of the capital:

> I did not know that we ought to ride on splendid horses and drive in magnificent carriages and be preceded by a procession and surrounded by applause and have everyone make way for us, as if we were wild beasts, and open out a passage so that our approach might be seen afar. . . . Elect another who will please the majority, and give me my desert, my country, and my God. . . . For they seek not for priests, but for orators, not for stewards of souls, but for treasurers of money, not for pure offerers of the sacrifice, but for powerful patrons. (42.24)[76]

The epilogue is an emotional farewell to the churches of the city, its Christian communities, the city itself, the world, and oratory:

> Farewell, ye lovers of my discourses, in your eagerness and concourse, ye pencils seen and unseen, and thou balustrade, pressed upon by those who thrust themselves forward to hear the word. Farewell, emperors and palace and ministers and household of the emperor, whether faithful or not to him I know not, but for the most part, unfaithful to God. Clap your hands, shout aloud, extol your orator to the skies. This pestilent and garrulous tongue has ceased to speak to you. Though it will not utterly cease to speak, for it will fight with hand and ink; but for the present we have ceased to speak. (42.26)[77]

In fact, it was soon after this, on his return to Cappadocia, that Gregory delivered what has usually been regarded as his oratorical masterpiece, Oration Forty-three, on what he describes (43.1) as "the grandest subject which

[76] Ibid., pp. 393-94.
[77] Ibid., p. 394.

has ever fallen to the lot of an orator," the Panegyric of Basil.[78] Basil had died in 379 while Gregory was in Constantinople; this speech was given, not at his funeral, but at some later memorial occasion. Basil is treated throughout as a saint and his intercession prayed for at the end. Since canonization was not a formal process in the Fourth-Century Church, it is possible that the occasion was a proclamation of his sanctification and included services at his tomb. The speech is, however, an *epitaphios*, which Menander had noted (III, p. 419 Spengel) was traditionally given "after some time" in contrast to a *paramythētikos* or monody, which reflects more immediate feelings of grief. Gregory generally follows Menander's rules for an *epitaphios*, but omits the consolation and adds an account of Basil's death and funeral which are in Menander's system characteristic of a monody. Unequal treatment is given to traditional headings depending on their importance for a Christian.[79] Progymnasmatic forms are introduced to amplify or ornament the thought, the most elaborate a synkrisis of Basil, patriarchs, prophets, and apostles (70-76). The tendency to avoid specific names of persons and chronological details is manifest, though not carried to the extreme of Byzantine times. Greek culture is treated with respect, even reverence; there are direct references to classical writers and constant employment of the periodic style

[78] For text, French translation, and introduction see Fernand Boulenger, *Grégoire de Nazianze, Discours funèbres en l'honneur de son frère Césaire et de Basile de Césarée*, Paris: Picard, 1908. English translations by Browne and Swallow, *SLN & PNF*, Second Series, VII, pp. 395-422, and by Leo P. McCauley, *Funeral Orations by Saint Gregory Nazianzen and Saint Ambrose* (The Fathers of the Church XII), Washington, D.C.: Catholic Univ. of America Pr., 1968, pp. 27-99.

[79] On the structure of the panegyrical orations of the Cappadocian Fathers see Johannes Bauer, *Die Trostreden des Gregorios von Nyssa in ihrem Verhältnis zur antiken Rhetorik*, Marburg: Universitäts-Bücherei, 1892, pp. 6-92, and Ruether, *Rhetor and Philosopher* (supra, n. 55), pp. 105-28.

and figures of speech of the sophists, but there is also a constant employment of biblical allusions and imagery.

Gregory's first objective is certainly to honor, and perhaps to canonize, Basil. He uses Basil's life, however, as a vehicle for preaching orthodox doctrine and for attacking Arianism. The speech is also an apology for Gregory's relations with Basil: long very close, they had become estranged at the time of the reorganization of the church in Cappadocia when Basil forced a bishopric on Gregory. Finally, but important for our study, the repeated allusions to eloquence and the extended descriptions of the life of Gregory and Basil as students of rhetoric in Athens seem to indicate that one goal of the speech, reflected also in its structure, allusions, and style, is the synthesis of classical and Christian cultural traditions into a harmonious whole. The length of the work suggests that the published version probably contains material, especially narrative material, not delivered in the original version.

The proemium begins with the themes of Basil and eloquence:

> It has then been ordained that the great Basil, who used so constantly to furnish me with subjects for my discourses, of which he was quite as proud as any other man of his own, should himself now furnish me with the greatest subject which has ever fallen to the lot of an orator. . . . I know not what subject I can treat with eloquence, if not this; or what greater favor I can do to myself, to the admirers of virtue, or to eloquence itself, than express our admiration for this man. To me it is the discharge of a most sacred debt. And our speech is a debt beyond all others due to those who have been gifted, in particular, with powers of speech. To the admirers of virtue a discourse is at once a pleasure and an incentive to virtue. (43.1)[80]

[80] See Browne and Swallow (supra, n. 78), p. 395.

Gregory has set out to create a masterpiece. As the Greeks had recognized since Homer, speech is a gift of God, but the oration will not only be eloquent as are speeches of sophists; it will be an exemplar of Christian virtue for all to follow. The appeal of panegyric to the world of later antiquity partly derives from the universality which it has and which transcends what is possible in judicial or deliberative oratory. Looking down from heaven, Basil will excuse Gregory's tardiness in praising him, and so must the audience, for they know the importance of what Gregory was doing in Constantinople and they know his frailty. Conventional protestations of unworthiness by the speaker are inherent in this passage, but presented with delicacy.

The main body of the speech begins at this point with praise of the homeland, ancestors, and parents of Basil (43.3-10). In Christian panegyric, including other works of Gregory, these matters are sometimes treated in aposiopesis: the orator mentions them only to say how unimportant they are. But in Basil's case, much could be said, and Gregory makes effective use of the headings to bring out Christian ideas: the modesty of Basil, the reality of his progenitors' great deeds in contrast with the infamous myths of the Pelopidae and Cecropidae and Alcmeonids and other famous families of classical Greece; the piety of his family. The point is made vivid by a narration (*diēgēma* is mentioned in section 8) of their adventures during the persecution of Maximinus, likened to those of the Children of Israel in the escape from Egypt (43.5-8). With considerable ingenuity Gregory makes a miracle out of the survival of Christians in the forests of Pontus, well-stocked with game, and scornfully compares myths of Orion, Actaeon, and Iphigenia. The section then concludes with praise of Basil's parents and their marriage.

A new beginning is then made (middle of section 10) with a return to the theme of Basil and eloquence:

I have now, in obedience to the Divine law which bids us to pay all honor to parents, bestowed the first fruits of my praises upon those whom I have commemorated, and proceed to treat of Basil himself, premising this, which I think will seem true to all who knew him, that we only need his own voice to pronounce his eulogy. For he is at once a brilliant subject for praise and the only one whose powers of speech make him worthy of treating it.[81]

The next traditional heading was the physical aspect of the subject. This is treated in a Christian aposiopesis:

Beauty indeed and strength and size, in which I see that most men rejoice, I concede to those who want them—not that even in these points he was inferior to any of those men of small minds who busy themselves about the body while he was still young and had not yet reduced the flesh by austerity—but that I may avoid the fate of unskilled athletes, who waste their strength in vain efforts after minor objects, and so are worsted in the crucial struggle, whose results are victory and the distinctions of the crown. (43.10)[82]

The athletic image was a traditional one in Greek epideictic since the *Panegyricus* of Isocrates, but was appealing to Christians because of its use by Saint Paul ("I have fought the good fight; I have finished the race," 2 Tim. 7) and because of the identification of contests in the arena with martyrdom.

Gregory duly turns to Basil's education (43.11-24), which he introduces with an encomium of *paideusis*:

not only this, our more noble form of it, which disregards rhetorical ornaments and glory and holds to sal-

[81] Ibid., p. 398.
[82] Ibid.

vation and beauty in the objects of our contemplation, but even that external culture which many Christians ill-judgingly abhor . . .[83]

In a long periodic sentence, built out of a series of comparisons and antitheses, he concludes:

. . . as we have compounded healthful drugs from certain of the reptiles, so from secular literature we have received principles of enquiry and speculation, while we have rejected their idolatry, terror, and pit of destruction.[84]

Basil's education, like Gregory's, far exceeds anything traditional among Christians. It is one of Gregory's purposes to show its value to the life of the saint.

Gregory proceeds stage by stage through Basil's education, which began in Pontus with *enkyklios paideusis*. In the context this seems to mean grammar, with study of the Greek poets, rhetoric, and religious instruction. He then went to Caesarea: "letters form our distinction here and are our badge, as if upon the field of arms or on the stage" (43.13). Presumably, he continued study of rhetoric with reading in classical literature and probably began a course in philosophy. At this stage Gregory describes Basil, whom he met at this time, as "an orator among orators, even before he studied with rhetoricians, a philosopher among philosophers even before he learned the doctrines of the philosophers. . . . Eloquence was his byword, from which he culled enough to make it an assistance to him in Christian philosophy, since power of this kind is needed to set forth the objects of our contemplation" (43.13). Then on to Byzantium and finally to Athens, "which has been to

[83] Ibid.
[84] Ibid., pp. 398-99.

me, if to anyone, a city truly golden and the patroness of all that is good" (43.14).

The mention of Athens causes Gregory to turn aside to a personal narrative of his friendship with Basil and their student life together in the 350s (43.15-24), perhaps a published addition to the delivered speech. The major study of the two young men was clearly rhetoric with the sophists, but they engaged in philosophical disputation (43.17), and they joined in a personal pact to devote their lives to Christian philosophy (19). It is in Pindar (*Olympian* 6.1) and not in the Bible that Gregory finds words to describe their friendship, "a well-built chamber with pillars of gold" (43.20). In the course of this section Gregory utilizes three separate synkriseis: the sacred with the secular (43.21), Gregory and Basil with Orestes and Pylades or Eurytus and Cteatus (43.22), and Basil's moral discipline with that of Minos and Rhadamanthys (43.23).

The next part of the speech (43.25-36) deals with the period when Basil returned to Caesarea and became a priest. His mode of life is treated first, then his actions. A series of comparisons amplifies the idea that the Church otherwise often preferred the influential and the ambitious to the worthy and experienced (43.26). Dramatic narratives present the conflict between Basil and Eusebius, bishop of Caesarea (43.28-29), the persecution of the orthodox under Valens (43.30-31), Basil's reconciliation with Eusebius (43.33), and Basil's work in alleviating famine (43.34-35). He did this not by prayer and a miracle, "since signs are for unbelievers, not for those who believe," but by *persuading* the rich to contribute supplies. The Church has thus moved into an age when rhetoric has new roles. Some of the narrative material in this part of the speech is perhaps an addition to the speech as delivered. The section ends (43.36) with a synkrisis of Basil and Joseph.

Next in order is discussion of the period of Basil's bishopric in Caesarea. There are several *synkriseis* here, of which the most interesting (43.45) is the comparison of the Arian emperor Valens and the Persian king Xerxes, allowing Gregory to introduce his own version of one of the most famous commonplaces of classical Greek epideictic, that describing the Persian invasion of Greece in 480 B.C.: "A strange land and sea were heard of, the work of the new creator; and an army which sailed over the dry land and marched over the ocean, while islands were carried off and the sea was scourged and all the other mad proceedings of that army and expedition, which, though they struck terror into the ignoble, were ridiculous in the eyes of men of brave and steadfast hearts."[85] An implied comparison of Basil and the Greeks at Salamis emerges (43.47), while the descriptions of Valens (46) and of the prefect Modestus (48), neither of whom is named, have elements of invective. Basil's hearing before Modestus is presented in dramatic dialogue (48-49), an example of prosopopoeia. Modestus uses external rhetoric, threatening confiscation of property, banishment, torture, and death; Basil demonstrates how little these efforts at intimidation mean to him. Modestus then returns to Valens and explains that Basil is "superior to threats, invincible in argument, uninfluenced by 'persuasion.' " The administration must either resort to violence or give in to Basil. Valens relents and we are treated to an ecphrasis of the scene when he visited Basil's church (43.52). This puts an end to the greater part of the persecution, so Gregory says, but Basil's banishment from his church was apparently a condition. A dramatic narrative recounts how Basil was ready to mount his chariot and depart, when suddenly Valens' son fell sick and Basil was appealed to to save him (43.54). The story is somewhat spoiled by the fact that the child dies, because—according

[85] Ibid., p. 410.

to Gregory—Valens also appealed to the Arians for their intercession, "blending salt water with fresh." Modestus himself is also stricken, but here Basil has greater success (43.55). Other incidents of the period are then narrated, including (59) the circumstances under which Basil forced Gregory to become a bishop. Gregory does not disguise his continued resentment about "the change and faithlessness of his treatment of myself, a cause of pain which even time has not obliterated," but he adds an apology for Basil.

This completes the discussion of Basil's actions, which is duly followed by an account of his virtues (43.60-69). Different men obtain success in different ways; he is best who has won his laurels on the widest field, or gained the highest possible renown in some singular particular; "such, however, was the height of Basil's fame that he became the pride of humankind" (43.60). His moral virtues are first considered: poverty (60), temperance (61), chastity (62), concern for the poor and the sick (63), with a synkrisis of the hospital which Basil founded to the wonders of the ancient world, including the pyramids and the Mausoleum. Allegations of pride are refuted (64). Then come the intellectual virtues: eloquence (65), followed by a synkrisis of the sun with Basil (66) and a description (67) of the effect of Basil's writings on Gregory, then in the climactic position, Basil's theological virtues. These are amplified and an exalted tone maintained by an extraordinary synkrisis which must have been very difficult of sustained delivery. Basil is compared to practically every great figure of the Bible, in chronological order, from Adam to Saints Peter and Paul (43.70-76). He surpassed or equaled each of them—and thus by implication deserves sainthood. The mood is then relaxed in a short passage (43.77) on the personal influence of Basil, followed by the final pathetic but triumphant narrative of his death (43.78-79) and ecphrasis of his funeral (43.80-81). This passage is characteristic of a monody rather than a panegyric and replaces the consolation which might have been expected. The emotional effect of the speech is of course greatly heightened. A short epilogue (43.81-82) concludes the oration, first recapitulating Basil's virtues and then returning to the opening theme of Gregory's efforts to praise him and a prayer to Basil in heaven, a sign that he has attained sainthood.

It is a remarkable speech, probably the greatest piece of Greek rhetoric since the death of Demosthenes, vibrant with sincerity despite its artificiality, continually imaginative and inventive in its use of commonplaces, possible only in an age and from an orator who united the passions of sophistry and Christianity, who had gone through the discipline of the rhetorical schools and found something important to say. It is a persuasive tribute to the theological, intellectual, and moral virtues of its subject, but rather hostile to Basil's work as a statesman of the Church, and it gives only passing reference to the two aspects of his career which have emerged as of greatest historical significance: his organization of Eastern monasticism and his reform of the liturgy.

Gregory's speeches include also funeral orations for his brother Caesarius (7), his sister Gorgonia (8), and his father (18), as well as panegyrics of Athanasius of Alexandria (21) and Cyprian (24). All show some influence of the structure and style of sophistic epideictic and progymnasmata, but none so completely as the speech for Basil. Since all are earlier works it is clearly not the case that Gregory began as a sophist and developed into a theologian. Nor did he move in the other direction. Eloquence and wisdom are inextricably combined in his work. The speeches for Gorgonia and for his father are about relatively unworldly people for whom traditional oratorical display was less suitable; Basil was regarded by Gregory as a great orator for whom it was eminently suitable. Caesarius, an educated physician, falls in between.[86]

In contrast, several other speeches are a uniquely Christian form of panegyric; though they show the influence of sophistry in stylistic ways, they lack classical structural elements and classical allusions. They are celebrations of Christian feasts and sometimes called homilies because of their simple structure and their application of Christian doctrine to Christian life, but they are not based on explication of a single scriptural text. Examples include Oration One on Easter, Thirty-eight on Christmas, Thirty-nine on the Epiphany, Forty on baptism, Forty-five on Easter, and Forty-six on Pentecost.[87]

Gregory became the great model for the union of Greek eloquence and Christianity and was so studied throughout the Byzantine period. It was his use of the Attic or high style which effectively established it as the official language of the Church in contrast to even the more elevated forms of *koinē*. John of Sicily, writing in the Ninth Century, says (VI, p. 99 Walz), "He excelled Plato in the virtues of speech as much as he did in theology and he made Demosthenes seem a mere child." Commentaries on Hermogenes came to cite examples of style from Gregory and commentaries on Gregory's speeches were written as early as the Sixth Century, suggesting that they were used as school texts.[88] Nine orations, but not including that for Basil, were trans-

[86] See Xavier Hürth, *De Gregorii Nazianzeni Orationibus Funebris*, Strassburg: Truebner, 1906.

[87] See Saint Grégoire de Nazianze, *Homilies XXXVIII, XXXIX, XL, XLV, XLVI*, introduction by Thomas Becquet, French translation by Edmond Devolder, Namur: Soleil Levant, 1961.

[88] See J. Sajdak, "Die Scholiasten der Reden des Gregors Nazianz. Ein kurzgefasster Bericht über der jetzigen Stand der Forschung," *BZ* 30 (1930), 268-74, and Friedhelm Lefherz, *Studien zu Gregor von Nazianz: Mythologie, Ueberlieferung, Scholiasten*, Bonn: Friedrich Wilhelms Universität, 1958.

lated into Latin by Rufinus of Aquileia around 400 and thus became known in the West.[89] There were also translations into Armenian, Syriac, Slavonic, Coptic, Georgic, Arabic, and Ethiopic.

Basil the Great and Gregory of Nyssa

Basil (c. 330-379) was himself more apologetic than Gregory of Nazianzus about his rhetorical studies, though his writing shows their influence.[90] In one of his letters (*Ep.* 223.2) he writes: "I had wasted much time on follies and spent nearly all my youth in vain letters and devotion to the teachings of a wisdom that God had made foolish. Suddenly I awoke as out of a deep sleep. I beheld the wonderful life of the gospel truth . . . and I prayed for a guide who might form in me the principles of piety."

Among Basil's surviving speeches the best known are the *Hexaemeron*, the series of homilies on Genesis 1:1-26 describing the first six days of creation.[91] Generally his style is far simpler, and often clearer, than Gregory's, and he disdains allegorical interpretation of scripture (see *Hexaemeron* 9.6). There are also sermons on vices and virtues

[89] Or. 2, 6, 16, 17, 26, 27, 38-40. See Wrobel, *Interpretatio* (supra, n. 69).

[90] See Quasten III, pp. 204-36; Leo V. Jacks, *St. Basil and Greek Literature* (Patristic Studies I), Washington, D.C.: Catholic Univ. of America Pr., 1922; James M. Campbell, *The Influence of the Second Sophistic on the Style of the Sermons of St. Basil the Great* (Patristic Studies II), Washington, D.C.: Catholic Univ. of America Pr., 1922; Margaret M. Fox, *The Life and Times of St. Basil the Great* (Patristic Studies LVII), Washington, D.C.: Catholic Univ. of America Pr., 1939; Robert C. Gregg, *Consolation Philosophy. Greek and Christian Paideia in Basil and the Two Gregories* (Patristic Monograph Series III), Philadelphia: Patristic Foundation, 1975; George L. Kustas, "Saint Basil and the Rhetorical Tradition," *Basil of Caesaria: Christian, Humanist, Ascetic*, ed. Paul J. Fedwick, Toronto: Pontifical Institute of Mediaeval Studies, 1981, pp. 221-79.

[91] English translation by B. Jackson in *SLN & PNF*, Second Series, VIII.

and on feasts of the Church. The one which comes closest to panegyric is that on the Forty Martyrs, but Basil says (19.2) "an address about the saints cannot be made to conform to the laws of encomium. The best encomium of the martyrs is to exhort the congregation to virtue."

Basil's treatise *To the Young on How They Should Benefit from Greek Writings* sets forth the utility of studying secular literature, but advises careful choice and warns against pagan mythology, atheism, and immorality. He deals with the content of writers like Hesiod, Homer, and Plato, but does not discuss orators, style, or sophistry.[92]

Basil's brother, Gregory of Nyssa (c. 335–c. 394), is the most profound thinker among the Cappadocian Fathers, deeply indebted to Plato and later Greek philosophers. His training in the sophistic schools led him to cultivate a prose style which is more artificial and less artistic than that of Gregory of Nazianzus.[93] His speeches include homilies, sermons on feast days, moral and dogmatic sermons, and panegyrics of Gregory Thaumaturgus, Theodore, and other martyrs, as well as three funeral orations: for Meletius, bishop of Antioch; Pulcheria, the daughter of Theodosius I; and Flacilla, wife of Theodosius.[94] These take the form of *paramythētikoi*, or consolations, rather than *epitaphioi*, and

[92] For text and commentary see N. G. Wilson, *Saint Basil on the Value of Greek Literature*, London: Duckworth, 1975; English translation by Roy J. Deferrari in Saint Basil, *Letters IV* (LCL), London: Heinemann, 1954, pp. 249-348. See also Fernand Boulenger, *Saint Basile, Aux jeunes gens sur la manière de tirer profit des lettres helléniques*, Paris: Les Belles Lettres, 1952.

[93] See Louis Méridier, *L'Influence de la seconde sophistique sur l'oeuvre de Grégoire de Nysse*, Paris: Hachette, 1906; E.C.E. Owen, "St. Gregory of Nyssa. Grammar, Vocabulary, and Style," *Journal of Theological Studies* 26 (1925), 64-71; Herbert Musurillo, "History and Symbol. A Study of Form in Early Christian Literature," *Theological Studies* 18 (1957), 357-86.

[94] Text in PG XLVI. See Quasten III, pp. 277-80. English translation by W. Moore and H. A. Wilson in *SLN & PNF*, Second Series, v, pp. 513-24.

are very close to the structure and *topoi* outlined by Menander. There is also an encomium of St. Ephraem Styrus and one of Basil.[95]

Two other preachers from Cappadocia in this period who show the influence of sophistry are Amphilocius of Iconium and Asterius of Amasea.[96]

John Chrysostom

If Gregory of Nazianzus is the greatest orator, John Chrysostom (c. 349-407) is the greatest homiletic preacher of the Greek Church. Socrates Scholasticus (6.3) describes his early life as follows:

> John was a native of Antioch in Coele-Syria, son of Secundus and Arthusa and descendant of a noble family there. He was a pupil of Libanius the sophist and of Andragathius the philosopher. Being on the point of entering a legal career,[97] and realizing that life in the law courts was hectic and unjust, he was moved to a quiet life and took it up in imitation of Evagrius, who had also studied with the same teachers but sometime earlier went over to the quiet life. Putting off his gown and his public appearance, he applied his attention to reading the Scriptures and frequented the church with zeal. Moreover, he persuaded Theodore (later bishop of Mopsuestia) and Maximus, who had been his fellow students with the sophist Libanius, to abandon the life of gain and to seek one of simplicity.[98]

---

[95] See Sister James Aloysius Stein, *Encomium of Saint Gregory, Bishop of Nyssa, on His Brother Saint Basil. Commentary, with revised text, introduction, and translation* (Patristic Studies XVII), Washington, D.C.: Catholic Univ. of America Pr., 1928.

[96] See Quasten III, pp. 296-301.

[97] Perhaps more likely the civil service, see A.H.M. Jones, "St. John Chrysostom's Parentage and Education," *Harvard Theological Review* 46 (1953), 171-73.

[98] Adapted from Zeno, *SLN & PNF*, Second Series, II, pp. 138-39.

Libanius always thought highly of John: asked on his deathbed who should succeed to his chair, he replied "John, if only the Christians had not stolen him" (Sozomen 8.2); John's opinion of Libanius is more difficult to define.[99]

For several years John lived an ascetic life, first at home, then in the mountains. After his health broke down under the regimen, he returned to Antioch and became a priest. It was in Antioch in the years 386-397 that he preached most of his surviving homilies. In 398, much against his will, he was made bishop of Constantinople, where he served under great strain in the corrupt and intrigue-ridden court. He made enemies by his imposition of Church discipline and by his criticism of the immorality of the empress Eudoxia. In 402 at the Synod of the Oak his enemies in the Church succeeded in deposing him and the emperor Arcadius exiled him to Bithynia, only to recall him the next day. He reentered Constantinople in triumph, but was exiled to Bithynia again in June 404. Since the Antiochenes kept coming there on pilgrimages to see him, he was further exiled to the east end of the Black Sea, where he died, September 14, 407.[100]

John's works are the most extensive among the Greek

[99] In Chrysostom's letters there are a few complimentary references to a Libanius, who may be the rhetorician: PG LII, 735, 737, 738. His encomium of Saint Babylas quotes and refutes the pagan thought of Libanius' *Monody for Julian*, but does not discuss its rhetorical qualities: PG L, 560-67. See A. J. Festugière, *Antioche païenne et chrétienne. Libanius, Chrysostome, et les moines de Syrie* (Bibliothèque des écoles françaises d'Athènes et de Rome CXCIV), Paris: Boccard, 1959, esp. pp. 409-10. On the use of similar arguments by Libanius and John see J.H.W.G. Liebeschuetz, *Antioch. City and Imperial Administration in the Later Roman Empire*, Oxford: Clarendon Pr., 1972, pp. 37-38.

[100] On Chrysostom's life and works see Quasten III, pp. 424-82; Chrysostomus Bauer, *John Chrysostom and His Time*, trans. M. Gonzaga, 2 vols., Westminster, Md.: Newman Press, 1959-1960; Donald Attwater, *St John Chrysostom. Pastor and Preacher*, London: Harvill Pr., 1959; Robert E. Carter, "The Chronology of St John Chrysostom's Early Life," *Traditio* 18 (1962), 357-64.

Fathers, extending for eighteen volumes in the *Patrologia Graeca*. The preservation of his writings almost in their entirety, though with the addition of some that are spurious, is due to the enormous respect in which he has always been held in the Greek Church for his piety, his sanctity, and his eloquence. He seemed to combine every theological, moral, and intellectual virtue known to the Christian tradition in a personality with both strength and gentleness. The rhetorical form in which he excelled is the homily: the great bulk of his works are sermons on biblical texts; but it may be convenient to begin consideration with a treatise in which he gives a picture of the functions he sought to perform.

The *Dialogue on the Priesthood* has been one of his best known works.[101] We have already seen that it is influenced by the apology of Gregory of Nazianzus.[102] The dramatic setting is almost certainly fictitious: John and an otherwise unknown Basil are being threatened with ordination to the priesthood and a bishopric against their personal desires for the contemplative life (1.6). John has deceived Basil into thinking he will accept, for he judges the latter well suited for the office. He himself escapes, but Basil is ordained and comes to reproach John in a passage which is a progymnasmatic *psogos* (1.7). John replies with a sophistic defense of the thesis "Timely deception used with right purpose is advantageous" (1.8-9, continued in Book Two). The moral justification for the deceit is essentially that advanced by Gregory, in his apology, that the speaker, unlike

[101] Text by J. A. Nairn in *Cambridge Patristic Texts IV*, Cambridge Univ. Pr., 1906. English translation by W.R.W. Stephens in *SLN & PNF*, First Series, IX, pp. 33-83, and by Graham Neville: Saint John Chrysostom, *Six Books on the Priesthood*, London: SPCK, 1964. Translations hereafter are from Neville.

[102] See also C. Nardi, "Echi dell'orazione funebre su Basilio Magno di Gregorio Nazianzeno nel prologo del *De Sacerdotio* di Giovanni Crisostomo," *Prometheus* 2 (1976), 175-84.

his friend, is unworthy of the exalted office. As often, John makes use of athletic and medical images. A number of passages discuss the priest as preacher and reveal John's attitude toward Christian oratory: Basil notes, for example, that Saint Paul was not ashamed of his poverty of speech when he wrote to the Corinthians, who were admired for their eloquence (2 Cor. 11:6). John replies that the pedantry of heathen rhetoric must be distinguished from presentation of the doctrine of the truth.

Paul did not say he was inexpert at both these qualities, only the former. To establish this fact he carefully made the distinction by saying he was "inexpert in speech, but not in knowledge." Now if I were demanding the polish, [*leiotēs*] of Isocrates and the grandeur [*ongkos*] of Demosthenes and the dignity [*semnotēs*] of Thucydides and the sublimity [*hypsos*] of Plato, it would be right to confront me with the testimony of Paul. But in fact I pass over all these qualities and the superfluous embellishments of pagan writers. I take no account of diction [*phrasis*] and style [*apangelia*]. Let a man's diction be beggarly and his verbal composition simple and artless, but do not let me be inexpert in the knowledge and careful statement of doctrine (4.6, pp. 121-22 Neville).

The references to Isocrates, Demosthenes, Thucydides, and Plato found in the *Dialogue on the Priesthood* are unusual in John. He clearly had studied these and other classical authors in his youth, but he does not ornament his sermons or illustrate his thoughts from pagan authors as does Gregory of Nazianzus.[103]

[103] See Paul R. Coleman-Norton, "St. Chrysostom's Use of the Greek Poets," *CPh* 27 (1932), 213-21; M. Soffray, "Saint Jean Chrysostome et la littérature païenne," *Phoenix* 2 (1947-48), 82-85; Robert E. Carter, "St. John Chrysostom's Rhetorical Use of the Socratic Distinction between Kingship and Tyranny," *Traditio* 14 (1958), 367-71; Festugière, *Antioche païenne* (supra, n. 99), pp. 211-40.

Eloquence in John's view conduces to salvation when handled by good men, but is a source of danger as well, for it requires them to devote an inordinate amount of attention to composing their sermons: "Most of those who are under authority refuse to treat preachers as their instructors. They rise above the status of disciples and assume that of spectators sitting in judgment on secular speechmaking. The audience is divided and some side with one speaker and others side with another. So in church they divide and become partisans, some of this preacher and some of that, listening to their works with favor or dislike" (5.1, p. 127 Neville). Throughout his career, but especially in Constantinople, John had the problem of applause in church, which he tried to prevent:[104] "When he [the preacher] has composed his sermons to please God (and let this alone be his rule and standard of oratory in sermons, not applause or commendation), then if he should be approved by men too, let him not spurn their praise" (5.6, p. 133 Neville). But if praise alone is what the preacher aims at, he is lost. Especially unhappy is the indifferent speaker of high rank who is constantly outshone by his ecclesiastical subordinates (5.8). Other problems of the eloquent preacher which John cites are allegations of plagiarism and the fact that successful sermons cannot be soon repeated, since the people listen for new treatments, not for contents and instruction. The fashionable preacher must exert contined effort. "For the art of speaking comes, not by nature, but by instruction, and therefore even if a man reaches the acme of perfection in it, still it may forsake him unless he cultivates its force by constant application

---

[104] See also the end of the thirtieth homily on Acts. The cult of the fashionable preacher reappears in seventeenth-century France and is the subject of François Fénelon's *Dialogues on Eloquence*, which show some influence of Chrysostom, see CR & CST, pp. 222-26.

and exercise" (5.4, p. 130 Neville). No allowances are made for bad days (5.5).

As the preacher in Antioch, and later in Constantinople, John had remarkable opportunities for leadership, not only of his congregation, but of the city.[105] His early reputation was apparently established by twenty-one sermons *On the Statues*,[106] delivered in the spring of 387 when the populace of Antioch had rioted over increased taxation and thrown down the statues of Theodosius and his late empress. Local magistrates immediately took repressive measures and the emperor threatened to destroy the whole place, but was eventually dissuaded. The sermons reflect the alternating fear and hope flowing through the city before Theodosius' first decision was known (it is announced in the last speech) as John sought to console and hearten the people and at the same time use their anxiety to instruct them and improve their morale. He explains why God allows suffering, calls on the people to refrain from slander, and repeatedly rebukes blasphemy, which he seems to regard as a basic cause of the suffering of the city. The sermons were preached in rapid succession at daily church services and were probably largely extemporaneous. Since John often builds his remarks around the scriptural reading of the day, they are basically homilies, though he goes beyond the homily form in his comments on contemporary events.

One of the most evident qualities of John's preaching is

[105] John's earliest sermon is addressed to God, "Who gave him his tongue and speech," *PG* XLVIII, pp. 693-700. On the language of John's early sermons see C. Fabricius, *Zu den Jugendschriften des Johannes Chrysostomos. Untersuchungen zum Klassizismus des vierten Jahrhunderts*, Lund: Gleerup, 1962.

[106] English translation by W.R.W. Stephens in *SLN & PNF*, First Series, IX, pp. 317-489, from which the versions below are taken. See Mary Albania Murns, *Saint John Chrysostom's Homilies on the Statues. A Study of Their Rhetorical Qualities and Form* (Patristic Studies XXII), Washington, D.C.: Catholic Univ. of America Pr., 1930.

his imagery, found in metaphor and simile. Some is drawn from the Bible, some from everyday life. Athletic images are commonest, reflecting the popularity of the games, but images from the sea, from military life, and from agriculture are common as well. The first sermon in the series *On the Statues*, which apparently slightly antedates the crisis, begins with a splendor worthy of Pindar. The text is Paul's advice to Timothy (1 Tim. 5:23), "Drink a little wine for thy stomach's sake."

> You have heard the Apostolic voice, that trumpet from heaven, that spiritual lyre! For even as a trumpet sounding a fearful and warlike note, it both dismays the enemy and rouses the dejected spirits on its own side, and filling them with great boldness, renders those who attend to it invincible against the devil. And again, as a lyre that gently soothes with soul-captivating melody, it puts to slumber the disquietudes of perverse thoughts; and thus with pleasure instills into us much profit. . . . Since then it is impossible to go through every part, what part of the text for today would you have us select for the subject of your address to your charity? For as in a meadow, I perceive in what has been read a great diversity of flowers; a multiplicity of roses and violets and of lilies not a few; and everywhere the various and copious fruit of the Spirit is scattered around, as well as an abundant fragrance. Yea rather, the reading of the divine Scriptures is not a meadow only, but a paradise; for the flowers here have not a mere fragrance only, but fruit too, capable of nourishing the soul. (1-2)

He then goes on to explicate and apply the text. As always, he avoids allegorical interpretation; it is characteristic of John to believe that things mean what they say. In so doing, of course, he also follows the tradition of the Antiochene School in which he had been trained.

CHRISTIANITY AND RHETORIC

These sermons, and John's preaching generally, make abundant, even excessive, use of the stylistic devices of the sophists, especially tropes and figures involving pleonasm, such as anaphora, or sound, such as paronomasia, or vivacity, such as rhetorical question or question and answer. Progymnasmatic forms appear, such as the ecphrasis of deserted Antioch (2.5-6) or of the works of creation (9.6; 10.5-6) or the human body (11.5). There are no citations of classical literature, but one passage (1.10) refers to the image of the soul in Plato's *Phaedrus*: "The steed that was unmanageable and restive he [Timothy] curbed with much vehemence until he had tamed him of his wanton tricks, until he had made him docile, and delivered him under entire control into the hands of that reason which is the charioteer." His view of the Greek gods is Euhemerism, that they were men who, after their death, came to be worshiped as gods by the ignorant multitude, though he adds the agency of the Devil (1.17).

As bishop of Constantinople after 398, John became deeply involved in public affairs at the highest level. As at Antioch he attempted to reform public morals, but he met much greater opposition, and the directness of his personality made clashes inevitable. His most dangerous opponent was the luxury-loving empress Eudoxia. Early in 404 John criticized those officials who allowed public games around the empress's new silver statue, which stood near the church:

> Now while it would have been proper to induce the authorities by a supplicatory petition to discontinue the games, he did not do this, but employing abusive language, he ridiculed those who enjoined such practices. The empress once more applied his expressions to herself as indicating marked contempt toward her own person: she therefore endeavored to procure the convocation of another council of bishops against him. When

John became aware of this, he delivered in the church that celebrated oration commencing with these words: "Again Herodias raves, again she is troubled; she dances again; and again desires to receive John's head in a charger." (Socrates 6.18)

It was this outbreak which led to his being tried and condemned by a synod and exiled to Bithynia for the second time. John's speech does not survive; the version found among his works (PG LIX, 485-90), to judge from style and contents, is not genuine, but it is hardly surprising that a later writer should have tried his hand at a prosopopoeia of John's most notorious speech.

John delivered encomia on figures of the Old Testament like Job, others on Christian saints like Babylas of Antioch. He does not, however, seem to have delivered funeral orations like those of Gregory of Nazianzus or Gregory of Nyssa. Although he uses the stylistic artifices of the sophists in these works, sometimes even to excess, he does not seek to imitate their structural forms and topics.[107] Among the early encomia are a series on Saint Paul, delivered on Saint Paul's day in successive years. These particularly well illustrate his use of progymnasmatic forms, especially synkrisis, but also show that the techniques of the stoic diatribe continued to be a popular influence on preaching.[108] The great bulk of John's surviving works are true homilies,

---

[107] See Thomas E. Ameringer, *The Stylistic Influence of the Second Sophistic on the Panegyrical Sermons of St. John Chrysostom. A Study in Greek Rhetoric* (Patristic Studies v), Washington, D.C.: Catholic Univ. of America Pr., 1921, and M. Simonetti, "Sulla struttura dei Panegyrici di S. Giovanni Crisostomo," *Rendiconti dei Istituto Lambardo di Scienze e Lettere* 86 (1953), 159-80.

[108] See Harry M. Hubbell, "Chrysostom and Rhetoric," *CPh* 19 (1924), 261-76; E. Amand de Mendieta, "L'amplification d'un thème socratique et stoïcien dans l'avant-dernier traité de Jean Chrysostome," *Byzantion* 36 (1966), 353-81; A. Cioffi, "L'eredità filosofica e retorica (diatriba e sentenza) nel *Quod nemo laeditur nisi a seipso* di Giovanni Crisostomo," *Nikolaus* 6 (1978), 3-45.

elucidations of the scriptural reading of the day for the theological and moral edification of his congregation. Homilies on Genesis, Kings, Psalms, and Isaiah survive, as do ninety on Matthew, eighty-eight on John, fifty-five on Acts, thirty-two on Romans, seventy-four on Corinthians, twenty-four on Ephesians, fifteen on Philippians, twelve on Colossians, sixteen on Thessalonians, twenty-eight on Timothy, and thirty-four on Hebrews, in addition to others of doubtful authenticity. Most of these homilies were delivered more or less extempore and apparently taken down by stenographers at the time. Some of the homilies exist both in a rather rough version and also in a more polished one, indicating later editing, possibly as late as the Tenth Century.[109]

An example of John's preaching is his Fourth Homily on First Corinthians, preached at an unknown date while he was still in Antioch.[110] The text is central to the relationship of Christianity with classical philosophy and rhetoric: "For the word of the cross to them that perish is foolishness; but to us who are saved it is the power of God. For it is written, I will destroy the wisdom of the wise and the procedure of the prudent will I reject. Where is the wise? Where is the scribe? Where is the disputer of the world?" (1 Cor. 1:18-20) Paradox is a dominant feature of Christian rhetoric: it is seen in the preaching of Jesus, is fully exploited in the text by Saint Paul, and naturally dominates John's homily.

John begins with a proemium designed to prepare the congregation to understand the text (1-3). He elaborates a

[109] See Blake Goodall, *The Homilies of St. John Chrysostom on the Letters of St. Paul to Titus and Philemon. Prolegomena to an Edition* (Univ. of California Publications: Classical Studies XX), Berkeley and Los Angeles: Univ. of California Pr., 1979, chapter 5.

[110] *PG* LXI, 29-40. English translation by Hubert K. Cornish and John Medley, revised by Talbot W. Chambers in *SLN & PNF*, First Series, XII, pp. 16-22, utilized below.

comparison between physical sickness, something known to everyone, and sickness of the soul, something less easily perceived by the sufferer, and he immediately introduces the theme to which he will return at the end, the application of the text: "So also in the case of the gentiles let us act; yea more than for our wives let us wail over them, because they know not the common salvation" (1). It is no wonder that the pagans use rational philosophy in criticism of Paul's passage, but "the things which transcend reasoning require faith alone" (2). Although the context of First Corinthians deals with pagan philosophical criticism of Paul's message, John probably also has in mind Christian rationalists like the Anomoians.[111] "Just so with regard to the things of God; should we desire to explain them by the wisdom which is from without, great derision will ensue, not from their infirmity but from the folly of men. For the great things no language can explain" (2). This doctrine is then applied to some of the greatest of Christian mysteries—for example, why did not Christ save himself from the cross? "He descended not from the cross, not because he could not, but because he would not. For him whom the tyranny of death restrained not, how could the nails of the cross restrain?"

In the second part of the homily (4-6) John reads and interprets portions of the text up through 1 Corinthians 1:25. At the end of the discussion of verse 20-21 we suddenly meet Plato: "It was [God's] good pleasure too by the foolishness of the Gospel to save; foolishness, I say, not real, but appearing to be such. For that which is more wonderful yet is his having prevailed by bringing in, not another such wisdom more excellent than the first, but what seemed to be foolishness. He cast out Plato, for example, not by means of another philosopher of more skill,

[111] See Quasten III, p. 445.

but by an unlearned fisherman. For thus the defeat became greater and the victory more splendid" (4). John here has in mind what develops as a Christian commonplace, found also in Gregory of Nazianzus (Or. 23.12) in the form "not like an Aristotelian, but like a fisherman."

Continuing with verse 22-24 John says, "The Greeks demand of us a rhetorical style and the acuteness of sophistry. . . . When therefore they who seek for signs and wisdom not only receive not the things which they ask, but even hear the contrary to what they desire, and then by means of contraries are persuaded, how is not the power of him that is preached unspeakable?" (5). This is amplified by comparisons: "As if to someone tempest-tost and longing for a haven, you were to show not a haven but another wilder portion of the sea, and so could make him follow with thankfulness. Or as if a physician could attract to himself the man that was wounded and in need of remedies by promising to cure him not with drugs, but with burning of him again" (5). John's fondness for forms of repetition and pleonasm is evident from the quotations; it must be remembered that he was primarily an orator and not a writer and that he was speaking to a congregation of varied intellectual abilities: he must dwell on his points if they are to be grasped. He also sometimes pauses to reevaluate his arguments.

At the end of the interpretive section John lists the doctrines which Christianity brought: the immortality of the soul, the resurrection of the body, the contempt of things present, the desire of things future. But the immortality of the soul was also a Platonic doctrine, and in the next section of the speech (7-10) he examines this objection, amplifying the Christian doctrine of immortality by contrast with the Platonic. Socrates drank the hemlock, but Christians have been enabled by their doctrine cheerfully to undergo torture and martyrdom. The apostles were "twelve ignorant men" (8), but they had the faith to change the world. Plato tried to change the government of Sicily and failed; Christ has changed the religion of all. Protagoras and others had eloquence and philosophy, but little effect. Socrates was executed "because in his discourses concerning the gods he was suspected of moving things a little aside." "How canst thou choose but be in admiration and astonishment when thou seest that the fisherman hath produced such an effect upon the world and accomplished his purposes, hath overcome all both barbarians and Greeks" (9). John's vantage point in the late Fourth Century, with the victory of Christianity secure, makes the power of Christianity evident to him.

The homily concludes with an epilogue (11) which exhorts Christians to apply their faith: "Let us show forth by our actions all excellencies of conduct." The light of the sun is great, but the light within is greater. And the darkness of heresy and superstition too is dreadful. Many disbelieve the resurrection; many consult horoscopes. Some trust amulets and charms. "But to these also we will speak afterwards, when we have finished what we have to say to the Greeks." "He that teaches about philosophy ought first to teach it in his own person and be such as his hearers cannot do without. Let us therefore become such and make the Greeks feel kindly toward us."

> Ye have given me vehement applause and acclamation, but with all your applause have a care lest you be among those of whom these things be said, Wherefore I beseech you all to become men, since so long as we are children, how shall we teach others manliness. How shall we restrain them from childish folly? Let us, therefore, become men, that we may arrive at the measure of the stature which has been marked out for us by Christ and may obtain the good things to come, through the grace

and loving kindness of our Lord Jesus Christ, with whom be to the Father, together with the holy and good Spirit, the glory and power for ever and ever. Amen.[112]

Theodore of Mopsuestia

The most important representative of the exegetical tradition associated with Antioch, admired in antiquity for both his learning and his eloquence, is Theodore, who was born in Antioch around 350, studied rhetoric with Libanius, became a friend of John Chrysostom, and became bishop of Mopsuestia in Cilicia, where he died in 428.[113] After his death his writings were criticized as showing the Christological heresies associated with Nestorius, and in 553 at the Second Coucil of Constantinople he was condemned as a heretic by the Greek Church. His works survive chiefly in Syriac, for they were highly honored by the Nestorian Church of Syria, Mesopotamia, and Persia. Most are philological and historical commentaries to books of the Bible. He was perhaps the first to apply literary criticism to the solution of textual problems. John was admired for his eloquence (Gennadius *De Viris Illustribus* 12), but this was difficult to judge until the Syriac text of his *Catechetical Homilies* was discovered in 1932.[114] These sixteen sermons constitute a unity which sets forth the Christian faith systematically in terms of commentary on the Nicene Creed; they may thus be regarded as credal rather than biblical homilies. On the basis of the French translation of the Syriac version of the Greek original, it appears that

[112] From Cornish and Medley (supra, n. 110), p. 22.
[113] See Quasten III, p. 401.
[114] See Raymond Tonneau and Robert Devreese, *Les homélies catéchétiques de Théodore de Mopsueste* (Studi e testi CXLV), Vatican City: Bibliotheca Apostolica, 1949; J. M. Vosté, "La chronologie et l'activité littéraire de Théodore de Mopsueste," *Revue biblique* 34 (1925), 54-81; D. Tying, "Theodore of Mopsuestia as an Interpreter of the Old Testament," *Journal of Biblical Literature* 50 (1931), 298-303.

Theodore's style was not unlike that of John Chrysostom: a high earnestness, a sense of mystery without allegory, and a use of classical figures of speech to maintain audience contact and enliven the style. Latin translations of his commentaries on the Psalms and the Pauline epistles became current in the Sixth Century and, despite his heretical views, exercised some influence on exegesis in Western Europe.[115]

The two generations from the middle of the Fourth Century to the beginning of the Fifth constitute the Golden Age of Greek Christian Eloquence. The leading figures resemble a spectrum which refracts the rays of classical rhetoric in varying degrees: Anthony and his monks take on almost none of its coloration; Athanasius adopts its techniques of invention, but not of arrangement and style; Basil shows the influence of the style of the sophists, but remains critical of them; John Chrysostom and Theodore of Mopsuestia occupy the center, easily utilizing both classical style and dialectic, but Christian to the core in thought and values; Gregory of Nazianzus and Gregory of Nyssa are both deeply attracted by classical philosophy and rhetoric, though both seek to merge them in Christian truth. At the extreme limits of Christianity stands Synesius of Cyrene, more of a classical orator than a Christian bishop. His criticism of the preaching of the monks and his vigorous defense of the needs of a Christian for intellectual satisfaction have been examined in Chapter One.

For the next thousand years these figures remain the major models of Christian eloquence, Nazianzus and Chrysostom the most, the others in varying degrees depending on the values and objectives of their successors. A great deal of subsequent Greek preaching not only imitates

[115] See M.L.W. Laistner, "Antiochene Exegesis in Western Europe during the Middle Ages," *Harvard Theological Review* 40 (1947), 19-31.

Gregory and John, but quarries phrases, sentences, and whole passages from their works. Their achievements were never surpassed and rarely equaled. Already in the Fifth and Sixth Centuries there is a falling off. The best Christian rhetoric of the Fifth Century, for example, is to be found in the writings of the Church Historians like Socrates, Sozomen, and Theodoret, not in speech. It is true that periods of great oratory are often brief: the fourth century before Christ in Greece, the first century in Rome, but in both those cultures the decline can be partly attributed to political changes. The achievements of Gregory and John result partly from their own genius, partly from their education, partly from the challenges they faced and the creative interworkings of classical and Christian forces in their time. No one of equal genius followed them. Although formal education in rhetoric remained strong in the Fifth Century, and accounts for the qualities found in the historians, it declined in the Sixth and Seventh. And the challenge facing the Christian orator declined as well. Gregory and John set a pattern, which their followers were content to imitate; the needs and conditions of the Church remained approximately what they were in 400. Audience expectations, clearly major factors in the preaching of Gregory and John, declined as well. The audience did not demand something new and the authoritarianism endemic to late antiquity and the Church asserted itself in style and content as it did in thought.

Isidore of Pelusium

The Fifth-Century Christian who probably best represents the synthesis of classical rhetoric and Christianity is Isidore of Pelusium (c. 350–c. 440), of whom some two thousand epistles survive.[116] Though an Egyptian monk,

[116] Text in *PG* LXXVII. See Quasten III, pp. 180-85.

he was well educated in the classics; he repeatedly refers to Demosthenes and in one letter (*Ep.* 4.205) not only discusses his career, but quotes Aristotle's *Rhetoric*. He greatly admired John Chrysostom as theologian, exegete, and stylist. To Isidore the Deacon he writes: "In his exposition of the Epistle to the Romans, O friend who shares my name, the wisdom of John the all-wise is treasured. I think—and let no one believe me to speak for favor—that if the divine Paul had chosen to express himself in the Attic tongue, he would have spoken no other than does this aforesaid famous man, so adorned is his style by enthymemes, ornaments [=figures], and choice of diction" (*Ep.* 5.32). Isidore's general view of secular learning is well encapsulated in the following short letter: "The truth adorns all arts and sciences. If it is lacking, they have no proper decorum. The philosophy of the Greeks, though they claim to seek the truth, has fallen away from it. Rhetoric concentrates on force and delicacy. Grammar boasts that she teaches the usage of words. If these arts are beautified by the truth, they deserve to be desired by the wise; if they take arms against her, they are rightly disenfranchised" (*Ep.* 3.65).

Cyril of Alexandria

The most important Christian orator of the Fifth Century is probably Cyril, who served as bishop of Alexandria from 412 to 444.[117] He resembles his distinguished predecessor Athanasius in his use of dialectic, but is given to a somewhat greater degree of ornamentation. Like Athanasius, he put a great deal of his energy into theological disputation, in Cyril's case not only against Arians but against Nestorians. Nestorius, who had been bishop of Constantinople, criticized use of the term *Theotokos*, or Mother of God, for the Virgin Mary. In Alexandrian theology the

[117] See Quasten III, pp. 116-42.

CHRISTIANITY AND RHETORIC

incarnation was, however, a mystical union of divine and human nature in Christ; Mary was the mother of both natures. Cyril wrote polemical works, dialogues,[118] and allegorizing commentaries on the Bilble.[119] Only a few of his sermons survive, the most famous being *Homily* 4, "On the Virgin Mary," though its authenticity has been questioned.

The Council of Ephesus

Cyril was a major influence at the Council of Ephesus of 431. Since this is the earliest ecumenical council of which we have *Acta*, or minutes, it is of special interest in seeing the form and function of rhetoric in such assemblies and in the Church generally.[120] The views of Nestorius of Constantinople, that the Virgin should not be called the Mother of God and that the infant Jesus should not be called God, awakened wide opposition and were condemned by Pope Celestine and a Roman synod in 430. Cyril was instructed to carry out a threat of excommunication against Nestorius unless he recanted within ten days of receipt of notice. Cyril sent Nestorius twelve theological propositions and demanded that he anathematize them. Although Nestorius eventually found a way to accept the term *Theotokos*, he refused to yield on the basic views which

---

[118] See Cyrille d'Alexandrie, *Deux dialogues christologiques*, ed. Georges Matthieu de Durand (Sources chrétiennes XCVII), Paris: du Cerf, 1964, and *Dialogues sur la trinité*, 3 vols. (Sources chrétiennes CCXXXI, CCXXXVII, CCXLVI), Paris: du Cerf, 1976-78.

[119] See Alexander Kerrigan, *St Cyril of Alexandria. Interpreter of the Old Testament* (Analecta biblica II), Rome: Pontificio Istituto Biblica, 1952.

[120] See *Acta Conciliorum Oecumenicorum*, ed. Eduard Schwartz, Tomus I, vols. 1-5, parts 1-8: *Concilium Universale Ephesium*, Berlin and Leipzig: de Gruyter, 1927. Selections, based on an earlier text, are translated by Henry R. Percival in *The Seven Ecumenical Councils of the Undivided Church*, SLN & PNF, Second Series, XIV, pp. 197-224.

THE COUNCIL OF EPHESUS

stood behind use of that term and received considerable support from followers of the Antiochene School.

The Council of Ephesus was called by Theodosius II. The emperor did not himself attend; Cyril presided in his place. It was a judicial assembly; the stasis was one of fact: had Nestorius performed the act of anathematizing the propositions as demanded? Some evidence of his refusal was introduced and he was condemned. The *Acta* seem to indicate that no discussion was given to the theological views involved and that the whole proceeding was dominated by the imposition of Church discipline. The basis of the judgment was a combination of Scripture and the tradition of the Church. At the opening session the gospels were "enthroned"; the Nicene Creed was read and proclaimed as authoritative; a chain of quotations from early Church Fathers was read as representative of orthodoxy.[121] After Cyril's letter to Nestorius was read, the *Acta* indicate that a series of bishops spoke in support of its orthodoxy. These and similar debates, if that is not too strong a word, take the form "X, bishop of Y, said . . . ," with one or two sentences, apparently comprising the gist of the remarks. Most frequently there is simply an assertion of agreement, but occasionally supporting reason is given from Scripture or tradition. At the end of the discussion there is a vote by acclamation: "All the bishops cried out together: whoever does not anathematize Nestorius, let him be anathema. Such a one the right faith anathematizes; such a one the holy synod anathematizes. Whoever communicates with Nestorius let him be anathema. We anathematize all the apostles of Nestorius. We all anathematize Nestorius as a heretic. Let all such as communicate with Nestorius be anathema."[122]

[121] See Person, *Theological Decision Making* (supra, n. 30), pp. 187-214.
[122] From Percival, *SLN & PNF*, Second Series, XIV, p. 199.

The point is thus made by emotional repetition. The general procedure may in fact be modeled on voting in the Roman senate. The form of an anathema is that of a formula in Roman law. For example, "If anyone shall say that Jesus as man is only energized by the Word of God and that the glory of the only-begotten is attributed to him as something not properly his, let him be anathema."[123] Subsequent synods could then judge the fact of what a preacher had said and apply the formula. Often, however, anathemas contain some supporting reason for their premises, taken from Scripture, and sometimes there is even an effort at logical reasoning. This is true of Cyril's first proposition to Nestorius, which became the first anathema of the Council of Ephesus: "If anyone will not confess that the Emmanuel is very God, and that therefore the Holy Virgin is the Mother of God, inasmuch as in the flesh she bore the Word of God made flesh, as it is written 'The Word was made flesh,' let him be anathema."[124] As rhetoric this is an epicheireme; from the Christian point of view it is even a syllogism, since it claims certainty.

Ephesus and other councils also adopted canons. These too are formulaic and use logical argument, but they do not cite authority. The authority of the Holy Spirit speaking through the bishops suffices. The first canon of Ephesus, directed against John of Antioch and his followers, may be taken as an example:

> Whereas it is needful that they who were detained from the holy synod and remained in their own district or city, for any reason, ecclesiastical or personal, should not be ignorant of the matters which were thereby decreed, we, therefore, notify Your Holiness and Charity that if any metropolitan of a province, forsaking this holy

[123] From ibid., p. 213.
[124] From ibid., p. 206.

and ecumenical synod, has joined the assembly of the apostates, or shall join the same hereafter, or if he has adopted, or shall hereafter adopt, the doctrines of Celestius, he has no power in any way to do anything in opposition to the bishops of the province, since he is already cast forth from all ecclesiastical communion and made incapable of exercising his ministry; but he shall himself be subject in all things to those very bishops of the province and to the neighboring orthodox metropolitans and shall be degraded from his episcopal rank.[125]

Like the language of laws in late antiquity, the decisions and decrees of the Church are rhetoricized: the choice of diction glorifies orthodoxy and ponderously seeks to crush its opponents, and for many ordinary citizens the syntax must have proved bewildering and intimidating.

The Tome of Pope Leo

To continue the study of the rhetoric of the Church and her Councils through the Fifth and Sixth Centuries would overwhelm the material of this book. Enough has probably been said to show how the theme might be approached. There is, however, at least one remarkable work of the Fifth Century, well known to historians of the Church, which deserves to be appreciated also by students of rhetoric and which will provide both a peroration to this chapter and a vivid illustration of some of the qualities of Christian eloquence. This work is the Tome of Pope Leo I, sent to the Council of Chalcedon in 451.

The theological issue of the Council of Chalcedon was the union of the divine and human natures in the person of Christ. It thus represented a third step toward an orthodox definition of the Trinity continuing the disputes inherent in Arianism and Nestorianism. As we have said be-

[125] From ibid., p. 225.

fore, problems of definition are central to the history of rhetoric, of dialectic, and of Christian doctrine in late antiquity. As usual, the issue was complicated by rivalries among the bishops, especially between Dioscurus, successor of Athanasius and Cyril as bisop of Alexandria, and Flavian, successor of Chrysostom and Nestorius as bishop of Constantinople, complicated also by court intrigue, by the role of the pope, by hostility between Alexandrian and Antiochene Christianity, and in this period by the intimidation created by bands of fanatical monks. These forces had come to a head at the so-called Robber Council of Ephesus in 449, dominated by Dioscorus through the use of terrorist methods. Pope Leo called for another Council and one was summoned by the emperor Marcian, who had recently succeeded Theodosius II, to meet at Chalcedon in the shadow of the court. The Council was exceedingly stormy. A central place in the discussion was taken by a letter which had originally been prepared by Pope Leo for the Ephesus Council of 449, but which had been suppressed there and was finally read and approved at Chalcedon. This letter was originally composed in Latin, but a Greek version was made for the Council; both survive.[126] Such dogmatic epistles become a regular feature of Councils both East and West and are traditionally known as tomes. *Tomos* in Greek originally meant "slice" and in classical times is used of a geometric section of a cylinder. From this it was applied to a cylindrical papyrus role and thus to a single volume within a series of documents.

The Tome of Pope Leo opens with a salutation to Flavian, bishop of Constantinople. It refers immediately to a letter from Flavian to Leo about the teachings of Eutyches

[126] Text in *Acta Conciliorum Oecumenicorum*, ed. Eduard Schwartz, Tomus II: *Concilium Universale Chalcedonense*, Berlin and Leipzig, 1933, vol. I, pp. 10-20; vol. II, pp. 24-33. English translation in Percival, *SLN & PNF*, Second Series, XIV, pp. 254-58.

asserting the single nature of Christ (monophysitism) and definitively condemns these and Eutyches himself. He should yield to persons wiser and more learned. He and others who do not apprehend the truth should have recourse to the prophets, the apostles, and the gospels, not to their own reason. There is thus insistence on Scripture, tradition, and the authority of the Church. If Eutyches did not know what to think and was not willing to search the Scriptures, he should have paid attention to the Creed in which the Faith is encapsulated. Leo returns to Eutyches and the specific matter of Church discipline at the end of the letter.

The greater part of the tome sets forth the orthodox theology of the union of the divine and human natures (not one, as the monophysites taught, but two) in the single person of Christ on the basis of Scripture. Leo avoids the unscriptural term "Mother of God," but clearly endorses the theology which it reflects. The Tome is a particularly clear example of one rhetorical problem of the Church: the description in words of an indescribable mystery. His solution, which proved effective in Christianity, is to insist on and to adorn the basic paradox of God and Man in one, much as Saint Paul and John Chrysostom had insisted on the divine foolishness of Christian wisdom. Leo constantly reiterates the paradox in variegated ways, so that it takes on an intensity inherent in the paradoxes of Christian thought and biblical language and reflects the sincerity of a writer who sets aside all other matters as trivial in favor of the enunciation of his one message of overriding importance. The following passage, which is the central highpoint of the epistle, illustrates this technique of scriptural reference, paradox, antithesis, and repetition.

For as we must often be saying, he is one and the same, truly Son of God and truly Son of Man. God, inasmuch as "in the beginning was the Word, and the Word was with God, and the Word was God." Man, inasmuch as "the Word was made flesh and dwelt among us," God, inasmuch as "by him were all things made and without him nothing was made." Man, inasmuch as he was "made of a woman, made under the law." The nativity of the flesh is a manifestation of human nature; the Virgin's childbearing is an indication of divine power. The infancy of the babe is exhibited by the humiliation of swaddling clothes; the greatness of the highest is declared by the voices of angels. He whom Herod impiously designs to slay is like humanity in its beginnings; but he whom the Magi rejoice to adore on their knees is Lord of all.[127]

The Tome of Leo sparked a controversial literature of which Photius gives some notice.[128] The theology of the Tome was attacked in polemical works by Timotheus and Severus and defended by Eulogius in a short *synēgeria,* or deliberative address. Photius says that Eulogius enunciated the law (*nomos*) that writings must not be judged on the basis of their parts. For example, the Bible must not be cited out of context to prove doctrines inconsistent with its overall message; that was what heretics did. This critical principle is also made a basis of exegesis by Augustine and is reminiscent of the insistence of Neoplatonists that Plato's writings, including his discussions of rhetoric and poetry, must be interpreted as a whole. Once the whole message of Plato or of the Bible is determined, the parts may be interpreted in terms consistent with that message.

[127] From Percival, *SLN & PNF*, Second Series, XIV, p. 256.
[128] Codex 225; see also 226, 228, 229, and 230.

CHAPTER FIVE

Rhetoric in Byzantium, 600-900

The empire which Justinian had created at great cost almost disintegrated in the late Sixth and early Seventh Centuries. Persian invasion from the East and Slavic invasion from the North reached to the outskirts of Constantinople. There was mutiny in the army, social unrest in the capital, and periods of collapse of the administrative machinery. Partial recovery was made under the rule of Heraclius (610-641), but the rise of Islam created an entirely new cultural and national force in confrontation with Byzantium. Muhammad died in 632; in the following decades Egypt, Syria, and parts of Asia Minor were permanently lost to the empire, and in 717-718 Constantinople itself was beseiged, but not taken, by the Arabs. The military threat was successfully met by Leo III (717-741), but was followed by the iconoclast controversy which wracked Church and society throughout the Eighth and Ninth Centuries. Iconoclasm is opposition to the worship of icons, or images in painting or sculpture. It had strong appeal in the East and was probably embraced by Leo as part of his attempt to hold Asia, but it had deep roots in puritanical Christianity and expressed itself also in Islam.[1]

[1] Some basic works for study of the Byzantine period include George Ostrogorsky, *History of the Byzantine State*, trans. Joan Hussey, New Brunswick, N.J.: Rutgers Univ. Pr., 1969; the handbooks of Hunger and Krumbacher identified in the bibliographical abbreviations; Hans-Georg Beck, *Kirche und theologische Literatur im byzantinischen Reich* (Handbuch der Altertumswissenschaft XII: Byzantinisches Handbuch 5. 2), 2 vols. Munich: Beck, 1978; *Byzantium. An Introduction to East Roman Cilvilization*, ed. N. H. Baynes and H. St.L.B. Moss, Oxford: Clarendon Pr., 1948; Salvatore Impellizzeri, *La letteratura bizantina*, Milan: Sansoni, 1975; Cyril Mango, *Byzantium. The Empire of New Rome*, London: Weidenfeld and Nicolson, 1980.

265

This period is known as the Byzantine Dark Ages: literature was neglected and those few writers who attained fame owe it to their religious views rather than their verbal art. Although the Attic style continued to be regarded as the appropriate idiom for official speech and serious writing, it was often ineptly practiced and imperfectly understood. Relatively few manuscripts were copied; historical sources are poor. The reasons for this decline are complex: one can point to the physical disruption of the period, the decline of population, and the infiltration of the empire by barbarians with little sense of the value of the classical tradition, but perhaps more significant is a realignment of society along more religious lines. Iconoclasm, which seemed to some the source of religious purification and safety, was inherently anticlassical, since the development of Christian art had been strongly influenced by classical models.[2] Yet opposition to iconoclasm eventually stimulated new efforts at expression and a new classicism in the Ninth Century, often called the Macedonian Renaissance from the Macedonian dynasty of emperors, founded by Basil I (867-886). Although uneducated himself, he insisted on the education of his heirs and encouraged learning. Events follow a somewhat similar course in Western Europe, where the Dark Ages of the Sixth and Seventh Centuries are followed by Charlemagne and the Carolingian Age, with a new interest in education and the classics.

[2] See Averil Cameron, "Images of Authority: Elites and Icons in Later Sixth-Century Byzantium," *Past & Present* 84 (1979), 3-35; Kurt Weitzmann, "Character and Intellectual Origins of the Macedonian Renaissance," *Studies in Classical and Byzantine Manuscript Illumination*, ed. H. L. Kessler, Univ. of Chicago Pr., 1971, pp. 176-223; idem, "The Classical Mode in the Period of the Macedonian Emperors," *The 'Past' in Medieval and Modern Greek Culture*, ed. Speros Vryonis, Malibu, Calif.: Undina, 1978, pp. 71-85. On the relationship between art and rhetoric see Henry Maguire, *Art and Eloquence in Byzantium*, Princeton Univ. Pr., 1981.

Early Byzantine Oratory

The forms and functions of rhetoric in the Seventh and Eighth Centuries remain those of later antiquity, but there is an evident increase in the use of external means of persuasion: application or threat of force, torture, or arbitrary imposition of authority. The legal system of the Sixth Century was revised and updated by Basil I and Leo VI, but preserved the main features of Justinian's time.[3] Orderly procedures, however, were sometimes neglected, and judicial oratory, the historic core of rhetoric, played a diminished role. One of the few trials about which we are well informed is that of Maximus the Confessor on charges of treason and heresy in 653. Maximus was born about 580 and, according to the *Vita* which survives from nearly contemporary times, had a thorough classical education in the *enkyklios paideusis*, attaining among other things "to the highest point in rhetoric and the art of speech" (PG XL, 69).[4] This would have been at the end of the Sixth Century. He served as secretary to Heraclius and later went to North Africa where he vigorously defended the orthodox belief in the two wills of Christ in opposition to the Monothelites. An account of his debate with Pyrrhus, the exiled monothelite patriarch of Constantinople, shows considerable dialectical skill (PG XCI, 287-354).[5] He later went to Rome and was then summoned back to Constantinople on charges that he had aided the Saracen conquest of Egypt

---

[3] See Louis Bréhier, *Les institutions de l'empire byzantin* (Le monde byzantin II) Paris: Michel, 1949, pp. 218-30; Panagriotes I. Zepos, "Die byzantinische Jurisprudenz zwischen Justinian und den Basiliken," *Berichte zum XI. Internationalen Byzantinisten Kongress*, Munich, 1958, fasc. 1.

[4] See Krumbacher I, pp. 61-64 and *New Catholic Encyclopedia*, s.v. "Maximus the Confessor."

[5] On the study of dialectic in this period see Mossman Roueché, "A Middle Byzantine Handbook of Logic Terminology," *Jahrbuch der österreichischen Byzantik* 29 (1980), 71-98.

and Lybia, had expressed treasonous views against the Emperor Constans II, and had subscribed to doctrines of Origen which had been declared heretical.

The *Vita* gives an extended account of Maximus' trial (PG XC, 87-96) and refers to a *hypomnēma* prepared by his disciple Anastasius, who was called as a witness against him. This *hypomnēma* also survives (PG XC, 109-30). Both sources are of course very favorable to Maximus and may somewhat exaggerate the arbitrary nature of the proceedings. Maximus was held in prison and allowed little or no contact with his supporters before or during the trial. The court consisted of the senate of Constantinople, with a large crowd of onlookers who were hostile to Maximus and were allowed, possibly even ecouraged, to interrupt proceedings. The prosecutor was Constans' *sacellarius*, or minister of finance, who is described as very eloquent and inventive of arguments, but as stooping to any wickedness to secure conviction. From reading the *Vita* one might conclude that the prosecutor delivered a speech in support of the first indictment, that Maximus then rebutted it, and that the procedure then moved on to the other indictments. From the *hypomnēma*, however, it is clear that although each of the indictments was taken up separately, there was no extended speech by either party. Rather, Maximus was relentlessly grilled by the prosecutor, egged on by the court, and at the end even beaten. He sought to defend himself calmly, to show that the witnesses used against him were not reliable, and that he had been inaccurately quoted. His rational argumentation was counterproductive, since it seemed to inflame the prosecutor and court; they had in fact already judged him guilty and what they wanted was confession and a plea for mercy. Representatives of the patriarch were sent to him in the prison at night to press him further, but without success. The decision of the court was to condemn him; punishment of exile was decreed in a conference between Constans and the patriarch, neither of whom apparently attended the trial. It is obvious that they desired to make a public example of Maximus and thought that the interests of state and Church required his abject defeat even at the expense of blatantly illegal and unjust methods of procedure. The trial is thus a good example of the "conflict of rhetorics," of the external rhetoric of intimidation against the rational rhetoric of the classical tradition. Signs of this conflict can, of course, be found earlier, but are especially characteristic of this period. Similar signs can be seen in the West, for example in the trial of Praetextatus of Rouen as described by Gregory of Tours (*Hist.* 5.18). Several factors contributed to the dominance of external rhetoric: the absolute power of rulers, the authoritative and dogmatic tendency of the age, seen especially in the Church's obsession with one true faith, the decline of education and an educated public, and a prevailing insecurity which created a lack of toleration of divergent views and an impatient desire for decisive action.

Opportunities for deliberative oratory show two conflicting movements. On the one hand, under Justinian's weak successors a greater voice in public policy was gained by the senate; it often participated actively in the choice of a new emperor and occasionally in the choice of a patriarch, and it provided a forum for the expression of the views of the aristocracy.[6] There is also evidence for the continued function of local senates. There were in addition occasional assemblies with a larger constituency convened to deal with specific issues, such as that which confirmed the Canons of the Sixth Ecumenical Council in 687 (*PL* xcvi, 427). We are ill-informed about speech in the senate or other assemblies, but opportunity for free debate occasionally existed, eloquence was respected, and skilled speakers

[6] See Charles Diehl, "Le sénat et le peuple byzantin aux VIIe et VIIIe siècles," *Byzantion* 1 (1924), 201-13.

certainly had an advantage over the mute or incoherent. On the other hand, powerful officials easily became impatient with debate and turned to external means of persuasion to attain their ends. This can be seen, for example, in the efforts of Leo III to persuade the public to accept iconoclasm. He sought to use public address and debated with his opponents, but was frustrated and impatient of results and turned to intimidation.[7]

After an apparent lapse of two centuries, secular panegyric was reintroduced in this period on the basis of classical models, but with some influence from popular saints' lives.[8] There are, for example, the funeral orations by Theodore the Studite for his mother and for his uncle Plato, who had resisted iconoclasm, delivered in 814 (PG xcix, 804-49). These were collected with other of his works in a book of panegyrics.[9] From the end of the period there is the funeral oration for Basil I by Leo the Wise delivered in 886.[10] Leo was eighteen at the time, and his speech shows the results of a Ninth-Century education. The traditional topics, including the lament, are included and the rules of Menander observed, but the true models for the speech are the Funeral Orations for Caesarius and Basil by Gregory of Nazianzus. Preaching remained a powerful influence.[11] Striking examples are the sermons on the nativity and on the assumption by John Damascene who lived

[7] See Paul J. Alexander, *The Patriarch Nicephorus of Constantinople. Ecclesiastical Policy and Image Worship in the Byzantine Empire*, Oxford: Clarendon Pr., 1958, p. 9.

[8] See Paul J. Alexander, "Secular Biography at Byzantium," *Speculum* 15 (1940), 194-209.

[9] See Beck, *Theologische Literatur* (supra, n. 1), p. 493.

[10] See *Oraison funèbre de Basile I par son fils Léon VI le Sage*, edited, with introduction and translation by A. Vogt and I. Hauscher (Orientalia Christiana xxvi, 1), Rome: Pontificale Institutum Orientalium Studiorum, 1932.

[11] See Beck, *Theologische Literatur* (supra, n. 1), pp. 454-59, 500-506, 542-57.

in the late Seventh and early Eighth Centuries.[12] They are important for the development of Mariology in the Church, and the feasts offered a Christian orator an opportunity for joyous encomium and colorful ecphrasis in this grim age, analogous to earlier sophists' celebration of the pagan gods or the beauty of spring. The imagery of nature had of course long been shared by sophists and preachers. Much of the language is drawn from the Bible, but the style is ornamented by classical tropes and figures of speech: "Who is the most pure creature ascending, shining as the dawn, beautiful as the moon, conspicuous as the sun? How sweet and lovely thou art, the lily of the field, the rose among thorns; therefore the young maidens loved thee. We are drawn after the odor of thy ornaments. The King introduced thee into his chamber. There Powers protect thee, Cherubims are hushed in joy, and Seraphim magnify the true Mother by nature and by grace of their very Lord."[13]

John's major works are the *Pēgē gnōseōs*, or *Source of Knowledge*, which includes a section on dialectics based on Porphyry, and, assuming it is genuine, the romance *Barlaam and Ioasaph*.[14] He was a vigorous opponent of iconoclasm and his independence was secured by the fact that he lived and wrote outside of the Byzantine empire under Arab rule in Syria. He came of a Hellenized Greek family, had a good classical education from a Sicilian monk named Cosmas who had been captured by the Saracens,

---

[12] See S. Jean Damascène, *Homélies sur la nativité et la dormition*, introduction, translation, and notes by Pierre Voulet (Sources chrétiennes lxxx), Paris: du Cerf, 1961.

[13] Translation by Mary H. Allen, *St. John Damascene, On Holy Images*, London: Thomas Baker, 1898, pp. 165-66.

[14] See *Dialectica: Version of Robert Grosseteste*, ed. Owen A. Colligan, St. Bonaventure, N.Y.: Franciscan Institute, 1953; St. John Damascene, *Barlaam and Ioasaph*, trans. G. R. Woodward (LCL), Cambridge: Harvard Univ. Pr., 1914.

and became chief councilor to the caliph of Damascus before retiring to a monastery.[15]

This is a convenient place to note the fact that Greek religious, educational, rhetorical, and literary traditions exercised influence on speakers and writers of Syriac, Armenian, and Arabic. In Armenian, Moses Khorenatsi (died c. 487), author of an important history of the country, had written a treatise on progymnasmata which partially survives and is said to be based on the writings of Theon and Aphthonius.[16] In Syriac, Anton of Tagrit in the Ninth Century composed panegyrics and consolations and a large rhetorical treatise in five books which survives in manuscript but has never been edited.[17] Arabic work on classical rhetoric derives ultimately from the studies of Aristotle in the School of Alexandria and by the Ninth Century produced translations of the *Rhetoric* and commentaries on it, of which the most important is that attributed to al-Farabi, translated into Latin by Hermannus Germanus in the Thirteenth Century.[18]

[15] See P. Joseph Nasrallah, *Saint Jean de Demas. Son époque, sa vie, son oeuvre*, Paris: Editions Universitaires, 1950, pp. 57-85.

[16] See Adolf Baumgartner, "Ueber das Buch Die Chrie," *Zeitschrift der deutschen Morgenlands Gesellschaft* 40 (1886), 457-515; H. Thorosian, *Histoire de la littérature armenien*, Paris: Araxes, 1951, p. 88.

[17] See Rubens Duval, *La littérature syriaque des origines jusqu'à la fin de cette littérature après la conquête par les Arabes au XIIIe siècle*, Amsterdam: Philo, 1970, pp. 299-301 and 389-90.

[18] See Moritz Steinschneider, *Die arabischen Uebersetzungen aus den Griechischen*, Graz: Akademie Verlagsanstalt, 1960, pp. 48-49, and for a survey with additional bibliography James J. Murphy, *Rhetoric in the Middle Ages. A History of Rhetorical Theory from Saint Augustine to the Renaissance*, Berkeley and Los Angeles: Univ. of California Pr., 1974, pp. 89-92. A native tradition of oratory existed in Arabic from an early time and stylistic theory was developed in the exegesis of the Koran, as it was by Christians for the Bible, see Regis Blachère, *Histoire de la littérature Arabe des origins à la fin du XVe siècle*, Paris: Adrin-Maisonneuvre, 1966, I, fasc. 3, pp. 717-36; S. A. Bonebakker, "Aspects of the History of Literary Rhetoric and Poetics in Arabic Literature," *Viator: Medieval and Renaissance Studies* 1 (1970), 75-95.

Early Byzantine Education

With the loss of Egypt and Syria, Constantinople came to dominate the intellectual life of the Greek world, and it is almost possible to write the history of Byzantine rhetoric without looking outside her walls. The history of higher education in Constantinople through the medieval period is, however, a vexed question; on the basis of what is currently known the most probable view can be summarized as follows.[19]

The "university" founded by Theodosius II in 425, with its grammarians, sophists, and philosophers, certainly continued to exist throughout the Sixth Century and offered important training for future intellectual leaders and administrative officials. The allegorical preface to Theophylactus Simocatta's *History*, written in the second quarter of the Seventh Century, describes the flight of philosophy from the royal stoa under Phocas, emperor from 602 to 610, but all this passage need indicate is that these were difficult years for the study of philosophy. Indeed, it is possible that classes had been interrupted and professors unpaid at times even earlier. Simocatta himself had had a thorough education and his work is one of the most rhetorical examples of its genre. He indicates that educational conditions improved under Heraclius. Sergius, patriarch of Constantinople from 610 to 638, apparently encouraged literary studies in general and Simocatta in particular. It was about this time that Stephanos of Alexandria arrived in the capital to become *oekoumenikos didaskalos*, a term earlier used of law professors at Beirut; it apparently became the title of

---

[19] The account here is based primarily on that of Paul Lemerle, *Le premier humanisme byzantin*, Paris: Presses Universitaires de France, 1971, pp. 74-108. See also works cited in Chapter 3, nn. 44 and 45 supra; Friedrich Fuchs, *Die höheren Schulen von Konstantinopel im Mittelalter*, Leipzig, 1926; reprinted Amsterdam: Hakkert, 1964; Mango, *Byzantium* (supra, n. 1), pp. 125-48.

officially appointed professors at the "university." There is no satisfactory evidence that the Patriarchal School of later times had yet come into existence.[20] Stephanus taught Plato and Aristotle, arithmetic, geometry, astronomy, and music, that is, he taught dialectic and the four subjects of the quadrivium as it was known in the West. It is not known who taught rhetoric, but its place in the curriculum seems clear from a number of references in biographies to the grammatical, rhetorical, and dialectical studies of individuals throughout this period.[21] For example, Germanus, patriarch of Constantinople from 715 to 730, wrote in a clear style according to Photius (*Bibliotheca*, Codex 233), made good use of figures of speech, expressed his thought cogently, and avoided irrelevant arguments. These qualities can be seen in his surviving works, which include a dialogue, letters, and two festival homilies (*PG* XCVIII, 440-53).

The "university" collapsed and *oekumenikoi didaskaloi* ceased to be appointed during the reign of Leo III (717-741). The story of how Leo burned the professors and their library when they opposed iconoclasm is probably a myth,[22] but it is likely that the iconoclast movement, with its distrust of Hellenism, is the basic cause of the neglect and death of the "university." Public support of education had always been connected with the training of administrators, and the increasing reliance on officials with military training in this period also contributed to, or reflects, the declining importance of public support of education. From writers of the Ninth Century it is clear that publicly supported education in a designated building with its own library was something vaguely remembered from former times

[20] See Lemerle, *Humanisme* (supra, n. 19), p. 85.
[21] Ibid., pp. 97-104.
[22] Source of the story is Georgii Monachi *Chronicon*, ed. C. de Boor, Leipzig: Teubner, 1904, II, p. 742. See J. B. Bury, *A History of the Later Roman Empire*, London: Macmillan, 1889, pp. 433-34.

and not a continuing institution. But education in rhetoric, as in other liberal arts, continued to be available from private teachers: references to a knowledge of rhetoric are consistently found in every period. For example, Theodore the Studite, born about 759, studied rhetoric as he did grammar and philosophy, but is said to have thought it wrong to form his character in a rhetorical manner and chose only those aspects of the subject useful to him, that is, composition and harmony (PG XCIX, 111 and 237). His writings and sermons show considerable eloquence.[23] Nicephorus, who became patriarch from 806 to 815, had studied *enkyklios paideia* and also had taken a course in the secretarial arts, presumably stenography, calligraphy, and letter writing.[24] Photius (*Bibliotheca*, Codex 66) describes his style as that of "the real and perfect orator."

The basis of the formal study of rhetoric in the Seventh and Eighth Centuries was certainly the Aphthonian-Hermogenic corpus, with the commentary material thereon composed in the Fifth and Sixth Centuries. There is no evidence for new commentaries until those attributed to John of Sardis. John is probably, but not certainly, to be identified as the bishop of Sardis to whom Theodore the Studite addressed a letter about the year 800 (*Ep.* 2.108 in PG XCIX, 1368-69) and is also the author of hagiographic works.[25] Certainly his commentaries antedate the Tenth Century since they do not show the strong Christianizing impulse which then became common. John's commentary on Aphthonius and the *Prolegomenon* to his commentary on invention survive.[26] At least some of the material which originally followed the prolegomenon is preserved by Dox-

---

[23] See Beck, *Theologische Literatur* (supra, n. 1), pp. 491-96.
[24] See Ignatii Diaconi *Vita Nicephori* in Nicephori *Opuscula Historica*, ed. C. de Boor, Leipzig: Teubner, 1880, p. 144.
[25] See Beck, *Theologische Literatur* (supra, n. 1), p. 510.
[26] See Ioannis Sardiani *Commentarium in Aphthonii Progymnasmata*, ed. Hugo Rabe, Leipzig: Teubner, 1928, and *PS*, pp. 351-60.

apatres.[27] Since the prolegomenon closely relates invention to stasis, it is likely that John had also written a commentary on stasis, and Rabe was able to show with some probability that John is "the other commentator" to whom is attributed *Prolegomenon* 21 in his collection and a commentary on stasis found in *Vaticanus Graecus* 1022, but still unpublished.[28]

John's work is a compendium of earlier material strung together. He sometimes utilizes material from commentaries on ideas in his discussion of progymnasmata. His sources include Sopatros and the Sixth-Century philosopher David's discussion of Aristotle's theory of virtues. John himself seems to have no independent ideas and is not even bothered if inconsistencies arise among his sources. Not surprisingly, John Geometres later criticizes his ignorance (VI pp. 576-77 Walz). The extant parts of his work do not discuss the utility of rhetoric nor reveal how he envisioned that a student should apply the material, but rhetoric is to him what he finds presented in his authorities, above all Aphthonius and Hermogenes, and that is what should be studied if one is to acquire a liberal education. The goal is apparently to be able to express oneself in Attic Greek, the high style, a knowledge of which is the mark of an educated man.

It is possible that John composed his commentaries after becoming bishop of Sardis and that they were intended for use in a school associated with his cathedral. The chief objection to this view is the very sorry condition of Sardis in the Eighth and Ninth Centuries as revealed by modern archaeologists.[29] It seems doubtful that many students could have been found there or that inhabitants of a province so

---

[27] See Gloeckner, pp. 12-22.

[28] See *PS*, pp. lxxxix-xciii; Hunger I, pp. 78, 82-83, and 87-88.

[29] See Clive Foss, *Byzantine and Turkish Sardis* (Archaeological Exploration of Sardis IV), Cambridge: Harvard Univ. Pr., 1976, pp. 53-66.

laid waste by Arab invasion would appreciate the opportunity offered to them. In later Byzantine times teachers in Constantinople sometimes became bishops, Leo the Philosopher being a Ninth-Century example, and thus John may have written his commentaries in Constantinople before taking up his appointment at Sardis. John's commentaries were well known to his Byzantine successors. However unusual in their own times, and however superficial they seem, they proved useful to others and were copied and studied during the next two centuries.

John's commentaries are probably to be regarded as an early sign of the resurgence of learning in the Ninth Century. A leading figure in this revival is Leo the Philosopher, or Mathematician.[30] He had studied rhetoric, philosophy, and arithmetic with "a learned man" on the Aegean island of Andros early in the Ninth Century (Theophanes Continuatus 4.29, p. 192 Bekker), taught the quadrivium at Thessalonika and Constantinople, and acquiring considerable fame, was given an appointment to teach publicly in the Church of the Holy Martyrs at Constantinople on a salary furnished by the emperor Theophilus (829-842) (Theophanes Continuatus 4.27). This seems to have constituted a personal chair, not a refounding of the "university," for we do not hear of any replacement when Leo moved on to become archbishop of Thessaloniki in 840.

Theophilus was succeeded by his three-year-old son, Michael III (842-867), for whom the queen mother Theodora and his uncle Bardas acted as regents. The new regime immediately reestablished the veneration of icons and further encouraged the study of the classics, or the "exterior wisdom" as it was called in contrast to the "interior wisdom" of the Church. Bardas personally sponsored the establishment of a new school of higher studies in the Palace of the Magnaura sometime after 843 (Theophanes

[30] See Lemerle, *Humanisme* (supra, n. 19), pp. 148-76.

Continuatus 4.26). This institution is often regarded as a refounding of the "university."[31] Leo, who had by now returned from Thessalonika, was put in charge of the school of philosophy. Others were appointed to teach geometry, astronomy, and grammar.[32] Rhetoric is not mentioned, but the inclusion of grammar, which is a more elementary discipline, suggests that it too was part of the curriculum. We do not know how long the School of Magnaura continued, but it had apparently collapsed at least by the time of Romanus I (920-944), for thereafter Constantine VII is said to have had to search out scholars to appoint as teachers.[33] There then follows a century of silence about higher education until the provisions made by Constantine IX in 1045. Public support of higher education in Constantinople was clearly dependent on the initiative of enlightened rulers.

Photius

The most important figure in the intellectual renaissance of the Ninth Century is Photius, who served as patriarch of Constantinople from 858 to 867 and again from 878 to 886.[34] As a young man Photius had remained in Constantinople on the exile of his father, a strong opponent of iconoclasm. No details are known, but he acquired a good education and a reputation for secular learning. Until his election as patriarch he remained a layman,

---

[31] See Paul Speck, *Die kaiserliche Universität von Konstantinopel*, Munich: Beck, 1974, pp. 1-13.

[32] Cometas, a specialist on Homer, was appointed to teach grammar, see *Anthologia Palatina* 15.36-40.

[33] The source is Cedrenus II, p. 326 Bekker. See J. M. Hussey, *Church and Learning in the Byzantine Empire, 867-1185*, London: Oxford Univ. Pr., p. 24.

[34] See *R-E* xx, 667-737; Francis Dvornik, "Patriarch Photius, Scholar and Statesman," *Classical Folia* 13, no. 2 (1959), 3-18; 14, no. 1 (1960), 3-22; Lemerle, *Humanisme* (supra, n. 19), pp. 177-204.

working in the imperial bureaucracy. He served on an embassy to Samarra, probably in 838, and rose to direct the chancery and to become a member of the senate. He never held an appointment as a professor, but he made of his house a small academy where he engaged in religious and philosophical discussions with friends and young admirers. In a letter to Pope Nicolas I he describes his reluctance to give up this way of life (*PG* cii, 597). His career as patriarch was a stormy one which twice led to his exile. Somewhat unjustly he has been regarded by the Western Church as the inspirer of schism, but modern studies in East and West have come to emphasize his orthodoxy, his enlightened leadership in the Church, and above all his learning, which probably exceeded anyone of his time in breadth and in integration of classical and Christian traditions.[35]

Of the numerous writings of Photius, the most important in the history of rhetoric are the *Lexicon*, the *Bibliotheca*, and the sermons. The *Lexicon* is probably an early work, expanded and published later.[36] Its original title seems to have been "An Alphabetical Collection of the Words by which the Labors of Orators and Prose Writers are Most Beautified," and it is thus a dictionary of Atticism, the vocabulary appropriate to the high style. Had it not been for the classical revival of the Ninth Century, it is likely that use of the high style, increasingly distinct from the spoken language, would have faded away except for ceremonial occasions in the Church. Photius' scholarship in the *Lexicon* and in other works and his personal authority helped to canonize and reinvigorate the tradition and to make it more easily available in a period which shows a

[35] See Francis Dvornik, *The Photian Schism, History and Legend*, Cambridge Univ. Pr., 1948.
[36] See Kyriakos Tsantsanoglos, *To Lexico tou Photiou, Chronologese, Cheirographe Paradose* (Hellenika Parartema xvii), Thessaloniki: Etaireia Makedonikon Spoudon, 1967.

new impulse toward artistic composition. The *Lexicon* was a major source for later handbooks such as the *Suda*. Photius' own sources are partly his reading of the classics and the classicizing writers of late antiquity, but much of the material is derived from lexicographers of the empire, some of whom he discusses in the *Bibliotheca* (145-58).

The *Bibliotheca*, or *Myriobiblos*, is a collection of 279 "codices," or descriptions of the works which Photius had read, slightly more than half Christian, the rest classical.[37] The longer accounts are analytical summaries or extracts, preserving the original language; shorter accounts sketch the compass of a work or cite only the author and title. In an introductory letter to his brother Tarasius, Photius indicates that he is going on a trip—presumably the embassy to Samarra—and that Tarasius has asked for summaries of the works read and discussed by Photius and his other friends at times when Tarasius was not present. Photius claims to have hired a secretary and dictated the summaries from memory. This may well be the genesis of the work, but the postscript speaks of the summaries as representing his reading over many years and the verbatim extracts in the manuscripts were probably copied out by a scribe at Photius' direction.[38]

The *Bibliotheca* is of great value for its inclusion of works now lost, such as considerable portions of the sophist Himerius, for its indication of what was available to a scholar

[37] See Photius, *Bibliothèque*, text and trans. by René Henry, 8 vols. Paris: Les Belles Lettres, 1959-77. For an incomplete English translation see J. H. Freese, *The Library of Photius*, New York: Macmillan, 1920.

[38] See Tomas Hägg, "Photius at Work: Evidence from the *Bibliotheca*," *GRBS* 14 (1973), 213-22, amplified in *Photios als Vermittler antiker Literatur. Untersuchungen zur Technik des Referierens und Exzerpierens in der Bibliotheke* (Studia Graeca Upsaliensia VIII), Stockholm: Almqvist and Wicksell, 1975; "The Preface of the Bibliotheca of Photius," ed. W. T. Treadgold, *Dumbarton Oaks Papers* 31 (1977), 343-49.

of the Ninth Century who was willing to hunt out manuscripts, and for Photius' own comments on the material he transcribes or summarizes and its literary qualities. He is primarily interested in prose works with which his contemporaries, even learned contemporaries, were not familiar. Thus Plato and Aristotle are entirely omitted. Demosthenes (265) and the other Attic orators except for Antiphon are included, which suggests that they were not widely studied at this time.[39] From the Ninth Century on, that study was to some extent resumed, as is shown by the copying of manuscripts and marginal scholia, based on commentators of late antiquity. Aelius Aristides and Libanius were also studied as models in the Byzantine period.[40] Photius certainly contributed to this development, as he did to the revival of Atticism in general, though he cannot be given all the credit. Another important development of this period, to which Photius did not personally contribute, is the recopying of manuscripts from uncial into minuscule script. This made it possible for large works or collections of works, such as the Aphthonian-Hermogenic corpus together with commentary material, to be conveniently assembled in a single manuscript.[41]

The *Bibliotheca* does not discuss rhetorical handbooks, but it reflects a knowledge of the Hermogenic theory of ideas. Photius consistently employs the terminology of *On Ideas* and its commentators in describing the style of both Christian and secular literature, but his own declared pref-

[39] See Rudolph Ballheimer, *De Photii Vitis Decem Oratorum Dissertatio Philologica*, Bonn: C. Georg, 1877; A. Vonach, *Die Berichte des Photios über die fünf älteren attischen Redner*, Innsbruck: Wagner, 1910.

[40] See the citations in the index to Hunger and Friedrich Walter Lenz, *Aristeidesstudien* (Deutsche Akademie der Wissenschaften zu Berlin: Altertumswissenschaft XL), Berlin: Akademie-Verlag, 1964.

[41] See L. D. Reynolds and N. G. Wilson, *Scribes and Scholars. A Guide to the Transmission of Greek and Latin Literature*, Oxford: Clarendon Pr., 1974, pp. 51-54.

erence is for a simplicity consistent with early Christian standards: in the case of classical authors he praises qualities which fall under Hermogenes' ideas of clarity, dignity, and the milder forms of ethos, while avoiding complimentary reference to asperity, florescence, vehemence, or sternness; the prose style which he most admires, as seen from his *Amphilochia* (PG CI, 601-2), is that of Saint Paul, which he regards as not derived from art but from a strength of mind given by God.[42]

As patriarch of Constantinople, Photius proved to be a powerful preacher. He adopts, as was to be expected, the typical Christian style with its combination of biblical imagery and sophistic figures of speech, but sometimes permits himself a greater degree of florescence or sternness than the criticism of the *Bibliotheca* would lead one to expect. A collection of eighteen of Photius' homilies is available in an excellent English translation and offers the best introduction to the preaching of this period.[43] These are not exegetical homilies, but sermons associated with the feasts of the Church year or with special occasions. Four (7, 10, 17, 18) were delivered before the emperor Michael III and are especially florid. The sermon on the annunciation (5) is given dramatic treatment, a popular genre of preaching in Byzantium which may have derived from Syrian sources.[44] The tenth homily contains an elaborate ecphrasis of the Church of Our Lady of the Pharos. The fifteenth and sixteenth are part of a series on Arianism, which is used as a warning against heretics of Photius' own time. The seventeenth was delivered on the occasion

[42] See George L. Kustas, "The Literary Criticism of Photius," *Hellenika* 17 (1962), 133-69.

[43] See *The Homilies of Photius, Patriarch of Constantinople*, English translation, introduction, and commentary by Cyril Mango, Cambridge: Harvard Univ. Pr., 1958.

[44] See George LaPiana, *Le rappresentazioni sacre nella letteratura bizantina*, Grottaferrata: S. Nilo, 1912, pp. 63-68.

of the unveiling of an icon of the virgin and thus relates to the iconoclast controversy.

In the proemium to the second homily Photius summarizes his views of preaching: greater preachers have gone before him whom he looks to as a choir of the blessed. These he will imitate to the extent of his rhetorical powers:

> I shall perform my duty in exhorting you to what is needful and inciting you to those deeds which are believed to keep our pact with God inviolate, which bring about victory over the Evil one, and yield the fruit of salvation in time of need.[45]

In the fifteenth homily he laments the stern role the preacher must play in contrast to his own earlier career:

> All was friendship and kindness, and my life was free of cares. Now, alas, the law of shepherds constrains me to grieve others to show myself severe . . . and to condemn (others)—me who from the beginning have avoided this rank and have consistently shown my aversion to it, although it did not prove possible to escape it, to have escaped which could be accounted a happiness.[46] (15.11)

It is thus his sense of the duty of the preacher which is responsible for introducing into his style that harshness which is essentially incongenial to him, but which at times gives him the tone of a prophet of the Old Testament. A good example is the opening of the third homily, which was delivered at the time of the Russian attack on Constantinople in 860.

> What is this? What is this grievous and heavy blow and wrath? Why has this dreadful bolt fallen on us out of the farthest north? What clouds compacted of woes

[45] From Mango, *Homilies of Photius* (supra, n. 43), p. 55.
[46] Ibid., p. 259.

and condemnation have violently collided to force out this irresistible lightning upon us? Why has this thick, sudden hailstorm of barbarians burst forth, not one that hews down the stalks of wheat and beats down the ears of corn, or lashes the vine-twigs and dashes to pieces the unripe fruit, or strikes the stems of plants and tears the branches apart (which for many has often been the extent of its most grievous damage), but miserably grinding up men's bodies and bitterly destroying the whole nation? Why or how have the lees (to call them no worse) of so many and great disasters been poured on us? Is it not for our sins that all these things have come upon us? Are they not a condemnation and a public parading of our transgressions? . . . We were delivered from evils which often had held us; we should have been thankful, but we showed no gratitude. We were saved, and remained heedless; we were protected and were contemptuous. (3.5-7)[47]

Ecclesiastical office also leads him to strong denunciation of the prettiness of classical mythology. In the ninth homily he attacks those who doubt the virgin birth, but delight in telling the stories of the Greek poets:

Tell us of the human poplars, from whose eyes drips the mythical amber, whence thou drawest thy wealth of silliness. Enumerate the laurel trees and palm trees, thy nightingales and swallows, thy musical swans and halcyons, and thy friendly dolphins. . . . I am silent about the rest. Nor is it, I think, proper for the unguent of faith to be mingled with the mire of error, . . . the murk of impiety. Wherefore, bidding a definite farewell to this tedious nonsense and chatter, and pitying for their folly those who are in a flutter about these things, while

[47] Ibid., pp. 82-83.

abominating their imposture, let us now proceed with the initial course of our speech. (9.6)[48]

In the work of Photius questions about the relationship of Christianity to rhetoric are faced again as they had been by the Cappadocian Fathers and answered in similar ways. The preacher is an orator; the Church has a use for rhetoric and for secular learning, but must exercise good judgment in terms of Christian values. Since rhetoric, even during the Dark Ages, was one of the basic skills, it may well be asked whether there were not subtle ways in which the theory of rhetoric affected the forms of thinking and expression of the Byzantines. George Kustas has suggested that the theory of ideas as set forth by Hermogenes, discussed by commentators of the Fifth and Sixth Centuries, and amplified by the aesthetic theories of Proclus and Alexandrian Neoplatonists, found a natural home in Christian mysticism with its love of symbol and allusion and its belief in a wisdom-not-of-this-world which can be apprehended, but not understood.[49] He contrasts this tradition in the East with the allegorical tradition in the West, where the theory of ideas was unknown, and feels that it paralleled the attitude toward religious art. Just as the icon becomes more than a mimesis of a human form with decorative aspects and comes to furnish a glimpse of a greater reality which cannot be otherwise grasped, so the logos is capable of meaning more than it says and of attaining an imitation of reality beyond the actual content and form of words. In this development the iconoclast dispute of the Eighth and Ninth Centuries may be a crucial stage. The defeat of the iconoclasts meant not only the acceptance of

[48] Ibid., pp. 170-71.
[49] See George L. Kustas, *Studies in Byzantine Rhetoric* (Analecka Vlatadon XVII) Thessaloniki: Patriarchal Institute for Patristic Studies, 1973, pp. 63-100 and 159-99.

the veneration of icons as representations of transcendent reality, but a philosophical belief in the validity of the Hermogenic ideas as equally transcendent, especially those aspects of Hermogenes' system which included obscurity and the quality known as *emphasis*, the technique of style by which words are made to mean more than they say. This view, emerging in the Ninth and Tenth Centuries, is given its most specific statement in the commentary on ideas by John Siceliotes in the early Eleventh. Siceliotes makes extensive use of examples of style from Christian sources, above all from Gregory of Nazianzus. In this way, classical rhetoric, in Kustas' view, is transmuted into a distinctive Byzantine rhetoric.

The appeal of the traditional Christian style, with its admitted obscurity and mystical quality, derives from its biblical authority and its use by the Fathers as an idiom distinct from classical rhetoric, but this style was refined and to some extent clarified by the application of classical dialectic and by the adoption of tropes and figures of speech taught by the sophists in attempts to appeal to an educated audience or to conform to an educated speaker's sense of how words should be used. It is certainly possible to apply the Hermogenic system of ideas to the description of characteristically Christian qualities of style, but that application was only partially perceived or conceptualized by Photius or even Siceliotes. Occasional references to obscurity as a virtue of style are perhaps more typical of the East than of the West, but they must be set against consistent references to clarity as a fundamental virtue. Byzantine rhetoricians continued to regard rhetoric as what it had been in the classical period, a civic art, and it emerged more clearly as such in the Middle Byzantine period. They continued to teach stasis theory as the core of the subject and they continued the association of rhetoric with dialectic as taught by Aristotle and the Neoplatonists. The theory of style was certainly studied and applied, but our limited knowledge of the Early Byzantine period probably exaggerates the identification of rhetoric with style. It is thus an example of the phenomenon of *letteraturizzazione*, which has obscured the history of rhetoric in many periods. Speech has been lost, only rhetoric cast in literature remains. Probably the most important way in which the theory of rhetoric affected the forms of thinking and expression of the Byzantines is that it tended to hold or draw back public address into classical forms of argument and arrangement, as well as style, and the most important feature of Byzantine rhetoric is not those small ways in which it developed a distinctive color, but the extent to which it transmitted unchanged the basic concepts of classical theory and practice.

Arethas

The most interesting Greek orator of the generation after Photius is probably Arethas of Patras (c. 860–c.935). He shows the influence of the new classicism and illustrates the Byzantine tension between clarity and obscurity.

Arethas' great importance in intellectual history is as editor, scribe, and scholiast who copied and commented on a large number of classical works.[50] He was also intimately involved in ecclesiastical and civil politics in the court and patriarchate of Constantinople and a number of his speeches are extant.[51] The most striking is perhaps his "After Dinner" speech delivered before Leo VI on July 20, 902, after a banquet which was part of a commemoration of Leo's

[50] See Lemerle, *Humanisme* (supra, n. 19), pp. 205-41.
[51] For the text see Arethae *Scripta Minora*, ed. L. G. Westerink, 2 vols. Leipzig: Teubner, 1968; 1972. For summaries and discussion see R.J.H. Jenkins, B. Laourdas, and C. A. Mango, "Nine Orations of Arethas from Cod. Marc. Gr. 524," BZ 47 (1954), 1-40. Cf. also P. Karlin-Hayter, "Arethas, Choirosphactes, and the Saracen Vizer," *Byzantion* 35 (1965), 453-81.

near escape from death (*Scripta Minora* 61, II, pp. 23-30 Westerink). Several other speeches by Arethas are also entitled "after-dinner speeches" (*dēmēgoriai epitrapezioi*); they are not entertainment pieces, as the title might suggest, but short Byzantine versions of the *basilikos logos* or other serious epideictic forms as known in late antiquity. This speech is in fact a panegyric of the emperor's character and actions, and its most unusual section (pp. 24-25 Westerink) seeks to identify the emperor with Plato's philosopher king:

> Plato, the son of Ariston, speculating with sharpness of mind about what was generally profitable for all men, demonstrated that life has its best qualities when philosophers are kings or when kings are philosophers. Now he expressed the ideal very wisely and systematically, but we are the first to make a trial of what he said. We see you as king, mixing philosophy with kingship, no easy thing for most men, and correcting the fault of each by the nobility of the other, so that kingship does not engage in discordant action through power, and philosophy, constrained by its love of quiet, does not sit and watch, idle and helpless. In this way you are a kingly philosopher rather than a philosophical king, greatly surpassing all kings before you, one by one, in the finest ways, just as they excelled their subjects in wealth.

The passage should not be dismissed as hyperbolic flattery. It may have been what Leo liked to hear, but in the beginning of the Tenth Century it also represented a significant revival of an ideal of enlightened monarchy inspired by a respect for classical philosophy.

Arethas is not a distinguished stylist, even by Byzantine standards: he has vigor of expression and some learning, but is often tortured and lacking in self-discipline. An unfamiliarity with classical theory was not, however, his problem. He rebukes Nicetas the Paphlagonian for an inappropriate mixture of styles in the latter's panegyric of Gregory of Nazianzus and in the process refers specifically to Hermogenes.[52] In another work he replies to his own critics, addressing an unknown friend:[53]

> Yesterday, about the time the cows come home, as they say, after some time in the city, you paid your debt of speech to us and claimed that there are those who mock my speeches for their lack of clarity, although they have no knowledge what obscurity is nor when it is appropriate nor to whom. If they were acquainted with technical authorities on the ancient culture and with those who have discoursed about speech, I would welcome the criticism rather than feel ashamed. For why would I not want deformity to be removed from my style? Since, if one believes Phocylides, a wise man corrects wisdom (in another) and a fellow artisan corrects art (in another). But no one would scorn me nor dishonor my speeches if he cared about culture and valued study more than drink. If any of those who think of speech as a matter of frippery (criticize me), soiling both speech and thought—"Hippocleides doesn't mind," as the proverb has it. For whom would they praise except those like themselves? (I, p. 186 Westerink)

There is an obvious elitism in Arethas' position, an elitism which characterizes most Byzantine practitioners of the Attic style. They are speaking to be appreciated by others educated in the classics and expect the ignorant mob to admire their works without comprehending them. To an educated audience, Arethas claims, his style is not obscure, but dignified, for it conforms to the standards of the

---

[52] I, p. 270 Westerink. For Nicetas' speech see *PG* cv, 439-88.
[53] See Kustas, *Studies* (supra, n. 49), pp. 84-85.

best Greek critics—he alludes to but does not name Hermogenes—and is modeled on the varied style of the most eloquent of the Fathers, especially Gregory of Nazianzus. Obscurity is a virtue only in the sense that a truly distinguished style will seem obscure to the vulgar.

CHAPTER SIX

Some Features of Rhetoric in
Byzantium, 900-1300

This chapter will not present a detailed picture of the many facets of rhetoric in Byzantium; its more modest objective is to continue the survey of the teaching of the Aphthonian-Hermogenic corpus and the writing of commentaries upon it. Since the main emphasis of that corpus was training in judicial and deliberative rhetoric, it is necessary first to say something about the functions of these primary forms in this period. Some reference will be made to the sophistic tradition of panegyric which is most evident in the literary remains, but the point needs to be made that panegyric was not the exclusive Byzantine interest in rhetoric.

The Tenth, Eleventh and Twelfth Centuries make up the Middle Byzantine period, in which Christian Greek culture of the Middle Ages achieved its most characteristic expressions in society, religion, the arts, and learning. The classicism which had emerged in the Ninth Century out of the iconoclast controversy and the studies of Leo, Photius, Arethas, and others remained a strong influence. Attic Greek strengthened its hold as the official language of learning, literature, and ceremony. The Church even sought to suppress saints' lives in the popular language or to replace them by more literary versions. Mastery of Attic required a classical education. Classical grammar, rhetoric, and dialectic were thus regularly taught in schools in Constantinople, and to a more limited extent in Thessalonika and other Eastern cities, even in Greek-speaking Italy and Sicily. The Aphthonian-Hermogenic corpus remained authoritative for the system of technical rhetoric, but new commentaries were written which sought to bridge the gap between classical and Christian values and to stress those ideas of style which were most congenial to the Byzantines. By the Tenth Century, Gregory of Nazianzus' works had been adopted as models side by side with those of Demosthenes and other classics, and they remained as models permanently. Plato's *Gorgias* and *Phaedrus* and Aristotle's *Rhetoric* were known to the more scholarly, keeping alive the tradition of philosophical rhetoric. The utilization of progymnasmatic forms is everywhere evident in literary composition, and some attention in the schools was given to declamation. Panegyrical and deliberative oratory flourished at the court and some speakers gained fame in the law courts as well. Although external means of persuasion were applied by officials, orderly judicial procedures became more common. The law began to be studied more seriously than had been the case in the immediately preceding three centuries. The fall of Constantinople to the Latins in 1204 disrupted education and speech traditions in the capital, but the exiled Greek court at Nicaea developed a strong sense of cultural unity which expressed itself in a new wave of classicism after the recovery of Constantinople in 1261. Commentators like Maximus Planudes sought to standardize and purify the rhetorical corpus, and efforts were made to write compendia of traditional learning, of which rhetoric was a part. As the Turkish threat to Constantinople increased in the Fourteenth and Fifteenth Centuries, communication between Byzantium and Italy became more frequent, and the final period of Byzantine rhetoric contributed to the rediscovery of the full theory of classical rhetoric in Renaissance Italy.[1]

[1] For basic bibliography, see Chapter 5, n. 1; also Robert Browning, "Byzantine Scholarship," *Past and Present* 28 (1964), 3-20, and his collection of essays, *Studies in Byzantine History, Literature, and Ed-*

The forms and functions of speech in the Middle Byzantine period are those traditional in Greek culture. Most conspicuous are the various epideictic or sophistic forms connected with the ceremonial of public life: panegyrics, funeral orations, both epitaphic and monodic, speeches of thanks, and the like. Such speeches were given a literary adornment and often published; many survive and were apparently read, admired, and imitated. Hunger has recently given a useful survey of them, which need not be repeated here.[2] Because of their obscure allusiveness, they are often frustrating sources for the historian; because of the inadequacy of published texts and the difficulty of their style, they have not yet attracted extensive study by scholars whose interests are primarily in rhetoric. As in late antiquity, it seems clear that such speeches often performed political and social functions by expressing national solidarity and stressing traditional values, but these objectives were not conceptualized by teachers or critics of the time any more than they had been earlier. Progymnasmatic exercises in encomia provided some training for the composition of such speeches, and the treatises on epideictic attributed to Menander were available in this period, but the art continued to be learned largely by imitation of earlier models, of which the funeral orations of Gregory of Nazianzus were the most admired. An important literary application of the structure and commonplaces of panegyric is found in the composition of saints' lives. These began in the Fourth Century, but were composed in all Byzan-

---

ucation, London: Variorum Reprints, 1977. On Byzantine legal procedure see the works listed in Chapter 5, n. 3.

[2] See Hunger I, pp. 92-196, and "Aspekte der griechischen Rhetorik von Gorgias bis zum Untergang von Byzanz," Akademie der Wissenschaften zu Wien, Philosophisch-historische Klasse, *Sitzungsberichte* 277, 3 (1977), 3-27.

tine periods and were perhaps the literary form with the widest public appeal. The most influential were in the literary language, but some show varying degrees of demotic.³

Stasis theory remained the core of formal rhetorical studies, although it is difficult to know how specifically that theory was applied in Byzantine courts. The legal system underwent some administrative modification, but preserved the main lines of procedure of earlier centuries.⁴ Except in trials before the senate or before a panel of bishops in ecclesiastical courts, there was a single judge who had considerable latitude in procedure; the principals might speak on their own behalf or be represented by advocates.

Trials, though often mentioned, are rarely described in enough detail to estimate the value of eloquence or rhetorical training, and few judicial speeches were published. They had of course ceased to be regarded as a literary form even in late antiquity. Michael Psellus, however, describes a trial over which he presided in August of 1056.⁵ An old monk had arranged a marriage for his adopted daughter, then still a child, with a young man of good family. The monk had influence at court and some wealth and had succeeded in getting honors for his prospective son-in-law,

³ See Cyril Mango, *Byzantium. The Empire of New Rome*, London: Weidenfeld and Nicolson, 1980, pp. 246-51.

⁴ See Louis Bréhier, *Les institutions de l'empire byzantin* (Le monde byzantin II), Paris: Michel, 1949, pp. 218-47. The *Peira* of Eustathius Romaius (second quarter of the Eleventh Century) contains the legal opinions which Eustathius delivered in a large number of trials. The procedure in court is not described, but it is possible to see what kinds of cases were prevalent, how the issues were defined, and how influence sometimes overshadowed the law. See Speros Vryonis, Jr., "The *Peira* as a Source for the History of Byzantine Aristocratic Society in the First Half of the Eleventh Century," *Studies in Honor of George C. Miles*, Beirut: American University, 1974, pp. 279-84. For the text see J. D. Zepos and P. I. Zepos, *Ius Graecoromanum* IV, Athens: Fexis, 1931.

⁵ See R. Guilland, "Un compte-rendu de procès par Psellus," *Byzantinoslavica* 20 (1959), 205-30; 21 (1960), 1-37.

including buying him the rank of protospatharius as part of the marriage agreement. Some years passed before the marriage and it became increasingly apparent to the monk that the young man would be an unsuitable husband for his daughter. Probably he was homosexual. The old monk, therefore, appealed to the empress Theodora to break the marriage agreement. She held a hearing, granted the request, and canceled the honors except for the appointment as protospatharius, but referred the question of damages to a court of which Psellus was appointed judge and in which scholars familiar with contract law participated as advisers. The old monk handled his own case; the young man was represented by an advocate. There was clearly an opportunity for oratory, but none in fact takes place. The stasis of the letter and intent of the contract could have been argued, but were not, for both litigants essentially threw themselves on the mercy of the court, the old monk because he was embarassed by the scandal and the young man's advocate because he saw little to gain for his client from protracted argument. The decision of the court was that the old monk owed the young man fifteen pounds for breaking the contract and the young man owed the old monk twenty pounds for his appointment as protospatharius. He must thus pay the five pounds difference. He claimed, however, that over time he had given the daughter at least five pounds in gifts, and the court accepted this plea and discharged the case. If the circumstances had been different, the procedure clearly provided opportunities for speech.

Some individuals gained fame as judicial orators, as is clear from Psellus' description in the *Chronographia* (6.178) of Constantine Lichudes. Lichudes had studied both rhetoric and law, and Psellus says that although he was a versatile speaker in all forms, he particularly excelled in judicial oratory, where his style was elegant and Attic. It seems clear that Attic was regarded as the appropriate diction for a formal speech before a court of law, just as Latin was in the West.

Ecclesiastical trials offered a situation more analogous to that of classical Greek courts in that decision lay with a jury of bishops rather than a single presiding judge, and prosecution and defense apparently relied more heavily on formal speech. A speech survives by Nicephorus Chumnus prosecuting Niphon (or Nephon), patriarch of Constantinople, on charges of simony in 1315.[6] It is addressed to a synod of bishops convened to hear the charge. Chumnus takes considerable pains to lay out canon law on the taking of money and other forms of corruption by Church officials, as well as citing the authority of the Bible and the Fathers. The stasis is one of fact: had Niphon actually engaged in the prescribed practices? In support of the charges, the evidence of witnesses and letters are introduced. The gravity of the charges is much stressed, and the speech as a whole has a strong emotional tone. The style may be described as *deinos*, but of practical necessity the speaker aims at clarity and is far more specific than epideictic orators, who avoid names and concrete details, but as in epideictic the language is Attic and there are reminiscences of classical literature and of Scripture. The speech is probably typical of what was heard from an able Byzantine orator speaking in an important case before an ecclesiastical court.

Michael Psellus

Michael Psellus (1018-1072 or later) is the most important orator and writer of the Middle Byzantine period and an important political figure, philosopher, and educator as well. His *Chronographia* is a major historical source for

[6] For the Greek text see J. F. Boissonade, *Anecdota Graeca e Codicibus Regiis* v, 1833; reprinted Hildesheim: Olms, 1962, pp. 255-83.

the Eleventh Century, recounting events in which Psellus took an important part as an adviser to emperors.[7] It is not only the most readable of his works, but probably the greatest piece of Byzantine literary prose which survives, far excelling the pedestrian summary characteristic of most Byzantine chronicles, yet equally avoiding the shallow imitation of Herodotus, Thucydides, or other classical historians seen in writers like Theophylactus Simocatta.

The *Chronographia* includes many references to speech, but few set orations, the most striking exception being an ethopoeia of the empress Zoe (5.2).[8] Psellus' tone throughout is quite personal; he often mentions himself, including his own speeches and his reaction to the eloquence of others, noting their ability at argumentation, style, and delivery (e.g., 4.7). He glosses over his own political defeats, exaggerates his influence and success, and reveals a personality given to enthusiasms, loyal to his friends, proud of his learning, and more philosophical than religious. In contrast to other courtiers who owed their power to family connexions or wealth, Psellus depended on his learning, his eloquence, and his wit, and not surprisingly he puts a very high, perhaps exaggerated, value on these qualities. Nevertheless, his work shows clearly that ability to argue cogently, to speak eloquently, and to adapt presentation to

[7] For the Greek text, French translation, introduction, and notes see Michel Psellos, *Chronographie ou Histoire d'un siècle de Byzance*, ed. E. Renauld, 2 vols., Paris: Les Belles Lettres, 1926; 1928. Passages are quoted from *The Chronographia of Michael Psellus*, translated from the Greek by E.R.A. Sewter, New Haven: Yale Univ. Pr., 1953. A revised version of this translation has been issued under the title *Fourteen Byzantine Rulers*, Harmondsworth, England: Penguin, 1966. See R-E, Suppl. XI, 1124-82, and C. Zervos, *Un philosophe néoplatonicien du XIe siècle: Michel Psellos. Sa vie, son oeuvre, ses luttes philosophiques, son influence*, Paris: Laroux, 1910; reprinted New York: Burt Franklin, 1973.

[8] See O. Schissel, "Die Ethopoiie der Zoe bei Michael Psellus," *BZ* 27 (129), 271-75.

the occasion and to the audience could be potent skills in the Byzantine court. Intrigue was rampant, and alliances continually shifted, but the ultimate decision-making process was oral and semipublic. Except when on military campaign or vacation, the Byzantine emperors spent much of their time sitting in state in a great hall with their council of advisers, listening to appeals and making administrative and policy decisions. The advisers were regularly called upon for their opinions (e.g., 7.47), and those who could express themselves well often won the day, but the situation encouraged flattery (7.1). At times the emperor himself spoke at some length and occasionally would address the senate or the people, as Michael V did, giving a dramatic account of his treatment of the empress Zoe (5.23). At trials the emperors could be arbitrary and unwilling to hear defenses, as was Constantine VIII (2.6) or Romanus III (3.11), and interrogation was a major element (e.g., 6.137), but sometimes even a conspirator was allowed to speak and at least one gained acquittal (6.147-49).

Another opportunity for eloquence was offered by embassies.[9] Psellus describes in detail an embassy which he undertook for Michael VI to Isaac Comnenus, who eventually gained the throne. A group of soldiers under Isaac's command came to seek promotion from the emperor. Psellus says that the emperor should have interviewed them individually, but instead he delivered an abusive speech against Isaac and refused to listen to those who defended him (7.3). As a result, the army sought to make Isaac emperor and won a battle against Michael's forces in Asia Minor. Psellus and two others were then sent by Michael to Isaac. "By my eloquence and powers of argument I was to soften him down and induce a change of attitude" (7.15). The ambassadors arrived in the evening and were cour-

[9] On other embassy speeches of this period see Hunger I, p. 149.

teously received, but any serious discussion was put off until the next day. This allowed Isaac to prepare a carefully staged reception; the use of ceremonial is an important device of persuasion throughout the Byzantine period. Isaac and part of his army assemble in an enormous tent, surrounded by a still larger force drawn up in concentric circles. The ambassadors are led through the ranks of troops, who stand in complete silence, up to the door of the tent, which is closed. After a dramatic pause it is suddenly drawn open. "The sight that met our eyes within was astonishing. It was so unexpected, and truly it was an imperial spectacle, capable of overawing anyone" (7.23). At this point the army outside broke into a series of carefully orchestrated cheers. Inside, Isaac sat on a couch covered with gold, on a high platform, wearing a magnificent robe, surrounded by his men in full armor. When the ambassadors advanced before him he asked for the letter which they bore from Michael and for the message which they brought.

Psellus was the spokesman and gives a description of his speech, bringing out its rhetorical qualities: "If the noise which was going on there had not scared me while I was speaking, and if it had not so frequently interrupted me that I forgot my long harangue, perhaps I would have recalled the actual words I had prepared beforehand. They would have occurred to me in their proper setting and sequence wherever I was developing my argument in periods, or stressing my ideas with a series of clauses rising to some climax" (7.26). This seems to suggest that he had planned to use a memory system such as that described by classical rhetoricians, though there is little evidence for study of memory by other Byzantines. "Nobody there noticed that there was subtlety in my plain speaking, but the fact was that by a careful imitation of Lysias in his use of common everyday speech, I took expressions known to the ordinary man and decked them out with delicate philosophical touches" (7.26). In other words, he used the high style, appropriate to his own position and the importance of the occasion and addressee, but he sought to be understood by all those present. Byzantine inclination to obscurity was in practice restrained in judicial and deliberative oratory and is primarily a phenomenon of epideictic and of literary composition.

Psellus goes on to say that his proemium was characterized by *deinotēs* and done artfully: he avoided all reference to guilty behavior and enumerated the honors given to Isaac and his men by the legitimate emperor. This was initially successful, but the crowd in the rear eventually cried out that Isaac must become emperor. Psellus countered this by urging an orderly progression by which Isaac would be made heir to the throne and eventually achieve it, reminding the audience how Constantine the Great had promoted his heirs. "Then, drawing together the threads of my argument, more in the manner of a syllogism, I made this comparison: 'That is how they treated their own sons, men of their flesh and blood. Isaac here is only a son by adoption . . .' and having thrown in the word 'adoption' I left the rest of the sentence in suspense" (7.30). Psellus' speech persuaded Isaac at the time to accept the offer of the rank of Caesar and heir to the throne, and Isaac was so impressed with Psellus that after the overthrow of Michael he made him his chief minister. The situation as a whole is an interesting example of what we have earlier called the clash of rhetorics, the confrontation of classical rhetoric with systematic use of external means of persuasion, seen here in the use of ceremony and the inhibiting effect of Isaac's army. The passage well illustrates the survival in Byzantium of primary deliberative oratory on a classical model and the limitations on its use.

In several passages in the *Chronographia* Psellus turns aside from his historical narrative to comment on the study

MICHAEL PSELLUS

of rhetoric or of philosophy or on the relationship between rhetoric and the writing of history. He notes that he had composed many panegyrics of Constantine IX in which he lavished praise on him. That praise was not undeserved, he claims, but it deliberately left aside the negative qualities of the emperor which must be described in historical writing (6.25; 6.161). Constantine was not himself an advanced student of literature or an orator, but he admired eloquence and invited to his court the finest speakers from all parts of the empire (6.35). Most of these were older men, but Psellus himself, then only twenty-five years old, was among them. He was at the time seeking to train his tongue by rhetoric to become a fine speaker and to refine his mind by systematic study of philosophy.

> I soon mastered the rhetoric enough to be able to distinguish the central theme of an argument and logically connect it with my main and second points. I also learned not to stand in complete awe of the art, nor to follow its precepts in everything like a child, and I even made certain contributions of a minor character. Then I applied myself to the study of philosophy [=dialectic], and having acquainted myself sufficiently with the art of reasoning, both deductive, from cause to immediate effect, and inductive, tracing causes from all manner of effects, I turned to natural science and aspired to a knowledge of the fundamental principles of philosophy through mathematics. (6.36)

He also mentions studying music and astronomy (6.39). In other words, he proceeded from the trivium of grammar, rhetoric, and dialectic to the quadrivium. Anna Comnena, describing her education in the Twelfth Century, similarly speaks (*Alexiad*, Preface 1) of studying grammar, rhetoric, Plato and Aristotle, and the quadrivium, though this was doubtless unusual for a woman.[10] Psellus says that philosophy was moribund in his time and the teachers ignorant, but one teacher eventually drew his attention to Aristotle and Plato, and from study of their works he went on to Plotinus, Porphyry, Iamblichus, and Proclus (6.37-38).

"Discourse has two branches," he continues (6.41):[11]

> One comprises the works of the orators, and the philosophers have arrogated the other. The first, knowing nothing of the deeper things, issues forth merely in a mighty torrent of noisy words; it concerns itself with the composition of speeches, sets forth certain rules for the arrangement of arguments on political subjects and for the various divisions of political orations, lends distinction to the spoken word, and in general beautifies the language of politics. Philosophy is less concerned with the embellishment of words. Its aim is rather to explore the nature of the universe, to unravel its secrets. . . . Now I had no mind to follow the example of most other men and emulate their experiences—men who study the art of the orator while despising the science of the philosopher, or else engross themselves in philosophy and enjoy the riches to be found in the marvels of thought, but contemn the glories of rhetoric and the skill required to arrange and divide the various parts of a speech. Thus, from time to time, when I compose an oration, I introduce some scientific proof, not without some elegance. Many persons have reproached me for this and they dislike the way I brighten a philosophic discourse with the graceful arts of rhetoric. My purpose in this is to assist the reader when he finds it difficult to abosrb some deeper

---

[10] See B. Lieb, "Quelques aspects de l'éducation à Byzance au XIᵉ siècle," *Byzantinoslavica* 21 (1960), 38-47.

[11] See Sewter, *Chronographia* (supra, n. 7), p. 129. I have substituted "discourse" for Sewter's "literature" as a translation of *logoi*.

thought, and so to prevent his losing the thread of philosophical argument.

He goes on to discuss "the new philosophy, based on the mysteries of our Christian religion" and his studies of theology (6.42).

Psellus thus embraces and seeks to apply the concept of philosophical rhetoric. He knew the *Phaedrus* well and wrote an exegesis of it, which contains extracts from the commentary of Hermeias,[12] and his views were influential on others. Like Gorgias, Psellus recognized the power of rhetoric, but like Plato he thought that power must be restrained. "If one were willing to bring into play the full force of one's powers of argument," he says (6.176), "it would be possible to convince any intelligent audience of anything. To me, however, such feats are not to be commended—I loathe the kind of clever dialectic that perverts the truth."

Psellus returns to the nature of rhetoric in a passage where he describes the loss of favor at court which impelled him to enter a monastery. Constantine IX was, he says (6.197), a man who easily tired of enthusiasms. In talking with him it was necessary to seek variety. Psellus would discourse to him on philosophy, but then,

> When I saw that he was becoming bored with these lectures, and that he wanted to change the subject to something more to his taste, I would turn to the muse of rhetoric and introduce him to another aspect of excellence, delighting him with word harmonies and rhythmic cadences, composition and figures of speech (which lend the art its peculiar force). The function of rhetoric is not merely to deceive by persuasive argument, or to deck itself out with ambiguous sentiments; it is an exact sci-

[12] For the Greek text see Psellus, *Scripta Minora* I, ed. Edward Kutz, Milan: Vita e Pensiero, 1936, pp. 437-40.

ence. On the one hand, it expresses philosophic ideas; on the other, by means of its flowery imagery, it beautifies them. The listener is equally charmed by both. Rhetoric teaches a man to think clearly, undisturbed by the association of words; to classify, to analyse, to make one's meaning plain without undue fuss. Its peculiar excellence lies in its freedom from confusion, its clarity, the way it suits itself to time or to circumstances. By dwelling on all these points I inspired him to a love of the art. But if I perceived that he was growing weary, I would alter my tactics and pretend that my memory was failing, or that my fire, after the manner of Hermogenes' heat, had almost burnt itself out through its own excess.[13]

He alludes of course to Hermogenes' collapse as a sophist after a brilliant early career, as described by Philostratus. The stress on clarity is important as a counterbalance to the view of some modern scholars that obscurity was the dominant value in Byzantine rhetoric.

From these passages and others it seems clear that primary rhetoric flourished in the Eleventh Century and that the discipline was not studied only as an aid to literary composition. The emphasis on stasis theory seen in the commentaries was intended to produce clarity of thought and intellectual rigor, and style was believed to secure varied and effective expression of ideas. It is the utility of rhetoric for speech which must be viewed as the basic reason the discipline survived with such strength. Application of rhetoric to literary composition in part derives from this, though it was certainly also influenced by Byzantine traditionalism and elitism.

Psellus had private pupils and was for a while the head

[13] See Sewter, *Chronographia* (supra, n. 7), pp. 193-94.

of a school of philosophy and rhetoric established by Constantine IX in 1045, another stage in the checkered history of the "university."[14] In this position he was apparently succeeded by his student John Italus (see Anna Comnena *Alexiad*, 5.8-9). Psellus also wrote several works on rhetoric which would be useful for students. One is a summary of Dionysius of Halicarnassus' treatise *On Composition*.[15] Another is a *Synopsis of Rhetorical Ideas* (v, pp. 601-5 Walz). A third is a summary of the rhetorical handbook of Longinus.[16] Still another is a versified summary of rhetoric in over five hundred lines, based on Hermogenes, but with references to Gregory of Nazianzus (III, pp. 687-703 Walz). Versification was presumably intended as a mnemonic device to assist the student in learning the system.

The influence of Gregory is very strong in this period. Psellus composed an essay on the styles of Gregory, Basil, Chrysostom, and Gregory of Nyssa, showing how they combined the Hermogenic ideas.[17] All of his own funeral orations show the strong influence of Gregory. These speeches are perhaps the finest Byzantine examples of the

[14] See Wanda Wolska-Conus, "Les écoles de Psellos et de Xiphilinos sous Constantin IX Monomaque," *Travaux et Mémoires* (Paris: Centre de recherches d'histoire et civilisation byzantine) 6 (1976), 223-43.

[15] See Germaine Aujac, "Michel Psellos et Denys d'Halicarnasse: le traité sur la composition des éléments du langage," *Revue des études byzantines* 33 (1975), 257-75.

[16] See Paul Gautier, "Michel Psellos et la rhétorique de Longin," *Prometheus* 3 (1977), 193-203.

[17] For the Greek text see Michaelis Pselli *De Gregorii Theologi Charactere Iudicium, accedit eiusdem De Joannis Chrysostomi Charactere Judicium ineditum*, Leipzig: Noske, 1912; A. Meyer, "Psellos' Rede über den rhetorischen Character des Gregorius von Nazianzus," *BZ* 20 (1911), 27-100. On Psellus' own style see Emile Renauld, *Etude de la langue et du style de Michel Psellos*, Paris: Picard, 1920; Gertrud Böhlig, *Untersuchungen zum rhetorischen Sprachgebrauch der Byzantiner, mit besonderer Berüchsichtigung der Schriften des Michael Psellos*, Berlin: Akademie-Verlag, 1956.

genre, but unfortunately not yet easily available in good texts or with aids to the nonspecialist reader.[18] We have, however, a good edition of the speech for Nicolaus of the Fair Source, with a detailed French résumé of its contents.[19] Psellus' most important funeral oration is probably that for Xiphilinus, with whom he was closely associated but then quarreled.[20] Xiphilinus was the greatest legal scholar of the age, and Psellus gives considerable attention to the law in this speech. All of Psellus' funeral orations emphasize the moral and theological virtues of their subjects and in so doing resemble encomiastic saints' lives. Similar, though not a funeral oration, is Psellus' encomium of John Mauropus, of which a structural analysis and Italian translation have been published.[21] An example of a monody by Psellus is his speech on Hagia Sophia, damaged in an earthquake.[22]

Middle Byzantine Rhetoricians

From the remarkable figure of Psellus we may turn to survey the work of more typical teachers of rhetoric in the Tenth, Eleventh, and Twelfth Centuries. They are characteristically commentators on the Aphthonian-Hermogenic corpus, which remained standard in the schools. Much of their work is a chain of traditional material drawn from earlier sources, though occasional new emphases can be detected. Much of it is also anonymous, such as the enor-

[18] For the Greek text see C. N. Sathas, *Mesaionike Bibliotheke: Bibliotheca Graeca Medii Aevi* IV, Paris: Maisonneuve, 1876; reprinted Athens: Gregoriades, 1972, pp. 301-462.

[19] See Paul Gautier, "Eloge funèbre de Nicolas de la Belle Source par Michel Psellos, moine à l'Olympe," *Byzantina* 6 (1974), 9-69.

[20] See Sathas IV (supra, n. 18), pp. 421-62.

[21] See Michele Psello, *Encomio per Giovanni, piissimo metropolita di Euchaita e protosincello*, introduction, translation, and commentary by Rosario Anastasi, Padua: CEDAM, 1968.

[22] See P. Würthle, *Die Monodie des Michael Psellos auf den Einsturz der Hagia Sophia* (Rhetorische Studien VI), Paderborn: Schöningh, 1917.

mous commentary found in *Parisinus Graecus* 1983 and other manuscripts which takes up the greater part of Volume Seven of Walz's *Rhetores Graeci*. Probably assembled from older material in the Tenth Century, it furnished a reference work for teachers to draw on in their classes. About some of these teachers we are reasonably well informed, though exact dates are rarely possible and many details obscure. A full history of Byzantine rhetorical studies will require patient study, not only of available texts, but of the manuscripts in which they are transmitted and of materials not yet identified or published which are contained in other manuscripts. The following account is roughly chronological and contains some notice of material other than commentaries which are of interest in the history of rhetoric. However, it is selective and does not attempt to discuss surviving examples of oratory, preaching, or literary composition of a rhetorical nature.

We may begin with John Kyriotes Geometres, who lived in Constantinople in the second half of the Tenth Century, taught rhetoric at some time in his career, and wrote commentaries on Aphthonius and to Hermogenes' *On Staseis* and *On Method*, perhaps also to other works in the Hermogenic corpus.[23] These do not survive as such, but material from them was incorporated into later commentaries, for example by Doxapatres (see II, pp. 123, 206, and 341 Walz). In the commentary to Aphthonius John inveighed against the ignorance of John of Sardis (VI, pp. 521-22 Walz) and insisted on the view that obscurity is sometimes a virtue (II, p. 226 Walz).[24] He also wrote an

---

[23] See Stephen Glöckner, *Ueber den Kommentar des Johannes Doxapatres zu den Staseis des Hermogenes*, Programm des Gymansiums zu Bunzlau, Kirchain: Schmersow, 1908, pp. 26-27; Theodor Gerber, *Quae in Hermogenis Scriptis Vetustiorum Commentariorum Vestigia Deprehendi Possit*, Dissertation Kiel: Boldt, 1891, pp. 29-41 on Doxapatres.

[24] See Kustas, pp. 24-25 and 90-93.

extant encomium of Gregory of Nazianzus and scholia to some of his speeches.[25] Although, as we have seen, scholia to Gregory were written in late antiquity and examples from Gregory are found in Sixth-Century handbooks of figures, this trend faltered in the Early Byzantine period. With Geometres and Siceliotes the Christianizing of rhetorical examples resumes vigorously. Six of Geometres' progymnasmata survive, of which two are *ekphraseis* and four encomia, praising the oak and the apple.[26] They combine allusions to classical literature and to Christian doctrine. John was a leading writer and churchman of his times whose other works include theological treatises, biblical commentaries, sermons, and poetry of considerable merit. His sermon on the Assumption is an excellent example of that tradition of preaching characterized by poetic imagery from the Old Testament.[27]

After an important civil career, when he rose to protospatharius, John became bishop of Melitene and finally retired to a monastery in Constantinople.[28] Approximate dates for his life are known from historical references in his poems, such as the epitaph on John I, who died in 976

---

[25] See Pietro Tacchi-Venturi, "De Ioanne Geometra eiusque in S. Gregorium Nazianzenum inedita Laudatione," *Publicazione periodica dell' Accademia di conferenze storico-giuridiche* XIV, Rome: delle Pace, 1893, pp. 133-62; Jan Sajdak, *Historia Critica Scholastorum et Commentatorum Gregorii Nazianzeni* (Melemata Patristica I) Cracow: Gebethner, 1914, pp. 89-95.

[26] For English translation see A. R. Littlewood, *The Progymnasmata of Ioannes Geometres*, Amsterdam: Hakkert, 1972; idem, "A Byzantine Oak and Its Classical Acorn: The Literary Artistry of Geometres, Progymnasmata 1," *Jahrbuch der österreichischen Byzantistik* 29 (1980), 133-44.

[27] See Antoine Wenger, *L'assumption de la T. S. Vièrge dans la tradition byzantine du VIe au Xe siècle* (Archives de l'orient chrétien V), Paris: Institut français d'études byzantines, 1955, pp. 185-205 and 363-415.

[28] See F. Scheidweiler, "Studium zu Johannes Geometres II. Leben und Schicksal des Johannes Geometres," *BZ* 45 (1952), 300-319.

(PG CVI, 903). Some of his epigrams reveal his scholarly interests, such as those on Sophocles, Aristotle, Porphyry, and Simplicius. One, on his departure to the monastery, implies that he has now put all worldly learning behind him:

> Trojans and Greeks fighting each other
> For the sake of one body (Helen) fell in battle for ten years.
> Wisemen have quarreled for ten thousand years
>   Over a word or a letter,
> But God has snatched me from arms and the tumult
>   To the knowledge and splendor of the Trinity.
> Some give great value to syllogisms, arguments, and words;
>   The One God has knowledge,
> He who is without beginning, is Spirit, and is Triune Light.
>
> (PG CVI, 921-22)

John Siceliotes may have been born in Sicily as his name suggests, but seems to have been a teacher of rhetoric in Constantinople in the early Eleventh Century, later than Geometres, but before Doxapatres, who made use of his work.[29] There survives an extensive commentary to Hermogenes' *On Ideas*, written in extremely tortured Greek (VI, pp. 56-504 Walz; Prolegomenon in *PS*, pp. 393-420). He also wrote commentaries on stasis and invention and scholia to Aelius Aristides.[30] Kustas sees in him the most original and characteristically Byzantine of the commentators.[31] Not only are obscurity and *emphasis*, or indirect

---

[29] On the possible date of the historical allusion of VI, p. 447 Walz, see Conrad Bursian, "Der Rhetor Menandros und seine Schriften," Akademie der Wissenschaften zu Munich, Philosophisch-philologische Klasse, *Abhandlungen* 16, 3 (1882), 13.

[30] See *PS*, p. 409-10, and Friedrich Walter Lenz, *Aristeidesstudien*, Berlin: Akademie-Verlag, 1964, pp. 97-99 and 113-17.

[31] See Kustas, p. 21.

expression, given high value, both in theory and practice, but the process of Christianization of the illustrative material and the critical principles already evident in Geometres is greatly advanced. Here is how Siceliotes begins his Prolegomenon:

> For those desiring political knowledge and eager, by means of great learning in this subject, to cleanse the intellectual faculty of the soul from material corruption, both (1) in the interests of an accurate discovery of what is effective by a change of hidden ignorance into a secure way of daily life, toward which we are moved from insensible and continuous satiation, and (2) in the interests of the diminution or tightening up of our capricious emotions and impulses in the direction of a measured and firm moderation and equality of conflicting extremes, in which process there occurs a kind of contest of the virtues and those things which are not virtues as praise and blame clash against each other, and in addition (3) in the interests of the attainment and the righteousness of justice, toward which those who are persuaded progress (in the interests of all of these), the secret rites and mysteries of civil rhetoric and the rituals of rhetorical methods, undisclosed to the accursed, are necessary. For of philosophy clearly the fairest part and first characteristic is that it seeks improvement through order (since we judge that God is constituted as by nature logical), both universally and particularly in the case of souls and bodies, households and cities, caring for the better by expulsion of what is perverted or borne along in a disordered or disorderly way by discordant forces; and more here than in the case of other sciences, what is logically divided advances upon the subjects in a practical way. For what is profitable in a few cases only does not prevail nor what is in turn comprehended in other

things, as letters are among signs and voices among sound intervals, but being the artisan of the foundation, the base, and the structure and disposing and managing and straightening the parts of our intellectual being, it [the philosophical principle] established them in order, after which, bringing forth political philosophers, it completes whole cities and towns, acting in accordance with the persuasion of the tongue. Such was Miltiades and he [=Themistocles] who in jealousy of the victories of Miltiades did not allow himself to sleep; despite many thousands of opponents by land and sea, under a modest banner they prevailed over Attica. Such was Demosthenes, the Nile of the Athenians rather than the Cephisus or Ilissus rivers, who opposed the machinations and bribes of Philip; who, if he had had power equal to his words in influencing the Athenians would have extinguished "the world-consuming brand of Olympias" [=Alexander the Great], and the Macedonians would have been washed away by the torrents of a Paianian, and the nations would have kissed the people of Erichthonius. Such were Basil and Gregory [of Nazianzus] and our golden ocean, sweet [of tongue] [=John Chrysostom], and all the stirrings of the great river [=the Fathers of the Church] by whom the churches of God are gladdened and souls and natures wicked and lawless are overwhelmed, hand to hand, in torrents pouring from blackness, and all the earth is changed and brought back to order and Truth. (PS, pp. 393-95)

Under this tortured maze of verbiage, with its Christian imagery and allusion to the thought of Plato and Aristotle, perhaps also of Isocrates, lie common late antique views of rhetoric and philosophy. Rhetoric is a form of knowledge, John is saying, with practical applications; its study and practice is a discipline which aids moral choice and the achievement of justice. It is a logical study which presupposes the dialectical process of definition and division; that is in accordance with God's will; historically, rhetoric has been an important factor in political evolution: the political leadership of Miltiades and Themistocles once saved Greece; the eloquence of Demosthenes almost did so again; Saints Basil and Gregory are the great models of Christian preaching. John seeks to give emphasis to the ideas and to imply a profundity of thought by the tortured form of expression. He writes for the few who understand and is providing a model for the kind of high-style rhetorical Greek a student should be able to write once he had completed John's course.

A third important Middle Byzantine commentator is John Doxapatres, often cited earlier since he sometimes preserves information not otherwise known about late antique rhetoric. From his references to the emperors Romanus III (1028-1034) and Michael IV (1034-1041) (II, pp. 309 and 508 Walz) Doxapatres can be dated toward the middle of the Eleventh Century in Constantinople. His *Rhetorical Homilies*, which take up much of Volume Two of Walz's *Rhetores Graeci*, are a commentary on Aphthonius. They frequently cite Geometres and show the Christianizing movement of the times, but are otherwise largely dependent on a collection of scholia of unknown authorship which also contributed to the anonymous commentary material in *Parisinus Graecus* 1983 and 2977.[32] Doxapatres also wrote commentaries to *On Staseis*, *On Invention*, and *On Ideas* which are unpublished except for their prolegomena (*PS*, nos. 20, 27, and 33).[33]

The alphabetical encyclopedia *Suda* (once thought to be the work of an author named Suidas) has been mentioned

---

[32] See Hugo Rabe, "Aus Rhetoren-Handschriften 3. Die Quellen des Doxapatres in den Homilien zu Aphthonius," *RhM* 62 (1907), 559-86.

[33] See Glöckner, *Doxapatres* (supra, n. 23).

several times in these pages and was compiled in Constantinople by an unknown author or authors about the end of the Tenth Century.[34] It is a mine of sometimes reliable information on classical and Christian writers, historical personages, unusual words, and Attic vocabulary. Apparently it was largely compiled from selections and abridgments of earlier works.[35] Numerous orators and rhetoricians are included, but only a few technical terms of rhetoric: *stasis* and *schēma* are omitted; *idea logou* is simply identified as *charactēr*. Probably rhetorical terminology was regarded as too well known to be given special treatment.

In Constantinople education in grammar, rhetoric, and other subjects was apparently readily available even before the reestablishment of the "university" under Psellus' direction. The Patriarchal School may also have existed in the Tenth or Eleventh Century, though details about it are not known until the Twelfth. Outside of Constantinople, rhetoric was largely studied in schools sponsored by local bishops or in a few monasteries where the authorities took an unusual interest in education. This was true not only in the East, but in Greek-speaking areas of Italy and Sicily. Some of the material in the anonymous commentary of Volume Seven of Walz can be attributed to Nilus the Monk, and he may in turn be Nilus of Rossano (in Calabria) who died in 1005 after a long life and is well known as the propagator of Greek Basilian monasticism in Italy and the founder of the monastery of Grottaferrata, near Rome.[36]

[34] Suidae *Lexicon*, ed. Ada Adler, 5 vols. Leipzig: Teubner, 1928-38. See Franz Dölger, *Der Titel des sog. Suidaslexikons*, Munich: Bayerische Akademie der Wissenschaften, 1936.
[35] See R-E IVA, 675-717.
[36] See Gloeckner, p. 4, and Venceslla Borzemska-Lesnikowska, "De Anonymo Hermogenis *Statuum* Interprete cum Nilo Comparato," *Travaux de la société des sciences et des lettres de Wrocław*, Series A, no. 42 (1950), 19-43. Nilus' life is in *Acta Sanctorum*, Septembris VII, pp. 259-320.

Certainly the material, which presupposes the Hermogenic commentators of late antiquity, cannot be attributed to Nilus of Sinai, who died in 430,[37] though there were other monks named Nilus. Nilus of Rossano, however, did found a Greek library and scriptorium, and study of rhetoric in tenth-century Italy is not unlikely.[38] The probability is strengthened by the work of Christophorus, who seems to have been a monk at Grottaferrata in the time of abbott Nicolaus II (1131-1140) and who also wrote a commentary to Hermogenes' On Staseis.[39] Both Nilus and Christophorus draw on George of Alexandria, which is unusual, and it is tempting to try to define a separate West-Greek tradition in the study of rhetoric. This study would, however, require a first-hand familiarity with the manuscripts and information about their history which is not currently available.

In Constantinople, around the end of the Eleventh Century, John the Deacon, logothete of Hagia Sophia, wrote commentaries to Hermogenes' On Ideas and to the treatise On Method. The latter work survives in a Fourteenth-Century manuscript and is apparently the oldest extant commentary on this part of the corpus. It draws, however, on a lost earlier source which was also used in the Twelfth Century by Gregory of Corinth.[40] The illustrative material is classical, not Christian, and includes quotations not otherwise known from several plays of Euripides.

[37] For his works see PG LXXIX.
[38] See Antonio Rocchi, *De Coenobio Cryptoferratensi eiusque Bibliotheca et Codicibus Praesertim Graeci Commentarii*, Tusculum: Tusculana, 1893.
[39] See Hugo Rabe, "De Christophori Commentario in Hermogenis Librum *Peri Staseon*," RhM 50 (1895), 241-49.
[40] See Hugo Rabe, "Aus Rhetoren-Handschriften 5. Des Diakonen und Logotheten Johannes zu Hermogenes *Peri Methodou Deinotes*," RhM 63 (1908), 127-51, and "6. Weitere Textquellen für Johannes Diaconos," ibid., pp. 512-17.

Gregory of Corinth was metropolitan of that Greek city in the first half of the Twelfth Century and the author of numerous theological and grammatical works.[41] One of these is devoted to classical Greek dialects,[42] another to syntax.[43] His commentary to the Hermogenic treatise *On Method* (VII, pp. 1088-1352 Walz) survives in both a longer and shorter version. The illustrative material is largely classical, but there are references to Gregory of Nazianzus (pp. 1138 and 1177).[44] A work on tropes attributed to Gregory (III, pp. 215-26 Spengel) and in some manuscripts to Trypho is probably by neither.[45]

Before becoming metropolitan of Corinth, Gregory taught in Constantinople and was apparently a member of the faculty of the Patriarchal School, which flourished there in the Twelfth Century.[46] To move from its faculty to a bishopric was a regular occurrence. The senior faculty was four in number, with assistants teaching in various churches in the city. These four were the teachers (*didaskaloi*) of the gospel, of the apostles, and of the psalter and the master of the rhetors. In addition to teaching, they were expected to deliver panegyrics, funeral orations, and other speeches.

---

[41] See *R-E* VII, 1848-52; Atanasio Kominis, *Gregorio Pardos, Metropolitano Corinto, e la sua opera*, Rome: Istituto di Studi Bizantini e Neoellenici, 1960; Daniel Donnet, "Précisions sur les oeuvres profanes de Grégoire de Corinth," *Bulletin de l'institut historique Belge de Rome* 36 (1966), 81-97.

[42] See Gregorii Corinthii et aliorum Grammaticorum *Libri de Dialectis Linguae Graecae*, ed. Godofredus H. Schaeffer, Leipzig: Weigel, 1811.

[43] See Daniel Donnet, *Le Traité Peri syntaxeos logou de Grégoire de Corinth. Etude de la tradition manuscrite, édition, traduction, et commentaire*, Rome and Brussels: L'institut historique Belge de Rome, 1967.

[44] On the sources see Gerber, *Commentariorum Vestigia* (supra, n. 23).

[45] See *R-E* VII, 1851.

[46] See Robert Browning, "The Patriarchal School of Constantinople in the Twelfth Century," *Byzantion* 32 (1962), 167-202, and 33 (1963) 11-40, esp. pp. 19-20 on Gregory.

Many were published and some have survived, especially in a codex in the Escorial written in the Thirteenth Century, which contains a large collection of speeches, chiefly from the late Twelfth Century.[47] One master of the rhetors was Nicephorus Basilices, who was removed from office for theological reasons in 1156. There survives a collection of progymnasmata by Nicephorus (I, pp. 421-525 Walz), including myths, narratives on classical subjects, a Christian and a classical chria, classical *anaskeuē*, *kataskeuē*, and *gnōmai*, and twenty-three ethopoeiae, mostly Christian. Examples of the latter include: what Hades said when Lazarus was raised from the dead; what the Virgin said when Christ turned water into wine; what Saint Peter said when about to be crucified by Nero.

Another person known to have been master of the rhetors in the Patriarchal School was Eustathius, who was named archbishop of Thessalonika in 1175. Many of his panegyrics and sermons survive, as well as his commentaries on Homer, Pindar, the geographer Dionysius Periegetes, and Aristophanes. In the Homeric commentary he makes considerable use of the Hermogenic ideas of style. He does not seem to have written commentaries on the rhetorical corpus.[48]

John Tzetzes (c. 1110–c. 1185) was a teacher of grammar and rhetoric and an irascible polymath who wrote commentaries on Homer, Hesiod, and Aristophanes, and versified surveys of classical learning. His verse lacks poetic merit and, like Psellus' summary of Hermogenes, was per-

[47] See Krumbacher, pp. 470-76.
[48] See Peter Wirth, "Untersuchungen zur byzantinischen Rhetorik des zwölften Jahrhunderts mit besonderer Berücksichtigung des Erzbischofs Eustathios von Thessalonike," Dissertation Munich, 1960, esp. pp. 119-41; Browning, *Byzantion* 32 (1962) (supra, n. 46), 186-93; Gertrud Lindberg, *Studies in Hermogenes and Eustathius. The Theory of Ideas and Its Application in the Commentaries of Eustathios on the Epics of Homer*, Lund: Lindell, 1977.

MIDDLE BYZANTINE RHETORICIANS

haps intended to provide a mnemonic aid to mastering the contents, but it better illustrates the ingenuity of the author in putting intractable material into meter. The most ambitious of Tzetzes' metrical efforts is commonly known as the *Chiliades* (ten thousand lines).[49] It devotes three separate sections to Hermogenic rhetoric: 6.79.743-817 describes the five-part corpus with some criticism and special attention to the ideas of style; 8.169.94-120 describes *paroidia* and *kollēsis* as found in the Hermogenic *On Method*; 11.369.102-358 again describes the whole system, with Tzetzes' comments. Tzetze's *Logismoi*, believed to be an earlier work, survives in large part in a variety of manuscripts, but only portions of it have ever been printed.[50] There is considerable similarity between the *Logismoi* and the passages on rhetoric in the *Chiliades*, suggesting that Tzetzes reutilized his own earlier material. He makes some use of the earlier work of Doxapatres and was in turn known to Gregory of Corinth.[51] A later epitomizer utilized the *Logismoi* for a versified account of his own (III, pp. 617-69 Walz).

Although the Aphthonian-Hermogenic corpus was the basis of rhetorical study in the Middle Byzantine period,[52] dialogues of Plato and works of Dionysius of Halicarnassus

[49] For the text see *Ioannis Tzetzae Historiae*, ed. P.A.M. Leone, Naples: Libreria Scientifica Editrice, 1968. See *R-E* VIIA, 1989-91; Wolfram Hörander, "Bemerkungen zu den *Chiliades* des Ioannis Tzetzes," *Byzantion* 39 (1969), 108-20.

[50] III, pp. 670-86 Walz, and J. A. Cramer, *Anecdota Graeca e Coddicibus Manuscriptis Bibliothecarum Oxoniensium* IV, Oxford Univ. Pr., 1837, pp. 1-148.

[51] See VII, pp. 1098, 1157, and 1186 Walz.

[52] The anonymous *Rhetorica Marciana* is the chief commentary on the Hermogenic corpus dating from this period. It replaces illustrative material from Demosthenes with citations of Gregory of Nazianzus and in the commentary on method borrows from Gregory of Corinth. A portion is printed in III, pp. 610-14 Walz. See Vittorio de Falco, "Trattato retorico bizantino (*Rhetorica Marciana*)," *Atti della società liguistica de scienze e lettere de Genova* 9, 2 (1930), 71-124.

and other rhetorical writers were known to some advanced students. We have already seen evidence for this in the case of Psellus. A letter by Michael Italicus, dated to about 1120, draws on the discussion of rhetoric in the *Gorgias* and *Phaedrus*.[53] Attention to the *Rhetoric* of Aristotle also increased. The best manuscript of the *Rhetoric* (*Parisinus Graecus* 1741) was copied in the Tenth Century, and John Italus made an epitome of the *Rhetoric* in the late Eleventh Century.[54] In the Twelfth Century, commentaries were written on several works of Aristotle to which there were no commentaries from late antiquity, including the *Politics* and the *Rhetoric*.[55] It is likely that Alexandrian scholars of late antiquity had lectured on the *Rhetoric* at least occasionally at the end of a course on the *Organon*, but no versions of their interpretations seem to have been published. From the mid-Twelfth Century, however, there are two commentaries on the *Rhetoric*, showing that it was a subject of study at that time.[56] The longer commentary, which is anonymous, contains a contemporary historical reference to events of 1126; the shorter commentary, which lacks the second half of Book Three, is attributed by the manuscripts to an unknown Stephanus and seems to have been written between 1151 and 1154 by a teacher of grammar, rhetoric, and philosophy in Constantinople.[57]

[53] See Ugo Criscuolo, "L'epistola di Michele Italico ad Irene Ducas," *Epetēris Hetaireias Byzantinōn Spoudōn* 38 (1971), 57-70.

[54] See Rudolf Kassel, *Der Text der Aristotelischen Rhetorik. Prolegomena zu einer kritische Ausgabe*, Berlin and New York: de Gruyter, 1971; Iohannis Itali *Opuscula Selecta* II, ed. Gregorius Cérétéli, Tiflis: Sachelmtzipho Universiteti, 1924, pp. 33-46.

[55] See Robert Browning, "An Unpublished Funeral Oration on Anna Comnena," *Proceedings of the Cambridge Philological Society*, no. 188 (1962), 1-12, esp. pp. 6-8 on references to commentaries sponsored by Anna Comnena.

[56] See *Commentaria in Aristotelem Graeca* XXI, 2: *Anonymi et Stephani in Artem Rhetoricam*, ed. Hugo Rabe, Berlin: Reimer, 1896.

[57] See ibid., p. ix, and *R-E* IIIA, 2364-69.

The two commentaries have a number of similarities. Both lack a prolegomenon as well as the beginning of the commentary on Book One, which might have told us something about their author's objectives, but both commentators clearly viewed the *Rhetoric* as a part of the *Organon* and to be studied primarily as a work on logic. Yet both commentators show an interest in rhetoric for itself and make an effort to integrate Aristotle's thought with the authoritative teaching of Hermogenes. For example, Stephanus has the following note on the last sentence of the Second Book of the *Rhetoric*: "We have been taught that one heading is that concerned with maxims, enthymemes, examples, and, in a word, the *ennoia* which we learned in the part of the "Rhetoric" of Hermogenes called *On Ideas*. We will (next) be instructed about the two remaining headings in the Third Book which is On Style. This is the second heading and the third is On Arrangement, which is like Method in Hermogenes" (p. 308 Rabe). This is incorrect, since *On Ideas* corresponds to Aristotle's discussion of style and Aristotle's discussion of arrangement to the Hermogenic *On Invention*. Nor, in another area, is it correct to say, as does the anonymous (p. 223 Rabe), that to Aristotle a syllogism has two premises, an enthymeme only one. Stephanus, but not the anonymous, refers to Aphthonius as well as Hermogenes and he provides visual diagrams to elucidate some of Aristotle's thought. Both commentators add examples from Christian sources. Gregory of Nazianzus is of course the major model, but the anonymous also refers to Basil and Stephanus to John Chrysostom. Despite their similarities and the fact that they are both preserved in the same Fourteenth-Century manuscript (*Vaticanus Graecus* 1340), the two commentaries seem largely independent of each other. Stephanus refers to earlier unidentified commentaries and sometimes corrects them; it is possible that one of these was the anonymous commentary. The latter may represent the writing out of what was originally marginal scholia in manuscripts of the *Rhetoric* with the lemmata incorporated in the text, whereas Stephanus has a personal tone and seems to be lecturing to a class. Like the late antique commentaries of Hermeias and Olympiodorus on Plato, the rhetorical content of medieval Greek commentaries on the *Rhetoric* deserves fuller study.

The Later Byzantine Period

We have seen that progymnasmata played an important part in Byzantine education and that model progymnasmata were composed in the Middle Byzantine period, for example, by Geometres and Nicephorus. A philosophical extension of such exercises is the double prosopopoeia of Michael Choniates, with a speech for the body and a speech for the soul, composed in the early Thirteenth Century.[58] Many of the forms, such as the ecphrasis, the encomium, and the ethopoeia, were of course regularly incorporated into other forms of writing and speech.

Declamation on judicial and deliberative themes (*meletai*) were also practiced in Byzantine schools. The passage from the Prolegomenon of John Doxapatres, cited earlier in this chapter, clearly refers to it, and the preservation throughout the Byzantine period of the declamations of Libanius and of works such as the *Diaereseis* of Sopatros also reflects an interest in themes for declamation. Original declamations were also composed and published increasingly in the Twelfth, Thirteenth, and Fourteenth Centuries. One example by Nicephorus Basilices is known[59] and two by George of Cyprus, who in 1283 became the patri-

[58] See Cyprien Kern, "La prosopopée de Michel Acominate," *Actes du VIe Congrès International d'Etudes Byzantines,* 1950; reprinted Nendeln: Kraus, 1978, pp. 261-78.

[59] See Antonio Garzya, "Una declamazione giudiziara di Niceforo Basilice," *Epetēris Hetaireias Byzantinōn Spoudōn* 36 (1968), 81-103.

arch Gregory II. The latter are replies to declamations by Libanius and included among his works.[60] There is in addition a collection of thirteen declamations by George Pachymeres (1242-1310), who is otherwise well known as the author of a history of the period 1242-1308 and of an exegetical compendium of Aristotelian philosophy in twelve books, as well as a textbook on the quadrivium.[61] Pachymeres also wrote progymnasmata (I, pp. 549-96 Walz). His themes are strictly classical, not Christian, which is a characteristic development of the Later Byzantine period. Additional declamations survive by Pachymeres' younger contemporary Thomas Magister and by later writers.[62]

The classicism of the Late Byzantine period seems actually to have been enhanced by political decline. In 1204 Constantinople and its European territory was captured by Latins. The Greek emperors set up their court in Nicaea, where the heritage of Orthodoxy and Hellenism was carefully nurtured. In 1261 Michael VIII, first ruler of the dynasty of the Palaeologi, regained the ancient capital and Byzantine culture entered its final flowering, though on a basis of political weakness, until the fall of the city to the Turks in 1453. Throughout this period of nearly two hundred years, classical scholarship flourished and education in it was regarded as essential for governmental and ecclesiastical position. It has been suggested that one of the reasons for the political weakness of the late empire was a preference in public life for scholars, interested in theology, philosophy, and literature, over more practically experienced administrators.[63] A symbol of the spirit of the times is that the word "Hellene," long used to refer to

[60] VI, pp. 52-82, and VII, pp. 142-79, Foerster.
[61] See P. Tannery, *Quadrivium de Georges Pachymere* (Studi e testi XCIV), Vatican City: Bibliotheca Apostolica, 1940.
[62] See Hunger I, p. 94.
[63] See Steven Runciman, *The Last Byzantine Renaissance*, Cambridge Univ. Pr., 1970, pp. 2-3.

classical Greek culture in contrast to Christianity, lost its pagan value and came to denote all those of Greek race and culture.[64] The "university" of Constantinople is commonly said to have been refounded by Michael VIII under the leadership of George Acropolites.[65]

Among the scholars of the Late Byzantine period there is a marked interest in the systemization and restatement of knowledge, signs of which have already been seen in Tzetzes and George Pachymeres. It is as though an effort were being made to write a concluding and summarizing chapter to Greek intellectual history as the end of the empire approached. Maximus Planudes, Joseph Rhakendytes, and Theodore Metochites are part of this development.

Maximus Planudes (c. 1260–c. 1310) was born in Nicomedia and moved to Constantinople, probably soon after it was retaken from the Latins.[66] There he taught grammar, rhetoric, mathematics, and other subjects for much of his life in a monastic school.[67] He seems never to have been appointed to the Patriarchal School. Unlike many scholars of his time, he lacked political ambition, but in 1297 he served on an embassy to Venice, and he engaged in theological controversy about the *filioque* clause in the Creed and the relationship of the Eastern and Western churches, which were political issues in his time. Planudes had an unusually good knowledge of Latin for a Byzantine, taught the language, and was the leading translator into Greek of works by major Latin authors: Ovid's *Metamorphoses* and *Heroides* (verse prosopopoeiae), Macrobius' commentary on

[64] See ibid., pp. 19-23, and D. M. Nicol, "The Byantine Church and Hellenic Learning in the Fourteenth Century," *Studies in Church History* 5 (1969), 23-57.

[65] See Friedrich Fuchs, *Die höheren Schulen von Konstantinopel im Mittelalter*, Leipzig, 1925; reprinted Amsterdam: Hakkert, 1964, pp. 54-76.

[66] See R-E xx, 2202-53.

[67] See Fuchs, *Höheren Schulen* (supra, n. 65), pp. 58-62.

Cicero's *Dream of Scipio*, Augustine's *On the Trinity*, and Donatus' *Ars Minor* were among these works.[68] The latter was the common Latin grammar of the Middle Ages. He also wrote orations, progymnasmata, commentaries on classical texts, theological and encyclopedic works, and a revised edition of the *Greek Anthology*. Rhetorical theory as commonly studied in the Middle Byzantine period had been collected for the use of teachers and students in large manuscripts such as *Parisinus Graecus* 1983 and 2977, both of the Eleventh Century.[69] Aphthonius and the Hermogenic corpus are the core of the collection, to which had been added various introductions, marginal scholia, and miscellaneous material. Planudes' major contribution to the teaching of rhetoric was to reedit this tradition. In his edition, commentary alternated with text on the page, rather than being written in the margin. The content of the commentary remained the traditional chain of notes built up over the centuries, but much that was irrelevant, repetitive, or inconsistent, was removed and the whole better organized. The result can be found in Volume Five of Walz's *Rhetores Graeci* (pp. 212-610). He wrote his own prolegomenon to the work (reedited in *PS*, pp. 64-73), though of a traditional sort, and he added some new material, including a synopsis of figures and ideas (III, pp. 704-11 Walz), Dionysius of Halicarnassus' work *On Composition*, and sixty-nine themes for judicial declamation (VIII, pp. 402-13 Walz), which were doubtless practiced in his school. His work has virtually no originality and, because of the editorial process, has removed some of the references of historical interest found in earlier commen-

---

[68] See W. O. Schmitt, "Lateinische Literatur in Byzanz. Die Uebersetzung des Maximos Planudes und die moderne Forschung," *Jahrbuch der österreichischen byzantinischen Gesellschaft* 17 (1968), 127-47.

[69] See Hugo Rabe, "Rhetoren-Corpora," *RhM* 67 (1912), 321-57.

tators, but it shows what was regarded as useful in the study of rhetoric at the end of the Thirteenth Century. Joseph Rhakendytes, or the Philosopher (c. 1280–c. 1330), is the author of a synopsis of rhetoric (III, pp. 465-569 Walz) which is actually the introductory part of a large encyclopedia of the liberal arts, including rhetoric, physics, anthropology, mathematics, ethics, and theology.[70] His discussion of rhetoric is unusual in devoting chapters to epideictic, derived from Menander (III, pp. 547-58 Walz), and to the epistle (p. 558) and also includes accounts of figures and tropes, which are published separately in Walz (VIII, pp. 671-93 and 714-25). The encyclopedia has a prose preface and introductory poem (III, pp. 473-77 Walz) in which Joseph describes his interest in divine and human learning, summarizes the content of his work, and tells something about his life. A few additional details are known from a memorial to him by Theodore Metochites and from letters by his contemporaries: he was born in Ithaca, became a monk and teacher in Thessalonika, and spent some years in Constantinople. Much admired by his friends, he was apparently offered, but declined, the patriarchate.

Theodore Metochites was a public official under Andronicus II (1282-1328) and one of the most learned of all Byzantine scholars. His chief work, the *Miscellany*, is a series of essays on philosophical, historical, and literary subjects, showing the influence of progymnasmatic forms and an admiration for Synesius of Cyrene. He is also the author of sophistic orations and an essay comparing the styles of Demosthenes and Aelius Aristides.[71]

[70] See M. Treu, "Der Philosoph Joseph," *BZ* 8 (1899), 1-64; N. Terzaghi, "Sulla composizione dell'Enciclopedia del filosofo Guiseppe," *Studi italiani di filologia classica* 10 (1902), 121-32; V. de Falco, "Sulla Rhetorica del filosofo Giuseppe," *Historia* 5 (1931), 635-38; Renato Criscuolo, "Note sull' Enciclopedia del filosofo Giuseppe," *Byzantion* 44 (1975), 255-81.

[71] See Theodorus Metochites, *Saggio critico su Demostene et Aristide*, ed. Marcella Gigante, Milan: Istituto Editoriale Cisalpino, 1969.

LATER BYZANTINE PERIOD

Synopses of rhetorical theory are attributed to Georgius Gemistus Pletho (VI, pp. 544-89 Walz) and his opponent Mathias Kamariotes (I, pp. 121-26, and VI, pp. 601-44 Walz), but they and others of the Fourteenth and Fifteenth Centuries, including George Trebizonius, are best left for consideration in a future study of the recovery of the full tradition of classical rhetoric in Renaissance Italy.[72]

The Byzantines provided few new insights into the nature of rhetoric; they preserved the heritage of antiquity in its technical, philosophical, and sophistic strands as these had been defined in late antiquity and they applied this to their own speech and writing in the high style. Through them, some aspects of ancient rhetoric not known in the West, especially the ideas of style, were transmitted to later times. Although their culture was less oral than had been that of the Greek city states and the Roman republic, speech retained important political and social functions, and study of rhetoric remained the entrance to public life and to advanced learning. In contrast to Western Europeans of the Middle Ages, they consistently gave a greater emphasis to rhetoric than to dialectic. Occasional signs of tension between rhetoric and Christianity are evident, as in the poem of Geometres quoted above, but even this is of a traditional nature, and the synthesis worked out by Gregory of Nazianzus and others in the Fourth Century was accepted by leading Byzantine churchmen. The Eastern Church never embraced rhetoric as the important tool for the exegesis of the Scriptures which Augustine and other rhetorically trained Latin Fathers bequeathed to the West.

[72] See John Monfasani, *George of Trebizond. A Biography and a Study of His Rhetoric and Logic* (Columbia Studies in the Classical Tradition I), Leiden: Brill, 1976.

Additional Bibliography

Some Works Published Since 1983

CHAPTER ONE

Greek Biography and Panegyric in Late Antiquity, edited by Tomas Hägg and Philip Rousseau. Berkeley: University of California Press, 2000.

Menander: A Rhetor in Context, by Malcolm Heath. Oxford University Press, 2004.

Power and Persuasion in Late Antiquity, by Peter Brown. Madison: University of Wisconsin Press, 1992.

The Private Orations of Themistius, translated by Robert J. Penella. Berkeley: University of California Press, 1999.

CHAPTER TWO

Canons of Style in the Antonine Age: Idea-Theory and its Literary Context, by Ian Rutherford. Oxford: Clarendon Press, 1998. Includes (pp.124–53) a translation of Pseudo-Aristeides, *On the Plain Style*.

Greek Declamation, by D. A. Russell. Cambridge: Cambridge University Press, 1983.

Hermogène, L'Art rhétorique: Traduction française intégrale, introduction et notes. Paris: L'Age d'homme, 1997.

Hermogenes on Issues, Strategies of Argument in Later Greek Rhetoric, translated by Malcolm Heath. Oxford: Clarendon Press, 1995.

Hermogenes on Types of Style, translated by Cecil W. Wooten. Chapel Hill: University of North Carolina Press, 1986.

Invention and Method; Two Rhetorical Treatises from the Hermogenic Corpus, translated with introduction and notes by George A. Kennedy. Atlanta: Society of Biblical Literature, 2005.

"Longinus *On Sublimity*," by Malcolm Heath. *Proceedings of the Cambridge Philological Society* 45 (1998), pp. 43-74.

"Porphyry's Rhetoric," by Malcolm Heath. *Classical Quarterly* 53 (2003), pp. 141–166.

ADDITIONAL BIBLIOGRAPHY

Progymnasmata: Greek Textbooks of Prose Composition and Rhetoric, translated by George A. Kennedy. Atlanta: Society of Biblical Literature, 2002. Includes works attributed to Theon, Hermogenes, Aphthonius, and Nicolaus.

The Chreia and Ancient Rhetoric: Classroom Exercises, ed. by Ronald F/ Hock and Edward N. O'Neil. Atlanta; Society of Biblical Literature, 2002.

"Theon and the History of the Progymnasmata," by Malcolm Heath: *Greek, Roman, and Byzantine Studies* 43 (2002-3), pp. 129–60.

Two Rhetorical Treatises from the Roman Empire: Introduction, Text, and Translation of the Arts of Rhetoric Attributed to Anonymous Seguarianus and to Apsines of Gadara, edited by M. R. Dilts and translated by George A. Kennedy. Leiden; Brill, 1997.

CHAPTER THREE

City and School in Late Antique Athens and Alexandria, by E. J. Watts. Berkeley: University of California Press, 2006.

Libanius, ed. and translated by A. F. Norman: Vol 1, *Autobiography and Selected Letters*; vol. 2, *Selected Orations*. Loeb Classical Library. Cambridge: Harvard University Press, 1992.

Man and the Word: The Orations of Himerius, translated, annotated, and introduced by Robert J. Penella. Berkeley: University of California Press, 2007.

CHAPTER FOUR

Encyclopedia of the Early Church, edited by Angelo Di Berardino. New York: Oxford University Press, 1979.

Greek Rhetorical Origins of Christian Faith: An Inquiry, by James L. Kinneavy. New York: Oxford University Press, 1987.

"John Chrysostom, Rhetoric, and Galatians," by Malcolm Heath. *Biblical Interpretation* 12 (2004), pp. 369–400.

New Testament Interpretation through Rhetorical Criticism, by George A. Kennedy. Chapel Hill: University of North Carolina Press, 1984.

The Rhetoric of the New Testament: A Bibliographical Survey, by Duane F. Watson. Blandford Forum UK: Deo Publishing, 2006.

CHAPTER FIVE

Byzantine Christianity, ed. by Derek Krueger. Minneapolis: Fortress Press, 2006.

Letters, Literacy, and Literature in Byzantium, by Margaret Mullett. Burlington VT: Ashgate, 2007.

ADDITIONAL BIBLIOGRAPHY

The Oxford Dictionary of Byzantium, ed. by Alexander P. Kazhdan. 3 vols. New York: Oxford University Press, 1991.
Rhetoric in Byzantium, ed. by Elizabeth Jeffreys. Burlington VT: Ashgate, 2003.
Scholars of Byzantium, by N. G. Wilson. London: Duckworth, 1996.

Index

Acropolites, George, 322
acta of Councils, 200-201, 258-61
adoxography, 36
advocates, 12, 13, 177, 294
Aeneas of Gaza, 169
Agathias, 13-18
Agricola, Rudolph, 60
akmē, 99
alētheia, 97, 100
Alexander, son of Numenius, 123-25
Alexandria, 178, 185, 208
al-Farabi, 272
allegory, 30, 39, 119, 141, 145, 184, 208, 212
ambassadors' speeches, *see presbeutikoi logoi*
Ammianus Marcellinus, 20, 21, 31
Ammonius, 119, 130
amphibolia, 83
anapausis, 98
anaskeuē, 58, 62, 68, 225, 316
Anastasius I, 174
Anastasius, sophist, 170
anathema, 19, 258-59, 280
Anatolius, 139-40
Anna Comnena, 301
antengklēma, 83, 84, 94
Anthony, Saint, 210-12, 255
anthypophora, 89
antilēpsis, 83, 84, 85
antinomia, 83
Antioch, 10, 149-63, 169, 242
Antiochene School of Exegesis, 185, 247, 254-55, 259
antiparastasis, 89, 90
antistasis, 83, 84
antithesis, 92-93, 181, 226
Anton of Tagrit, 272

ap' archēs achri telous, 85, 91
apheleia, 100
Aphthonius, 54, 59-66, 102, 103, 116, 272, 275-76, 291, 306, 307, 312, 319, 323
aposiopesis, 231, 232
applause, 9, 245
Apsines, 9, 87, 90, 94, 95, 110, 112
Aquila, 79, 103, 110, 115
Arabic rhetoric, 272
Arcadius, 37-39
Arethas, 287-90
argumentation, *see* enthymeme; epicheireme
Arianism, 188, 192, 197-208, 213, 216, 230, 236
Aristides, Aelius, 70, 96, 101, 104, 132, 141, 152, 154, 174, 281, 309, 324
Aristotle, 49, 52, 61, 68, 73, 75, 106, 114, 116, 117, 120, 128, 129, 132, 165, 209, 221, 257, 272, 302-3, 309, 311, 318, 321; commentaries on the *Rhetoric*, 318-20
Arius, 197-99, 202-3
Armenian rhetoric, 272
art, description of works of, 172-74
Asterius, 207-8
asystaton, 82
Athanasius, bishop of Alexandria, 202-12, 255
Athanasius, sophist, 112, 115, 120
Athens, Schools of, 135-49, 167-68, 177-79, 233-34
Atticism, 45-49, 152, 175, 184, 238, 266, 276, 279, 281, 291, 295-96, 300, 313

331

INDEX

Augustine, 134, 183
axiōma, 99

Bardas, 277-78
barytēs, 100
Basil the Great, 151, 214, 215, 228-37, 239-40, 255
Basilicus, 112
basilikoi logoi, 27-31, 37-39, 288
Beirut, Law School of, 7, 178
Bemarchius, 164
biaion, 89
bonus orator, 108

Caecilius of Calacte, 123
Callistratus, 173
ceremony, 9, 18, 203-4, 299-300
Chalcedon, Council of, 261-64
characters of style, 44, 52, 64, 65, 96
Choniates, Michael, 320
Choricius, 175-77
chria, 55, 56, 57, 58, 59, 61, 67, 146, 147, 210, 219, 316
Christophorus, 314
Chrysostom, John, 221, 241-54, 257, 311
Chumnus, Nicephous, 296
Cicero, 52, 55, 71, 75, 80, 106, 108
clausulae, 49
commonplaces, see topoi
consolation, see paramythētikoi logoi
Constans I, 139
Constantine I, 19, 20, 27-31, 33-34, 186, 191-97, 203-6
Constantine IX, 303-5
Constantinople, 151, 163-67, 216, 242, 248, 272-75, 277, 287, 292, 308, 309, 313, 318, 322; Patriarchal School of, 315-16; "university" of, 12, 166-67, 178, 272-75, 278, 313, 318, 322
Constantius I, 165

Constantius II, 138
Cyril of Alexandria, 257-58, 262

Damascius, 121, 126, 167, 168
declamation, see meletai
deinotēs, 64, 97, 100, 102, 300
delivery, 43-44, 118-19
Demetrius, 71, 96, 122
Demosthenes, 49, 88, 89, 94, 97, 98, 99, 100, 103, 106, 118, 119, 122, 123, 133, 137, 142, 151, 162, 163, 170, 176, 238, 244, 257, 281, 311-12, 324
diaeresis, 41, 53, 66, 80, 82, 99, 105, 108, 109, 312
dialectic, 53, 74, 183-85, 189, 194-96, 199, 202, 208-10, 214, 225, 257, 267, 271, 273, 291, 301, 303, 312
dialexis, 143, 167, 171, 175
diatribe, 177, 182, 249
diēgēma, see narrative
diēgēsis, 16, 29, 61, 88
dikaiologia, 76, 81
Dio Chrysostom, 36-37, 39-45
Diocletian, 134, 163
Dionysius of Halicarnasus, 26, 93, 96, 108, 110, 112, 113, 167, 305, 317, 323
Diophantus, 137, 140, 141, 150
disputation, see dialectic
Doxapatres, John, 66, 117, 118, 120, 275-76, 307, 312, 317, 320,
drimytēs, 91, 92, 100

ecphrasis, 56, 58, 65, 146, 155, 170, 171, 172-73, 177, 191, 193, 221, 222, 225, 226, 235, 236, 248, 271, 282, 308
emphasis, 94, 286, 309
encomium, 25, 26, 36-37, 56, 57, 58, 63, 64, 68, 153, 154, 169, 171, 174, 175, 191, 210, 218, 249, 271, 306, 308

INDEX

enstasis, 89, 90, 145, 195
enthymeme, 88, 90, 91, 145, 148, 195, 257, 319
Ephesus, Council of, 258-60
epicheireme, 36-37, 88, 89, 90-91, 92, 145, 148, 260
Epiphanius of Salamis, 202
Epiphanius, sophist, 137, 140
epistolography, 21, 31-32, 70-73, 324
epitaphioi logoi, 23, 158, 175, 229, 240, 305-6
epithalamioi logoi, 68-69, 143, 147-48, 175
erga, 52, 68, 77, 105, 114
ergasia, 42, 61, 62, 88, 90, 91, 145, 195
ethopoeia, 59, 64, 71, 172-74, 297, 316. *See also* prosopopoeia
ēthos, as idea of style, 97, 148-49
Eunapius, 9-10, 22, 77, 105, 136-42, 149
Eunomius, 188, 224
Eusebius of Alexandria, 139
Eusebius of Caesarea, 175, 186-96, 203-5
Eusebius of Nicomedia, 199
Eustathius of Thessalonika, 316
Eustathius, sophist, 21-22, 115
Evagoras, 79, 103, 110
Evagrius, 189
exegesis, 53-54, 182-85. *See also* Antiochene School
external rhetoric, 4-5, 20, 45, 199, 203, 235, 267, 269, 270, 299-300

figured problems, 30, 93-94, 164
figures of speech, 92, 98, 119, 123-26, 183, 191, 248, 303, 324
flattery, 5, 12, 18, 25, 38, 193, 298
funeral oratory, *see epitaphioi logoi*

Gaza, 169-77
Geometres, John, 276, 307
George of Alexandria, 103, 104, 112, 115-16
George of Cyprus, 320-21
glykytēs, 100
gnōmē, 10, 59, 61-62, 67, 72, 212, 316
gorgotēs, 97, 100
Gregory of Corinth, 314-15, 317
Gregory of Nazianzus, 24, 32, 72, 125, 141, 214-39, 243, 252, 255, 270, 286, 292, 293, 305, 308, 311-12, 315, 319
Gregory of Nyssa, 240
Gregory Thaumaturgus, 185
Gubazes, 14-17

hagiography, 210, 270, 275, 291, 293-94
Hecebolius, 164
Hephaestion, sophist, 138
Hermagoras, 52, 74
Hermeias, 126-29, 303
Hermogenes, governor of Achaea, 143-47
Hermogenes, sophist, 20, 54, 58-59, 60, 62, 73, 74, 76-103, 107, 108, 109, 110, 111, 112, 114, 116, 121, 122, 123, 125, 132, 167, 238, 275-76, 281-82, 285-86, 289, 291, 304, 305, 306, 307, 309, 312, 314-17, 319, 323. *See also* ideas of style; stasis
Himerius, 24, 49, 68, 104, 140-49, 280
historiography, 31; Christian, 186-90
homily, 182-84, 207, 208, 217, 224, 240, 246-47, 250-54, 274, 282
homoousios, 198, 205
horos, 15, 74, 84
hymns, 28, 63, 68
hypodiairesis, 91, 195

333

INDEX

Iamblichus, 78, 112, 126, 302
ideas of style, 44, 52, 72, 96-101, 110-12, 119, 121-22, 146, 148, 223, 282, 285-86, 309, 313, 314, 316
imitation, 21, 64, 121
invective, see psogos
irony, 181
Isaac Comnenus, 298-300
Isidore of Pelusium, 256-57
Isocrates, 18, 34, 61, 153, 174, 219, 232, 244, 311
Italicus, Michael, 318
Italus, John, 305

John Damascene, 270-72
John of Gaza, 170
John of Sardis, 66, 103, 275-77, 307
John the Deacon, 314
Joseph Rhakendytes, 324
Julian of Caesarea, 9, 137-38
Julian the Apostate, 21, 27-32, 34, 135, 141, 151, 156-58, 164, 169, 214, 221-23
Justinian, 8, 12, 14-17, 18-19, 177-78

kallos, 97, 100
kataphora, 93
kataskeuē, 58, 62, 68, 88, 225, 316
katastasis, 88, 131
katēgoria, 6
Khorenatsi, Moses, 272
koinē, 46-47, 184, 187, 188, 209, 213

Lachares, 66, 95, 167-68
Lactantius, 164
lalia, 69, 72, 143, 144
lamprotēs, 99
Latin, 153, 164, 194, 204, 322
letter and intent, 17, 74, 83, 84, 226

Leo I, 261-64
Leo III, 270, 274
Leo the Mathematician, 277
Leo the Wise, 270
Leontius, sophist, 169
Libanius, 7, 18, 34, 49, 56, 59, 60, 71, 133, 134, 136, 140, 149-63, 164, 169, 176, 241-42, 254, 281, 320, 321
Lichudes, Constantine, 295
logikē, 83, 84
Lollianus, 75-76, 107, 108, 113, 134
Longinus, Cassius, 77-78, 87, 167, 305
Lydus, John, 12-13, 71
lysis, 87, 90, 195

Malchion, 143, 185
Marcellinus, 104, 112, 116, 118, 119, 120
Marinus, 167, 168
Maximus the Confessor, 267-69
megethos, 97, 99
meletai, 28, 53, 65, 81, 93-95, 104, 133-79 *passim*, 161-63, 171, 175
memory, 299
Menander Rhetor, 21, 25-26, 27, 63, 68-70, 133, 147, 174, 229, 241, 270, 293, 324
metalēpsis, 74, 76, 83, 84, 85
metastasis, 83, 84
method, 97, 101-3, 314, 315, 317
Metochites, Theodore, 324
Metrophanes, 102, 110, 115
Minucianus, 76-77, 102, 103, 107, 110, 115
monarchy, 32, 38, 113, 119, 192, 226
monks of Egypt, 40-42, 210-13
monody, 69, 143, 154, 158, 229, 237
myth, as progymnasmatic form,

INDEX

58, 60-61, 67, 144, 145, 146, 147, 316
mythology, 30, 36, 39, 141, 143, 175, 225, 231, 284

narrative, as progymnasmatic form, 55, 56, 57, 58, 61, 86-87, 222, 231, 316
Neoplatonism, 40, 77-78, 79, 98, 99, 106, 108-9, 113, 114, 119, 121-22, 124, 126-32, 133, 135, 137, 158, 178, 194, 209, 264, 285
Nestorius, 254, 257-58
Nicaea, 151; Council of, 19, 200-207, 321
Nicephoros Basilices, 316, 320
Nicolaus, 66-69, 71
Nicomedia, 149, 154, 163
Nicostratus, 101
Nilus, 313-14
noēsis, 52, 68, 105
nomikē, 83, 84, 85, 86
nomou eisphora, 65-66

obscurity, 286-87, 290, 300
oekoumenikos didaskalos, 273-74
Olympiodorus, 129-32
ongkos, 99
Origen, 184-85, 189, 196

Pachymeres, George, 321
paignia, 36
Palladius, 213
panathēnaikoi logoi, 69
panegyric, 23, 26, 68, 92, 100, 107, 151, 177, 185, 190-94, 209, 213, 217, 231, 270, 288, 293, 301, 315, 316
paradox, 181, 226, 263
paragraphē, 76, 83, 84
paramythētikoi logoi, 70, 176, 229, 237, 240
Parnasius, 138
Paul, Saint, 180-83, 202, 212, 232, 244, 247, 249, 250, 257, 282
Paul ho panu, 116
Paul of Samosata, 185
peribolē, 99
periodic style, 93, 167-68, 229
Philip of Side, 188
Philostorgius, 188
Philostratus, 59, 72, 75, 79, 102, 110, 149, 304
Phoebammon, 115, 120-26
Photius, Patriarch, 47, 142, 143, 168, 175, 264, 274, 275, 278-85
Photius, sophist, 115
Planudes, Maximus, 66, 79, 117, 292, 322-24
Plato, 18, 37, 49, 98, 99, 109, 114, 122, 149, 165, 176, 189, 192, 196-97, 213, 225, 238, 240, 244, 251, 252-53, 264, 288, 301-2, 311; Gorgias, 100, 101, 106, 113, 114, 129-32; Phaedrus, 41, 44, 100, 170, 171, 219-20, 248, 303, 318
Plutarch of Athens, 109
pneuma, 92-93, 145
poiotēs, 16, 74, 83, 84
Porphyry, 45, 53, 66, 77-78, 107, 108, 110, 112, 114, 115, 117, 121, 302, 309
pragmatikē, 76, 81, 84, 85, 86
preaching, 182-83, 270-71, 282-85, 308, 316
presbeutikoi logoi, 20-22, 298-300
probolē, 77
Proclus, 71, 109, 126, 167, 285, 302
Procopius of Gaza, 170-76
progymnasmata, 25-26, 53, 54-70, 133, 155, 161, 191, 192, 224, 272, 308, 316, 320, 321, 323, 324
Prohaeresius, 9, 138-41, 215
prokataskeuē, 88, 146

335

INDEX

prolegomena, 54, 67, 112-14, 116-22, 275-76
propemtikoi logoi, 143
prosopopoeia, 56, 58, 59, 64, 176, 210, 212, 235, 249, 320. See also ethopoeia
prosphōnētikoi logoi, 68-69, 143, 144, 157
protheōria, 26, 147-49, 154, 161-62, 168, 176
Psellus, Michael, 129, 294-306
psogos, 25, 63, 59, 60, 68, 146, 224

quadrivium, 301, 321
Quintilian, 52, 55-57, 77, 108, 116, 119, 121, 122, 124

rhythm, stress, 48-49, 143, 168
Rufinus of Aquileia, 221, 239

saphēneia, 97, 98
schoinotēs, 93
semnotēs, 99
senate, 19, 34, 166, 268, 269
shorthand, 7, 15, 72, 142
Siceliotes, John, 120, 238, 286, 309-12
Simocatta, Theophylactus, 272
Simplicius, 178, 309
sminthiakoi logoi, 69
Socrates Scholasticus, 120, 188-89, 197-98, 201, 206
Sopatros, 103, 113, 114, 115, 142, 276, 320
sophistry, 133-79
Sopolis, 138
Sozomen, 189, 202
sphodrotēs, 99
stasis, 15, 52, 73-86, 110, 119, 140, 203, 224, 226, 259, 276, 294, 296, 304, 309
stenography, see shorthand
Stephanus of Alexandria, 272-73
Stephanus of Constantinople, 318-20

stochasmos, 15, 74, 83-85, 225
Stoics, 75, 106
stress accent, see rhythm
strongylos, 92
Suda, 57, 77, 103, 120, 167, 168, 170, 280, 312-13
Superianus, 168
syllogism, 40, 83, 300, 319
synēgoria, 65, 264
Synesius of Cyrene, 12, 22-23, 35-45, 255, 324
syngnōmē, 83, 84
synkrisis, 25, 31, 41, 58, 64, 146, 193, 221, 227, 229, 234, 235, 236, 249
synthesis, 98
Syriac rhetoric, 272
Syrianus, 79, 95, 98, 102, 103, 104, 109-12, 167, 168

tasis, 93
technē, 105-6, 110, 113, 218, 219
telika kephalaia, 63, 65
Themistius, 9-10, 19, 21, 32-35, 45, 165, 192
Theodore of Mopsuestia, 241, 254-55
Theodore the Studite, 270, 275
Theodoret, 189
Theodorus of Gadara, 68n
Theodosius I, 11, 159, 246
Theodosius II, 19, 134, 165, 259
Theon, 20, 55-58, 69-70, 272
theotokos, 257, 258
thesis, 65, 209
Thomas Magister, 47, 321
Tiberius, *On Figures*, 123
topoi, 21, 26, 62, 69, 73, 88, 90, 91, 236, 237, 241
torture, 5, 10, 45, 235
trachytēs, 99
Troilus, 120
troops, addresses to, 19-20
Trophonius, 120
Tzetzes, John, 316-17

336

Ulpian, 138, 149
Valens, 10, 235
virtues of narration, 61
Xenophon, 210
Xiphilinus, 306

Zacharias Scholasticus, 169-70
Zeno, sophist, 115
Zosimus, historian, 10-12, 19, 20, 21
Zosimus of Ascalon, 103, 120, 170

www.ingramcontent.com/pod-product-compliance
Lightning Source LLC
Chambersburg PA
CBHW070011010526
44117CB00011B/1508